Governing as Governance

Governing as Governance

Jan Kooiman

SAGE Publications
London • Thousand Oaks • New Delhi

Jan Kooiman 2003

First published 2003

SAGE Publications Ltd
6 Bonhill Street
London EC2A 4PU

SAGE Publications Inc.
2455 Teller Road
Thousand Oaks, California 91320

SAGE Publications India Pvt Ltd
32, M-Block Market
Greater Kailash - I
New Delhi 110 048

British Library Cataloguing in Publication data

A catalogue record for this book is available from the British Library

ISBN 0 7619 4035 9
ISBN 0 7619 4036 7 (pbk)

Library of Congress Control Number 2002104221

Typeset by C&M Digitals (P) Ltd., Chennai, India
Printed in India at Gopsons Papers Ltd., Noida

SUMMARY OF CONTENTS

CONTENTS

ACKNOWLEDGEMENTS

Governance, or as the Dutch say *besturen*, has interested me for many years. It featured in my dissertation *Besturen is Beslissen* (To Govern is to Decide 1970), in an introductory text *Besturen* (1980), and in the edited volume *Modern Governance* (1993). In this book this interest is fully explored. Its inception began about seven years ago as a Research Report, in which I summed up not only my own ideas on governance, but also the work of my collaborators and PhD students at the time. The result of this common effort was promising enough for me to commit myself to transforming this material into what is published here. In the last few years several colleagues in the Netherlands and abroad were willing to look at drafts of the book in the making, for which I am immensely grateful. Henrik Bang, Jan Berting, Matthias Finger, Rainer Greca, Hubert Heinelt, Flip Idenburg, Nick Huls, Svein Jentoft, Walter Kickert, Frans van Nispen, Stephen Osborne, Roger Pullin, Charles Raab and Roger Sibeon took the trouble to go through the whole manuscript or parts of it. Not only were the comments they gave on the text of great help, but their encouragement and support for the project was of even greater value. In the book I also make use of the work of many of my students, some implicitly, others explicitly. Here I especially mention Margaretha (Inez) van Eeden and Jeroen Warner, both of whom have been of great help during the whole process. I express my gratitude to all of those at Sage Publications who contributed to a professional and congenial way in bringing this book to completion. I also would like to thank all those colleagues and friends who in the course of the past few years told me that they are looking forward to this book. I hope I don't disappoint them.

I dedicate this book to Cornelia and to the memory of Rienkje.

GOVERNANCE, GOVERNING AND INTERACTION

PART 1
GOVERNANCE, GOVERNING AND
INTERACTION

1

SETTING THE STAGE

Social-political governance

This study advances ideas presented in *Modern Governance: Government-society Interactions* (1993),[1] in which attention was drawn to interactions with a 'co-' public-private character, offset against a 'do-it-alone' government perspective. This study maintains this line of thinking, but broadens it by seeing governance as a societal quality made up of public as well as private 'governors', hence the term social-political. The essence of the argument is that governance of and in modern societies is a mix of all kinds of governing efforts by all manner of social-political actors, public as well as private; occurring between them at different levels, in different governance modes and orders. These mixes are societal 'responses' to persistent and changing governing 'demands', set against ever growing societal diversity, dynamics and complexity. Governing issues generally are not just public or private, they are frequently shared, and governing activity at all levels (from local to supra-national) is becoming diffused over various societal actors whose relationships with each other are constantly changing. There has, judged against traditional public governing activities, been an increase in the role of government as facilitator and as co-operating partner. As such it is more appropriate to speak of shifting than of shrinking roles of the state. However, a reshuffling of government tasks and a greater awareness of the need to interact with other societal actors does not render traditional government interventions obsolete. It merely implies a growing awareness of the limitations of traditional governance by the state on its own.

Responses to diverse, dynamic and complex societal issues require approaches involving previously uninvolved partners, looking not only at the market as seems to have been an almost universal response in recent years, but also looking at 'civil society' actors, as serious governing partners. The 'why' of modern governance can be best explained by an awareness that governments are not the only actors addressing major societal issues; that besides the traditional ones, new modes of governance are needed to tackle these issues; that governing arrangements will differ from global to local and will vary sector by sector. In diverse, dynamic and complex areas of societal activity no single governing agency is able to realise legitimate and effective governing by itself. Such governance is achieved by the creation of interactive, social-political structures and processes stimulating communication between actors involved, and the creation of common responsibilities next to individual and separate ones. There is a need to restructure governing responsibilities, tasks and activities, based upon differentiation and integration of various concerns and the agents representing them. In a world characterised by – possibly – increasing diversity, dynamics and complexity, social-political issues are the result of various interacting factors that are rarely wholly known and not caused by a single factor; technical and political knowledge is dispersed over many actors; and governing objectives are not easy to define and are often submitted to revision. The challenge for anyone involved in governing and governance is to make governing interactions productive. This requires a social-political perspective on those interactions, instead of seeing them exclusively as a matter for 'traditional' public governors.

In the past few years the literature on governance has grown tremendously in many different areas and disciplines.[2] In the next section I attempt to define it.

Defining governing and governance

Governing is varied, and the aim of this book is to conceptualise it in such ways and terms as to encompass limited governing action by individual citizens, as well as large scale efforts by interested public and private actors to influence major social-political developments. To some degree, governing can be seen in models, in practice, governing can be observed everywhere. Social-political governance is a fact of life, and by defining governing in terms of interactions, in which societal diversity, dynamics and complexity are expressed, I seek to make social-political processes analysable and interpretable. For instance, creativity, intuition and experience are just as important as goal-directness, criteria of efficiency and working 'according to rules'. Emotions play a part, as does power, calculation as well as coping with uncertainty. But this breadth of response does not mean that 'anything goes'.

A working definition of 'social-political' or 'interactive' governing and governance, or simply governing and governance – the elements of which will be clarified in the course of the book – looks as follows:

> **Governing** *can be considered as the totality of interactions, in which public as well as private actors participate, aimed at solving societal problems or creating societal opportunities; attending to the institutions as contexts for these governing interactions; and establishing a normative foundation for all those activities.*

> **Governance** *can be seen as the totality of theoretical conceptions on governing.*

I call the conceptual perspective for this book **social-political governance**. Social-political governance means using an analytical and normative perspective on any societal governance that is 'collective'. Collective not in the sense that the care and development of these activities is looked upon as a public task (the 'state'), a responsibility of the private sector (the 'market'), or of the third sector ('civil society') in isolation, but as a shared set of responsibilities. Public governing carried out with an eye to 'private carrying capacities'; and private governing carried out with an eye to 'public carrying capacities'. Some of those activities are of a self-governing nature, others are considered to be co-governing, and there is also a place for authoritative or hierarchical governing.

The perspective of this study also can be called **interactive governance**. This adjective might be used because conceptually interaction plays a dominant role and because forms, models and modes of governing interactions are key conceptual elements in this book. Interactions as a social phenomenon, and governing interactions as a specific type of them, are a rich source for analysing and synthesising insights into many facets of governance. In particular, in governing interactions the diversity, dynamics and complexity of governance issues in modern societies can be expressed. Interaction thus becomes a 'linking pin' between societal attributes and governance qualities. As such, the governability of social-political entities is decided by the quality of its governing interactions. The totality of these interactions in all their diversity, dynamics and complexity is the start of the analysis and at the same time its end. These ideas are, broadly, the theme and subject matter of this book.

Crossing boundaries

Governance as a concept is not new, but currently it is being treated more systematically, and this might be expected to continue. In previous analyses the state was the central governing actor; in newer ones state-society relations are the focus.[3] There is great scope for a governance paradigm to arise, to be championed, lauded and debated as a subject of inter-scholarly rivalry, inevitably to be replaced by a newer, rival theory. We are still in a period of creative disorder concerning governance, optimistic that: 'governance theory has tremendous potential in opening up alternative ways of looking at political institutions, domestic-global linkages, transnational co-operation, and different forms of public-private exchange'.[4] Whether this potential will be fulfilled depends on certain conditions being met. In particular a number of boundaries will have to be crossed: conceptual boundaries, boundaries between theory and practice and last but not least between 'world views'.

It is commonplace to say that many, if not all, major issues facing us these days cannot be properly seen within one dimension. However, in practice this is what many governors and governed alike would have us believe: if we just do this or that a problem will be solved or an opportunity seized, but this is not what a diverse, dynamic and complex world looks like today. If governance is going to make an impression as a societal practice and as a scholarly activity it has to be multi-faceted. Scholarly work discussing, supporting or criticising governance of whatever kind has to be multi- or interdisciplinary in nature. However, crossing disciplinary boundaries as an individual can only be a limited activity. In order to develop systematic ideas on governance I restricted myself to such social science disciplines as political science, public administration/management, sociology, international relations and some institutional economics. When I discuss complexity, diversity and dynamics I make use of some recent insights from the natural sciences: already 'translated' for social science use by others.

In the book I refrain from the term 'theory' for what I am trying to do, instead conceptualising or conceptual perspective are employed. This is a deliberate choice, because I am of the opinion that the two are different scholarly activities. In this book governance is examined through an exploration 'in breadth' of its many aspects and manifestations, rather than as a systematic theoretical exercise 'in depth'. The relation between concepts and theory is perhaps double-sided, maybe even paradoxical: without theory there are no concepts; without concepts there is no theory. 'The proper concepts are needed to formulate a good theory, but we need a good theory to arrive at the proper concepts'[5]. I will cautiously proceed, treading a fine line between conceptualising, analysis and advancing theory. The following chapters are the first necessary step on the borderline between concept formulation and theory development. The result of which can be found in the various statements (in tinted boxes throughout the book), which both summarise the discussion on aspects of governance, and also can be considered as the beginning of a systematising of insights on governance as a theoretical construct, especially in Part V of the book. The application of the governance perspective to empirical situations has been published or will be reported elsewhere.[6] It has always been my conviction not only that conceptual ideas need empirical testing, but also that experiences in real-life governing and the examination of them go hand in hand. This belief in the iteration between practice and reflection found its first expression in the late 1960s, when during a four-year period as assistant to the leader of the Dutch Parliamentary Labour Party, I had the opportunity to look at day-to-day political governing 'from the inside'. This resulted not only in a study on the Dutch Parliament, it also profoundly strengthened my idea that theorising on governing and governance can only be developed when interaction between theory and practice occurs. Since then, wherever possible, I have looked for occasions to put my ideas on governance to the test. Many of the doctoral dissertations I have had the privilege to supervise, and much of the contract or other forms of applied research I have participated in, used elements of the governance perspective in their conceptual base. I consider this book a conceptual outcome of this iterative process and as such a product of a boundary-crossing and interactive process.

The governance approach focuses on the interactions taking place between governing actors within social-political situations. These interactions give human actions their irreversible and unpredictable character as attempts are made toward understanding the diversity, complexity and dynamics of these situations. In doing so there is scope for influencing societal features that occur between the 'modern' and the 'post-modern'. In this respect I find a kindred spirit in Toulmin, who has identified two philosophical traditions that contributed to modernity: one based upon the principle of rationality, the other based upon principles of humanism.[7] I call a combination of elements taken from these two traditions 'cross-modern'; elements of both traditions may, I believe, lead towards an improved governability of 'cross-modern' (Western) societies. This implies a growing awareness and acceptance of different modes of governance, including 'self-governing' capacities of social systems, 'co-governing' arrangements and 'hierarchical' governing; each contributing in single and mixed modes to questions of governability in a broader sense. Pragmatic (meta) principles such as openness to difference, a willingness to communicate, and a willingness to learn are important criteria in coping with societal diversity, dynamics and complexity. Substantive criteria on which basis actors are willing and able to interact with each other and accept each other's boundaries are also needed.

Because of the lack of an overall and overarching social-political ideal, the only other way to establish such criteria is to accept the 'cross-modern' character of Western democracies. That is to say, not only to accept the 'rational' and the 'humanistic' roots of our societies, but to develop new substantive criteria on the basis of the juxtaposition and combination of both. This is the inherent richness on which our democratic societies are built: a wellspring that has not yet dried up. To pursue scientific endeavours is to put one foot in the past and one in the future. This is what my perspective on governance does. Therefore, I use terms that are familiar (cybernetics, problems) and some that are promising but less familiar (emergence, opportunities). In 'cross-modern' situations it seems preferable to apply useful concepts from more than one tradition.

Many things in life are not either-or, but and-and. Global standardisation may be useful and necessary; the same applies to local variety and autonomy. To accept that insights and truths are always inter-subjective is not to deny that – inter-subjectively – some insights are more useful than others, and some truths seem better than others. Replacing a 'this is true' statement by 'this could also be true' makes diversity of opinion the lifeblood of social-political science and of social-political governance. If insight and truth is in the eye of the beholder, then what we need are social-political governing processes (and structures) that take both inter-actions and actors seriously.

Interactions shape actors and actors shape interactions; they are 'equal' as basic units of analysis and theory development in terms of 'and-and', not of 'either-or'. The governance perspective starts from the diversity, dynamics and complexity of the societies to be governed – and the govern-ing themselves. These societies need order, but nothing can change with-out dynamics. They require similarity to enable communication, but diversity to gain new insights. They need standards to reduce uncertainty and risk, but complexity to solve problems and create opportunities. As such, thinking on governance needs to be diverse but consistent, complex but elegant and dynamic but orderly. The 'both-and', instead of the 'either-or', is a key characteristic of this exploration.

Overview of the book

This book will explore the utility of the governance concept as an instru-ment for conceptualising issues on the boundary between the social and the political, or in current terminology, between state, market and civil society. Many governing challenges cannot be handled by each of these societal realms or institutions in isolation. The character and nature of these challenges – either problems or opportunities, is such that they 'tres-pass' traditional boundaries between them. Thinking about modern governance in a systematic manner, requires a set of concepts that show each of them to be parts of such governing, forming a coherent framework that enables a picture of governance as a societal quality to emerge. The conceptual framework advanced in this study aims at presenting a 'rich' picture of the totality of such governing without losing sight of the parts and aspects it consists of. To accomplish this, several steps will be taken.

In this book interaction is a central concept. Governing is, after all, interaction in some way or another. First, it seems proper to begin by specifying what this concept might mean, and to elaborate on the impor-tance it assumes in the governance perspective; with the help of the inter-actions concept, social-political reality can be observed in its various manifestations. Social-political governance – in terms of interactions – should be placed in the context of the diversity, dynamics and complexity of modern societies. These societies derive their strength from these fea-tures, continually presenting these societies with opportunities. But they also present them with problems. These opportunities and problems themselves are also complex, dynamic and diverse. This also applies to the structural conditions under which opportunities are created and used

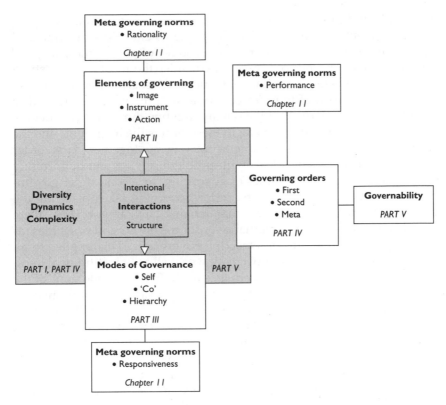

Figure 1.1   Scheme of analysis

and problems formulated and solved. Separately, but especially in their inter-relatedness, these three aspects are the second key building block of my thinking about social-political governing, governance and governability. Only if we take these three basic features and their influence on all governing activities within modern societies seriously can we begin to conceptualise how they can be used in the governance of those societies.

To make full use of the conceptual potential of interactions I distinguish an intentional and a structural aspect within it, plus the relation between these two levels. Doing so, the analytical as well as the synthetic capacities of the interaction concept can be fully exploited. These distinctions within interactions as a concept will be utilised throughout the study and especially in relation to governing interactions.

In Figure 1.1 this is expressed in its different parts. In Part II the intentional level of governing interactions is presented in three different elements: images, instruments and action. The idea is that both public and private governors, in their governing interactions, make systematic use of these elements in their governing. They have images about what their governing is about, they apply instruments to reach what they want to accomplish, and they use a certain amount of action (potential) to bring these instruments into place. In Part III of the scheme the structural level of governing is represented. Here, three modes of governance, self, 'co' and hierarchy are introduced, which I consider the most integral structural characteristics of governing interactions. All societal governance can be looked at as mixes of those three modes and the way they related to each other. Then, in Part IV of the scheme I define three further orders of governance, first, second and meta. In these orders the intentional and the structural level of governing interactions come together. First order governing and governance deals with problem solving and opportunity creation, the day-to-day activities of governing. In second order governance the institutions in which first order governing takes place are the object of governance: their design, maintenance and care for. Third, there is meta governance. In this governance order the norms and principles for governing as a whole are the object of governance. This applies to all problem solving and opportunity creation as well as to institutional questions, and in fact also to meta governance itself. In the scheme some of the major concepts used to give meta governance substance are indicated.

The book follows in principle this scheme. Part I closes with a chapter on interactions. This concept, and the three societal features of diversity, dynamics and complexity belong to the core of the approach generated. Part II is devoted to the three governing elements images, instruments and action. Part III takes up the conceptualisation of the three governance orders, self, 'co' and hierarchical governance. In Part IV the three orders of governing and governance are discussed. The book closes with two chapters in which governability is the central theme. One might say that Parts II, III and IV highlight analytical parts of the study, while in Part V all the discussed governing and governance aspects are brought together by synthesising them in the governability of social-political systems. In governability I emphasise the quality of these systems, to which all other aspects contribute.

Notes

1 Kooiman, 1993.

2 See Kooiman, 1999 for a survey of governance approaches, and also the substance of this section is broadly discussed. While my point of view is partly in line with other recent ideas on governance, it also differs in important aspects. Besides accounting on my own explorations in this book, summaries of my line of thinking on governance have been published elsewhere. See Kooiman, 1999, 2000, 2002, Kooiman, in press.

3 Peters, 2000.

4 Pierre, 2000, p. 241.

5 Kaplan, 1964, p. 53.

6 Kooiman, 2000b; Kooiman, Vliet van, Jentoft, 1999; Pullin, Bartley and Kooiman, 1999. In 2004 or 2005 two major publications can be expected from an EU sponsored worldwide project 'Fisheries Governance and Food Security' based upon this governance perspective. For references: 'MARE', Center for Maritime Research, University of Amsterdam. E-mail mare@siswo.uva.nl or jkooiman@xs4all.nl

7 Toulmin, 1990.

2

INTERACTION

The interaction concept has a central place in the governance perspective.[1] Governance issues arise in interactions between 'the' political and 'the' social, and are also handled in governing interactions. With these terms I refer to the multi-lateral relations between social and political actors and entities (individuals, organisations, institutions). In the governance perspective it is assumed that governing interactions also have to be reflected in its conceptualisation. From an interaction perspective the observer will experience the cohesion and disjunction of societal governance issues more clearly and systematically. Day-to-day governing occurrences appear to be complex, layered interaction processes enacted between a variety of unpredictable actors with discrepant interests and ambitions. In these interaction processes all kinds of tensions and conflicts are articulated, manifest or latent. Thus, in the interaction perspective the immense diversity, complexity and dynamics of social reality becomes visible and conceptual tools become available to deal with them.

The governance approach also assumes that many of these inter-relations are based on the recognition of inter-dependencies. No single actor, public or private, has the knowledge and information required to solve complex, dynamic and diversified societal challenges; no governing actor has an overview sufficient to make the necessary instruments effective; no single actor has sufficient action potential to dominate unilaterally. The classical way to handle such a situation was to first design a new institutional framework, and later find out what kind of governing work it was capable of. In recent years there is more openness to looking at social-political questions such as governing interactions at the outset. The more hierarchical patterns of governance are not yet out of date. Governments still intervene in the daily lives of citizens, firms meddle in what their competitors do, and voluntary bodies influence the behaviour of their members. This is also part and parcel of societal governance. In my governance perspective such interventions are also seen as inter-actions, if of a special kind.

All this calls for a closer look at governing and governance as patterns of interactions. I will do this in three steps. I begin with a short introduction detailing how I look upon interactions. This is followed by taking an important step in the analysis of (governing) interactions: distinguishing an intentional and a structural level within them. These two levels are also related, providing us with an opportunity to look also at interactions in a synthetic manner. I end the chapter by launching three forms of societal interactions, interferences, interplays and interventions. They are a means for me to reduce the complexity, diversity and dynamics of social-political life, but they also facilitate thinking about modes of governance, as I will show later on in the book.

> In governing interactions the versatility of governance issues can be made visible, and at the same time these interactions serve as conceptual media to come to grips with those issues.

Interactions

Although numerous social science scholars have used interactions as a concept and many theories have been developed around it, the subject of interactions related to the conceptualisation of structure, culture and behaviour is a neglected area in social research.[2] Interactions are predominantly seen as useful at the 'micro' analytical level of social relations, and less so in other societal contexts.[3] Social interactions as we find them in families, friendships or informal groups, will not abound in governance literature. However, insights from social interaction studies, using concepts as (self) perceptions, (self) confirmation, trust, security, and defence, but also identity, interpretation, signalling, framing, and their (in)consistencies may play a role in studying social-political governance. They are important in understanding the less formal and personalised aspects of governing interactions. Biographies of leading 'governors', both past and present, give evidence of this.

Quite a different view on governing interactions can be found in International Relations, which examines the relations between states as patterns of interaction. Some of the same variables, such as trust, security and defence, reappear their substance differing quite radically from those in social interaction studies. Also, in the study of international interactions, other concepts appear such as dominance, accommodation, retaliation, vigilance and reciprocity. Again, theorising with the help of concepts such as these can be useful in analysing governing interactions in domains other than international relations.

There are many other areas of social inquiry that directly or indirectly use interactions as a major tool. Even a well-known 'action' theory, such as Habermas' theory of communicative action, in which 'subjects capable of speech and action co-ordinate their conduct', is more a theory of interaction than of action.[4] So, for a study of governing interactions, we are not completely empty-handed. Designing an interaction concept serving the different purposes I envision will occasionally require making use of what the divergent literature using interactions has to offer.

An interaction can be considered as a mutually influencing relation between two or more actors or entities. In Dutch the word *wisselwerking* is used, having a nice connotation of mutuality, *wissel* meaning 'to and fro', and *werking*, translated as 'having effect'. In this book interactions are considered as predominantly between human actors with social-political governing roles, but interactions between man and nature, as in the exploitation of natural resources, are also relevant in governing terms.

In an interaction an action or intentional level and a structural or contextual level can be distinguished, i.e. each interaction can be said to consist of processes and structures. Processes are the outcome of the capacity of governing actors or entities to act, while the structure of interactions points at the material, social and cultural contexts in which interactions come about. With the aid of structure and process elements, we can break down an interaction into its constituent elements, allowing for interactions to be conceptualised as an object and as a subject of governing. Any conceptualisation of social structures necessarily involves a conception of its constituent actors,[5] likewise, any theory of social interaction implies its structural components. It should be made clear from the outset that many factors are involved in the mutual influence of intentional and structural levels of governing interactions. The interaction concept allows insight into such factors, such as the diversity, dynamics and complexity of societal situations, trends and patterns.

> Distinguishing an intentional and a structural level in governing interactions articulates that governing actions and governance structure (culture) cannot be understood without each other.

Interaction as an analytical concept

The intentional or actor level of interactions

My ideas about actors and their intentions in interactive governing fit with so-called inter-actor theory.[6] This theory focuses on actors and their relations and is general and abstract enough to be applicable to actors as individuals, but also to collectivities, as organisations, or even nation-states. The basic unit of analysis in inter-actor theory is an 'actor-in-situation'. Situations can generate, define, and determine the course of an interaction process, but actors in inter-actor situations also have the capacity to control some of the variation in their own actions.

In governing interactions individual citizens can be the focus of analysis. However, more common will be governing situations, where the actor is not simply an individual, but is better seen as a 'corporate actor'. Mayntz, for instance, speaks of interacting organisations, of those who represent or can commit an organisation, as being corporate actors.[7] Corporate actors usually have a broad array of resources at their disposal, at the same time they are often constrained in the scope of their interactions, exactly because they represent organisations. Actors will usually be identifiable by their varying capacities and the roles they play: actors as individuals, actors as corporate representatives, or actors as governing entities – such as states.

Action implies intention, which relates to consciousness and identity. We see a constant oscillation between the need for predictability to keep interactions going, by reinforcing identity both at the individual and collective level, and indeterminacy due to the complexity of governing experiences and a necessary adaptation to the ever-changing conditions of the natural and social environment of these interactions.[8] Role theory may help in analysing such difficulties not only in oscillations between identity (predictability) and experience (complexity), but also between tensions within other role expectations in governing interactions at their intentional level.[9]

At the intentional level of governing interactions issues such as goals, interests and purposes of individual or corporate actors are at stake. However, individual, organisational, or group goal-oriented interactions can be non-goal-oriented in their consequences.[10] Such unintended effects will often be the result of (systems) complexity and dynamics of governing situations at hand, assuming processes to be linear when in fact they are non-linear.[11] Effects such as these abound in all governing interactions, making them both more complex than many of the rational models of political interaction, and more realistic and rich in content. The same applies to the often-supposed unity of actors or entities in governing inter-actions, as in interactive game theories, where whole states are considered to be unitary 'actors'. This is not the way I want to look at governing inter-actions, although it is true that formalised analyses on governing inter-actions such as in game theories have a contribution to make.

> Unintended as well as intended consequences are inherent in governing interactions due to tensions within and between roles of actors involved and situational factors.

The structural level of interactions

Intentional interactions do not take place in a void; they are always contextually situated. This is what I call the structural dimension of interactions. The question of what exactly this means is more easily put than answered. Structure is a concept used by many, but defining it is not an easy matter. Even writers who have made it the subject of systematic analysis admit that it is one the most 'elusive terms in the vocabulary of current social science' and 'the metaphor of structure continues its essential if somewhat mysterious work in the constitution of social scientific knowledge despite theorists' definitional work'.[12] I will refrain from a formal definition, but extend the above metaphor by adapting a term from a delightful book on structures in everyday life: 'structures, or why things don't fall down or apart'.[13] Therefore, the structural element in governing interactions are the stable and enduring patterns, contexts or conditions ensuring that they don't 'fall down or apart'. The structural dimension of governing interactions point to the material, social and cultural contexts in which interactions come about and into effect. It consists of those circumstances that limit, broaden and at the same time condition its intentional level: institutions, general social constructs, patterns of communication, material and technological possibilities and societal power distributions. This makes for a potentially great choice of factors that can be considered relevant, in that structural dimensions in a particular interactive governing situation are a question of purpose and taste. Determining this purpose and taste is one of the major objectives of the governance perspective. The richness, and also the elusiveness of the structural component of governing interactions will become apparent, as the book unfolds.

> Governing actors will consider the structural components of the interactions they participate in as relatively constant/predictable in the short term, while in the long term they will see them as changeable, partly due to their own activities in them.

Interaction as a synthetic concept

In the analysis of interactions it became apparent how governing actors relate to each other through the intentional level of governing interactions. How societal (sub) systems, of which these actors are part, work, was detailed as at the structural level of those interactions. These levels of governing interactions also influence each other, be it in different time frames. For instance, looking at actions within these interactions, we keep their structure 'constant' in the short term, while if studying their structural level we detract from actor's activities in the short run. Therefore, as much as the analysis of interactions consists of actors and structures, the relations between these elements merits attention; interaction can be seen as a concept for synthesis.

Relations between actor and structure in interactions

Through their interactions, governing actors structure and restructure the systems they are part of, and in doing so they also influence social developments. Different theories relating to actor (agency) and system (structure), emphasise different aspects and work on different levels of interactions. For governance purposes three major lines of thought have a contribution to make in this context.

The structural aspect of social-political interactions refers to the cultural, material and power conditions that constrain and enable the intentional or actor level of these interactions. Writers such as Giddens (and somewhat differently Foucault) emphasise an enabling aspect in contrast to others who see structure mainly as constraining. Giddens also sees structures not as unchangeable but as potentially mutable, even as a process.[14] Structuration means that social systems are produced and reproduced by actors in interaction, who draw upon rules and resources in the complexity of action contexts. The structural properties of social systems are both means and outcome of the practices they organise. Although structures always both constrain and enable in time and space, they are beyond the control of any individual actors. Structuration theory stresses that broader structural contexts shape individual action, but also argues that these actions in turn shape structure in an interactive and recursive way.

Actor-System Dynamics (ASD) theory highlights in particular the tensions between the action level and the structural level of governing interactions.[15] These tensions are the consequence of system preserving and system changing forces that are at work in every interaction at the same time. ASD theory speaks of a dialectical tension between on the one hand structuring processes of systems with their own dynamics of change and conservation, and on the other hand the intentional forces caused by human goal-oriented action to lead those dynamic forces, and doing so continuously to renew or maintain structures. Using ASD theory we might say that social-political interactions should not be abstracted from the typical individual social and psychological features of human interactions. Actors with enduring relationships are likely to take one another into account and by employing self-regulating mechanisms actions such as cheating, exploitation and betrayal are avoided: 'The weaker the commonality of interests and endogenous controls among the actors, the more social control must be accomplished through external mechanisms, for instance, making collective decision making, such as voting, obligatory and its results binding'.[16]

Bourdieu's *theory of symbolic power* is an effort to show how cultural resources, processes and institutions dominate individuals and groups inter-generationally in competitive and self-perpetuating systems of domination and/or differential distribution.[17] The relation between actors, structure, culture and power, is a dialectical one, based upon the insight that the individual and society are not separate entities, but relational in two dimensions of the same social reality, expressed in key concepts as habitus and field. Habitus is best seen as an interiorised set of master perceptions with an habitual and an improvising quality. Internalised successes or failures are reproduced in structures of life chances and thus become part of cultural reproduction. Habitus is an element in the adaptation and continuation of social stratification and power structures: 'Habitus then represents a sort of deep-structuring cultural matrix that generates self-fulfilling prophecies according to different class opportunities'.[18] Field is the structure within which habitus operates, and is organised around specific types of capital. Thus, the intellectual field is the matrix of organisations, institutions and markets where writers, academics and artists compete for symbolic capital and reflect their power relations. Struggles within fields centre around specific forms of capital. Culture is a specific form of power with partially autonomous rules and mechanisms for its development and reproduction. In this strive for autonomy symbolic power is important because it legitimises existing social arrangements.

> Actors in governing interactions will make use of the enabling as well as constraining, the conserving as well as dynamic, the cultural as well as power elements of the interactions they participate in.

Societal diversity, dynamics, complexity and interactions

In the governance perspective emphasising interactions and, particularly, governing-as-interaction(s), it is essential not to lose sight of the actors, diverse as they may be. Indeed, actors cannot be separated from the role they play in the interactions that occur. We are used to considering individuals and other entities as being independent from the interactions they participate in. They interact and, seemingly, can stop at will. But actors are continuously shaped by (and in) the interactions in which they relate to each other. The actors constitute, as it were, intersections in interaction processes. Taking a closer view, actors may themselves consist of interactions, and the boundaries from which they derive their identities are relative and often ambiguous. This applies to social systems, but also to organisations, groups and even individuals. Insight into the diversity of participants in social-political interactions can only be gained by involving them in the governing process, giving them the opportunity to act out their identities; Ashby formulated a famous 'law', saying that 'only variety can destroy variety'.[19] Applied to governance this might mean that it takes a variety of actors to tackle the diversity of governing situations. In this post-modern age with its emphasis on the diversity of individuality and cultural expression, diversity in governing interactions are a prime candidate for serious consideration.

In the interaction concept tensions between the action and the structural level of an interaction can be considered to be the expression of societal dynamics. Rhodes has labelled my approach to governance (among others) as 'socio-cybernetic', emphasising the dynamics of societal situations and their governance.[20] Authors such as Deutsch[21] and Etzioni[22] have made us sensitive to the dynamical qualities of governing processes, and more recently Prigogine[23] has made insights on irreversibility and non-linearity accessible for non-natural science readers. Dynamics is decisive because of the nature and direction of the interactions involved. It gives the tensions within and between the intentional and structural level its specific features, and importantly, characterises the choice between change and conservation of social-political interactions as a central issue. At the action level of interactions this choice shapes the central aspirations of actors by serving special and joint interests, as well as satisfying the system-internal and system-external needs. The more space an interaction creates the more freedom there is for actors to select the values, goals and interests they want to strive after. Conversely, the more inhibiting and controlled an interaction, the more it will influence action contrary to the aspirations of those participating in it. In strongly controlled interactions, the values, goals and interests of actors and the degree with which they can aspire to, are influenced by structural components of the interactions rather than the actors exerting influence on these interactions. This might be a source of strong dynamics and high tensions.

Furthermore, in every interaction another tension can be recognised. Structures can usually be characterised by a tendency for closure, in particular if we compare them to action processes. Closed systems are liable to experience a loss of energy (entropy). All physical, natural and social systems can do to fight this entropic tendency by counterbalancing this loss of energy (negentropy), by creating new sources or forms of energy or they will disintegrate and finally disappear. Etzioni sees any social order as being a counter-entropic arrangement: 'Societal entropy occurs when the societal structure breaks down and there occurs no societal actualization…'[24] Under the influence of the tension between the structural and the intentional level, a tension can be noted within the structural level of interactions between entropic and negentropic forces, between the decay and building of structures.

The complexity of social-political systems can be seen in the fact that a multitude of interactions take place in many different forms and at different intensities. Indeed, most interactions in governing will occur concurrently and inter-dependently of others. Such interactions can only be influenced if aspects of complexity are sufficiently understood. To govern social-political problems and opportunities requires clarity about the nature of interactions involved in a problem to be tackled or an opportunity to be created, the way these interactions interrelate, and their characteristic patterns. Complexity is an issue many branches of science struggle with. Simon[25] and Luhmann[26] both place complexity as an issue central on the agenda of the social sciences.

I will return to diversity, dynamics and complexity in Chapter 12, but I chose these three major concepts to characterise societal conditions, situations and developments. They cannot be considered only as basic governing challenges, but instead as central features of governance itself. In analytical terms, they can be seen as main variables in my governance analysis, and in most chapters I will pay attention to them. Although these three societal characteristics have been part of my thinking almost from the beginning (see *Modern Governance*), here they function as 'working' concepts. The way in which they contribute to the whole will become apparent in the course of the book, and I will bring these results together in the final part.

> In governing interactions insight can be gained in the diversity, dynamics, and complexity of modern societies, and the way these features appear in governance issues.

A model of interactions

In summary, I consider a (governing) interaction as a mutually influencing relation between two or more entities. All interactions consist of an intentional and a structural level. At the intentional or action level two processes are at work, those between the special interests of those participating in the interaction, and a common interest. At the structural level entropic and negentropic forces work simultaneously. The action and the structural level mutually influence each other. The activities of governing actors co-influence the structural conditions within which they govern by changing or conserving them, while these structural conditions co-determine these governing activities by enabling or controlling them. A governing interaction concept can also help in coping with the diversity, dynamics and complexity of 'the world-to-be-governed' and 'the governing-world'. In the entities between which the interactions occur, the diversity of social-political reality comes into being. In the tensions at work within interactions the dynamics of governing issues are expressed. In the mutual cohesion between the many interactions, the complexity of the interacting world of governing is realised.

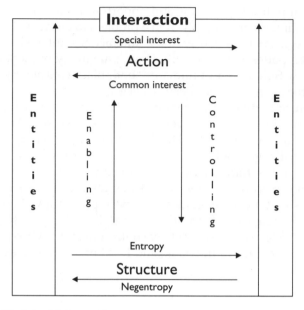

Figure 2.1   Model of interactions

Varieties of societal interactions

In modern society, not only an enormous variety of interactions can be observed; a striking phenomenon, from a governance perspective, is that much societal governance takes place 'by itself'. This is fortunate: if this were not the case, the fundamental freedom to establish patterns of social and social-political interactions would be immensely restricted. However, there are also formal modes of interactions, Mediated by official rules and regulations, with positive or negative provisos attached. Governments are often involved in these forms of interactions, but not exclusively: in the professions and the business world much interaction is formalised and sometimes backed up by rules and regulations – sometimes with official status but this is hardly a hard and fast rule. Also, all around us the build up and growth of networks of private, semi-private and public organisations occurs. Networks and networking are among the 'buzzwords' of our time. For good reason modern societies could be labelled as 'inter-organised societies', anyone familiar with workplaces like universities and hospitals, but also banks and governmental bureaus, will be aware that within them exist all kinds of interactions: unofficial and freely organised ones, semi-organised and semi formalised ones, and finally those one finds on organisation charts.

These observations alert us to different forms of societal interactions. The choice of how to ascertain varieties of interactions is a conceptual one, although distinctions also serve analytical purposes in reducing the complexity of what can be found in the field of social-political interactions (see also Chapter 13).

> To comprehend governance issues in modern societies, the division of societal interactions in different types (interferences, interplays and interventions) is a major analytical tool.

Interferences

Interferences can be seen as the interactions forming the 'primary' societal processes: to maintain a family, take care of the sick, produce or sell a product, teach a school class, play in a string quartet. The form and substance of these activities are in principle unlimited, and this principle also applies to the interactions in and around them. Technical, economic, social and cultural primary processes each have their particular style of direct interferences around them. One can systematically scrutinise such processes and generalise their characteristics into a feasible number of interferences and find out how these are distributed across or between societies.

Alternatively, you could start at the other end and differentiate societal domains such as state, market and civil society according to the occurrence of this form of interactions. Throughout this book I will predominantly follow the latter course. Although interferential interactions are basically the least organised kind of societal interactions, they also occur in quite formalised work processes such as in banks, public administration, or the judiciary. Patterns can be determined in the varying degrees interferences are deployed as societal interactions and the way they are structurally used as societal media. Comparing them (sub) sector by (sub) sector can contribute to our knowledge of the structural conditions and cultural traditions of primary interactional processes (see Chapter 6).

Interplays

Interplays can be considered as interactions with a typical 'horizontal' character. In principle there is no formal authority, domination or subordination within them. Interplays aim to reach goals by engaging actors in collective, rather than independent action, and on a generally equal basis. Although interplays can be found within organisations, from a social-political governance point of view, interplays between organisations require attention. The importance of interplays as forms of interaction can be attributed to the growing specialisation and differentiation of modern societies on the one hand and the need for inter-relations to counter these tendencies on the other. These tendencies occur in all societal sectors and levels, a fact of which Durkheim expounded upon. For governance, individuals interacting in interplays are interesting, but horizontal interactions between groups, organisations and other entities are more important. In these interplays, tensions between striving for individual and collective interests, always present in interactions, relate mainly to differences in organisational goals (see further Chapters 7 and 13).

Interventions

Interventions are the most formalised kind of societal interactions. They are interactions aimed at directed exertion of formalised influence, often with provisos attached. Interventions can be found in all sectors of societies, although public ones are the most conspicuous. A relatively simple way of conceptualising interventions is to take formal rules as the starting point. This not only refers to public rules, which are surrounded by, and based upon, carefully defined sets of procedures, usually expressed as rules themselves, but also to many of the interventionist kinds of interactions within and around private organisations, for instance those formalised in bylaws, instructions and formal procedures. They only bind those who explicitly agree to be bound by them, who thus accept these interventions in their behaviour, either individually or as a collective.

If we look at interventions as a 'one-way' relation between an intervening and an intervened entity (as is quite often the case in the literature on public interventions), we miss out on an important aspect; the interaction one. Interaction means a mutual relationship where entities influence each other. This also pertains to interventions, in which both the intervening actor and the object of intervention are bound. The relation between the structural level and the application of concrete interventions at the intentional level, become more apparent in interventions than in either interferences or interplays. Not only do actual interventions usually have a formal nature, such as rules and regulations, but also at a structural level, authorities are allowed to introduce and implement interventions. Indeed the relation between the two levels exists through sets of formal rules and regulations: 'rules to make and execute rules'. This is the consequence of the formalised character of interventions, and the guarantees surrounding them.

Types of interactions and modes of governance

Not only do these three types of interactions have a descriptive value in reducing the complexity of societal interactions, distinguishing them also has a two-fold analytical function: they can serve as a basis for defining differences between the societal institutions of state, market and civil society, and they can help in formulating qualities of variance between modes of governance. These subjects will be treated more extensively later in the book, here I will only introduce them.

We can say that in the state, the market and in civil society domains all three types of interactions can be found, but not in the same manifestations, proportions or mixes. So for instance in the state domain we find high proportions of highly formalised interventions, but an abundance of interplays and interferences are also apparent to a lesser degree. In the market domain the most common interaction will be interplay, although there is no lack of interventions as well, while interferences are also quite common. In civil society interventionist interactions are the least likely, and interferences and interplays dominate; interventions occur, but relatively rarely (see Chapter 10, and Part V).

The distinction between the three types of interactions is also important in relation to modes of governance: interferences to self-governance, interplays to co-governance, and interventions to hierarchical governance. They are the object of governing, but at the same time can be seen as forms of governance themselves; an interplay in a work situation is a form of work organisation that thus governs the activities of the workers. At the same time, probably at another level in the organisation and by means of co-governance, 'interplay as structure', and 'work-interplays' can be influenced. The same might happen at still another governance level, where interplays between representatives of trade unions and employers in a co-governance mode might result in 'horizontal' general agreements on how to co-govern interplays in the workplace. The exercise works equally when applied to interferences and interventions. This sounds complicated, but for a proper analysis of social political governance these 'layered' forms and interactions and modes of governance are not only facts of life, but analytical tools that cannot be neglected.

The dual character of the interaction concept itself, with its distinction between an intentional and a structural level, might also assist us. Intentional interactions do not take place in a void, but within their particular contexts or structures. This dualistic element of social-political interactions is also relevant when applied to the three disaggregated forms of them. The intentional level of interferences as the least organised dimension of societal interactions matches its structural dimension of governance, of self-governance. The same can be said for the intentional level of interplays: these forms of (highly) organised societal interactions – either in, or between, the market, the state or civil society – can be viewed from their structural features; this structural dimension of interplays will be called 'co'-governance. Finally, in the state domain we find highly formalised interventionist interactions (found also in the market). Following the above line of reasoning this structural angle on interventions will be designated as the hierarchical mode of governance.

> Governing actors have a choice of different types of interactions to participate in at the intentional level of governing interactions; by doing so they explicitly or implicitly contribute to the structural features of these types of interactions as modes of governance.

Conclusion

The survey presented in this chapter serves as an introduction to the interaction concept. Interaction is a central conceptual tool in my approach to governance, and aspects of it run as a *leitmotif* through all the chapters to come, forming a binding element between them. I have given interaction a prominent position for two reasons. First, because the basic assumption of this book is that all social-political-governance revolves around interaction. In fact the term 'social-political' is the expression of this assumption: without social governance there is no political governance, and without political governance no social governance. *Wisselwerking* between the social and political is the essence of the governance perspective. This first aspect of interaction as a central concept is related to a second one; that interaction is a means to deal with the diversity, complexity and dynamics of modern societies. In the chapters to come the interactive character of social-political governance will be discussed in relation to these three societal features, which will be summarised in the last part of the book. Therefore my first argument for the central place of interactions, and especially governing interactions, is a 'substantive' one: interaction as the concept to deal with the substance of social-political governance. Second, the importance of the interaction concept is an analytical and synthetic one. In the analysis and the synthesis of social-political governance as a subject of systematic inquiry interaction also plays a major role. Fortunately interaction, *wisselwerking*, not only has great substantive value, but also has turned out to be a concept of great analytical and synthetic power. Much of what I have brought to bear in this chapter, as an introduction to the concept, can be seen in this light. Its analytical and synthetic possibilities will slowly become apparent in the conceptual stages to follow, and – again – will be rounded off in the last two chapters of the book.

Two aspects of this first encounter with interaction can be mentioned in particular, because I will use them time and again throughout the book: the distinction between an intentional level and a structural level, and the distinction between three different types of (governing) interactions: interferences; interplays; and interventions.

The levels aspect of interaction, or 'structure-agency', takes up a broader discussion in the social sciences. By conceptualising interactions in two related levels, I make use of elements in this discussion, while giving an interpretation aimed at developing the governance perspective. As I hope to show in the book, this 'levels' distinction is a rewarding one. Analytically it offers an opportunity to draw attention to intentional and structural elements of governing interactions. As a synthetic concept its usefulness becomes especially clear in the relations between these two levels, and in the possibility to incorporate societal diversity, complexity and dynamics and governance in the approach.

The three types of interactions; interferences, interplays and interventions, play an important role in the way the perspective on governance can be defined. The distinction should also be seen as an intermediary and exploratory step in positioning governance within its societal context. The distinction is not intended as a step in designing a broad theory of societal interactions. It is an aid in creating some order in the great variety of social interactions, and it functions as a base to develop some ideas on modes of governance. Much of this is more an exploration than a definition. The value of the interaction concept and the way I cultivate it will become apparent in the chapters to come.

Notes

1 This chapter is partly based on Eeden van and Kooiman, 1995

2 Eisenstadt, 1989.

3 Turner, 1988; Ritzer, 1992.

4 Habermas, 1984, 1987; Campbell, 1996, pp. 14–19.

5 Whitmeyer, 1994.

6 Berger, et al., 1989.

7 Mayntz and Scharpf, 1995, pp. 9–51; Mayntz, 1999.

8 Crespi, 1992, esp. Chapter 1.

9 Classics are Dahrendorf, 1964; Kahn et al., 1964; Gross et al., 1964.

10 Giddens, 1984, pp. 25–26.

11 Jervis, 1993, pp. 25ff

12 Sewell, 1992, p. 1–2.

13 Gordon, 1978.

14 Giddens, 1984.

15 Burns et al., 1985.

16 idem, p. 107.

17 Bourdieu, 1991; Swartz, 1997; Calhoun et al., 1993.

18 Swartz, 1997, p. 104.

19 Ashby, 1958.

20 Rhodes, 1997, pp. 50–51.

21 Deutsch, 1963.

22 Etzioni, 1968.

23 Prigogine and Stengers, 1984.

24 Etzioni, 1968, pp. 95–96.

25 Simon, 1962.

26 Luhmann, 1982, 1984, 1995.

PART II

ELEMENTS OF GOVERNANCE

3

GOVERNING IMAGES

Governing is inconceivable without the formation of images. Anyone involved in governing, in whatever capacity or authority, forms images about what he or she is governing. Such images can be extensive in scope and based upon thorough analysis, but they can also be limited, and informed by personal experiences. Images can be clear and made explicit, or hover implicitly in the background. All sorts of inner and outer data can be part of a governing image: visions, knowledge, facts, judgements, presuppositions, wishes, goals, hypotheses, theories, convictions, and even metaphors or parables. In governing, images are often built on more or less implicit ideas of man and society. Those who govern social-politically are as prejudice-ridden as anyone else. When confronted with governing challenges, philosophies of life are at stake and emotions are also involved. Even implicit images govern those who govern. Governing images are always there; however, they can certainly be (re) created and changed. During image formation, governing challenges will be defined and formulated as governing issues. Information will be gathered, opinions will be collected and selected. In the governing process, images are the main frame of reference. Governing images and the way in which they are formed have an important, even decisive, influence on the unfolding of governing processes.

The importance of explicit image formation in governance is twofold. In the first place there is the contribution to effective governing. When images are made explicit, they can indicate where and how possibilities and limitations of dealing with situations involving governing can be found. Images are also the point of departure for the selection of governing instruments and taking governing action. By checking governing images and the processes in which these are formed, we can control and criticise them. Second, it is necessary to make images explicit in light of the legitimacy of governance. In image formation problems definitions are confronted with potential solutions, and opportunities are scrutinised, capacities assessed, and normative governance ideas raised, discussed and tested. This is the basis for their potential understanding and acceptance in democratic governance.

A basic assumption of the governance approach is that social-political governing in modern societies needs to be well-structured, open and flexible enough to cope, with among other things, their diversity, complexity and dynamics. Therefore, we need an image concept that conforms to these requirements. In this book, the outlines of such an input will be drawn. As always in the governance perspective, this starts with interactions. Image formation as an observation process for governing purposes comes about in the form of interactions. As in all interactions in this process we can ascertain an intentional and a structural level. In this case, the intentional level refers to actors who observe the governing phenomena they are confronted with, and on the structural level the social and cultural circumstances under which this observation takes place can be found. In the following section, the intentional level of these observing interactions will be discussed as presumptions, knowledge and learning. After that I address the structural level of image formation under the heading of factual and evaluative systems and their influence on governing. The relation between the intentional and the structural level in these image formation interactions is conceptualised as the public sphere. This is the arena in which governing images are formulated, discussed, tested and disseminated. It is also the arena in which governing images find their way in the daily practice of governing, and are moulded into broader issues becoming part of governance culture.

Assumptions, knowledge and learning

In image formation, information about social-political issues is transformed at the intentional level of governing interactions. Knowledge and learning are important inputs in this process. Learning is the conversion of information into manageable and transferable knowledge. For actors, perception and observation of governing subjects and objects never takes place in a void: there are always pre-visions, pre-images, shaping the perception of new governing information. In turn, new information also influences those pre-images. Governing images and pre-images contain factual and evaluative elements. Together these form subjective governing knowledge. As a (new) message enters the governor's mind several things can happen: the image may remain basically unaffected; the image may change in a regular way, or it may change more radically. The result depends on the internal consistency of existing pre-images.[1] Stability or resistance to change in governing images depends greatly on their internal consistency and arrangement, which contain logical and non-logical qualities. Image formation for governing happens in the (sub) cultures in which they are developed.

Governing images are created, sustained or changed by dialogical communication between governing actors within the broader context of governing culture or cultural spheres.[2] Their latent nature directly effects the quality of image formation. Unconscious image formation processes proceed according to their own logic.[3] Each new observation, conscious or latent, is appreciated for the effect it will have on already existing images. When the observer is not aware of the cognitive operations that precede the construction of meaning, and the new information is threatening the present images, the new information will be resisted, in the form of denial, suppression, displacement, or projection. If new information confirms already present (pre) knowledge or (pre) conceptions, the stability of the image will increase, and greater resistance against 'hostile' information will accrue. The image becomes, as it were, more self-confident. An image will only change drastically when new information is very penetrating and is repeated. Existing preconceptions and knowledge are decisive in observations. When one is unable or unwilling to examine images within them, the tendency to repeat a self-image will always be stronger than the opportunity to renew it. This points to the necessity of making governing images transparent in interactions. Traditionally, the knowledge acquiring process is usually excluded from observation in image formation, and a bias towards the products of the knowledge process occurs. However, in interactive image formation the act of observing is part of the experience.[4]

Assumptions

In the field of International Relations (IR), images and other types of belief systems (operational codes, cognitive maps) have played an important role in research and analysis. All of these focus basically on the same factor: the nature of the filtering device of existing beliefs concerning empirical and normative data.[5] Stereotypes are also part of such image studies because they are multi-dimensional phenomena; they are social constructions of reality in which individual as well as structural components play a part.[6] Studies dealing with presumptive images or other belief systems in IR, in particular those dealing with mutual 'enemy images' and associated spiralling processes, stress the re-enforcing nature of image formation. 'Negative' beliefs that parties in a conflict harbour against each other are treated as 'fact', and actors will always find 'evidence' to support their own negative beliefs. It is quite probable that because of the competitive character of much governance, the images governing actors employ in their interactions will be loaded with assumptions that must not be neglected. Because of the influence of assumptions in the formation of images, it is important that this kind of implicit knowledge is made explicit and controllable. For instance, self-reflection can be utilised to form a part of governing interactions, in which latent images, influencing the creation of new ones, become transparent. If new information isn't turned into knowledge, image formation will be stuck in presumptions.

> Governing actors actualise in their interactions conscious as well as unconscious, explicit as well as implicit, revealed as well as hidden, assumptions about the diversity, dynamics and complexity of the governed and the governing world.

Knowledge

A large proportion of image formation in governing centres around knowledge. The production and utilisation of governing knowledge can be seen as a vast social process in which not only scientists, political and other opinion leaders, but also 'ordinary' people play a role. During knowledge production and dissemination, misinformation and false knowledge also enter the frame. Enlightenment or confusion might be the outcome. Knowledge production proceeds along broad, diffuse and open-ended patterns of (both cognitive and evaluative) interaction, adding to factual and value elements in the images of those involved in governing. Knowledge is also a source of power, so there is great interest in obtaining insight in knowledge production and its distribution.

To make such processes transparent, distinctions between types of knowledge, between data, ideas and arguments, are useful. Each has its own arenas or communities of interactions, creating and handling special sorts of knowledge. The societal actors for *data* are usually specialists in academic or other professional circles. Each has its own methods or rituals that determine what is relevant and what is not.[7] Governing *ideas*, are mainly created and exchanged by people of mixed status at crossroads; interaction between governments and the academic or professional world in advisory roles is an example of this. These interactions are characterised by coping with uncertainty, as brokerage and as risk taking. Knowledge formation and utilisation as *argument* in governing is more 'political' because it involves reasoning and convincing others. This type of knowledge is usually created in public domains: either in explicitly defined roles, as between politicians and mass media commentators, or in less formalised arenas, as between members of 'advocacy coalitions'.[8] All these modalities of interactive knowledge creation and testing are of importance in the formation of governing images.

> Governing actors will determine the sort of knowledge they use according to the character of the interactions they participate in: data will be used in 'professional' interactions, ideas in 'creative' interactions and arguments in 'convincing' interactions.

Learning

Learning is the process in which information becomes knowledge.[9] Governance allows for mutual, interactive learning in image formation. Learning occurs in all aspects of governing, from practical problem solving, to institutional learning and learning at the 'meta' level of governance. Learning can take two forms, single-loop learning and double-loop learning.[10] Single-loop learning is considered to be learning of the common type, while double-loop learning is 'learning how to learn'.

Single-loop learning in governing interactions takes place when mismatches between intentions and results are discerned and corrected. Communication is aided in these interactions if participants are able to see the backgrounds, assumptions and aims of others. 'Learning does not take place among complete strangers. Informal contact and a strategy of "no surprises" establishes the level of interpersonal communication and the trust necessary for the recipients of new information to incorporate that information'.[11] In governing, logical reasoning, empirically verifiable facts, controllable experiences and interpretations open for discussion, are important single-loop learning elements. However, actors may also express different rationalities with high probabilities that different insights and perspectives are deemed irrational, thus blocking learning and communication in the formation of governing images.

Double-loop learning occurs when the basic variables and conditions that create disparity at the first level are identified and changed. Argyris argues that greater emphasis should be placed on double than on single-loop learning: 'Although single-loop actions are the most numerous, they are not necessarily the most powerful. Double-loop actions, i.e. the master programs, control the long-range effectiveness, and hence, the ultimate destiny of the system'.[12] However, that is easier said than done. Double-loop learning requires us to question and scrutinise fundamental assumptions and values. Such an exercise may be seen as threatening for governing actors, who may be inclined to evade or resist it.

Interactive learning is a process in which participants learn from each other and from each other's learning. For learning to become a permanent feature of the governance process rather than sporadic and *ad hoc*, second- and third- order, or meta-learning, is essential. In interferential forms of interactions, single-loop learning is relatively easy, but can be brief because of its spontaneous and informal character. Successful double-loop learning opportunities are not as easily achievable, but their likelihood is better in interplays because of their more organised and semi-formalised form of interactions. In interventionist societal interactions, beginning the learning processes may be difficult, but once introduced – especially the double-loop variety – they may become institutionalised. How learning proceeds throughout an institutional process as both a cause and effect and as a force shaping the change process itself is also an important governance question. Is the range of options broadened or narrowed as a consequence of learning? At first glance, one would expect the former, because learning is supposed to broaden our perspectives. However, as in the case of changes in scientific paradigms, learning may often have the opposite effect: we may discard what we already know.

> Governing actors wanting to change governing images, can choose between 'common type' learning with short-term substantive effects, or 'learning how to learn' affecting processes in which those images come about, with long-term results.

Factual and evaluative systems

Now turning to the structural component of image formation in governance: the term 'factual and evaluative systems' will be used to refer to this aspect of governing interactions. This term indicates rather well what I want to express, namely that facts and their evaluation usually are interrelated in systematic, collective representative ways.[13]

Images guiding governing always operate in contexts, varying from broad notions of what governing is to be done, to expectations in specific situations. What we have seen at the actor's cognitive level as resistance to new information also occurs at the structural level of image formation interactions. (Pre-) conceptions and (pre-) knowledge on governance can be considered to have systemic qualities. Factual and evaluative (knowledge) systems grow continuously and reproduce according to circular patterns structuring and typifying them. A living factual or evaluative system defines its own domain, and engages in interactions when the possibility of losing its identity are not at stake. Breaking through the resistance against the renewal of basic images in factual and evaluative systems can only be realised when their basic circularity is broken. Boulding argues that the only way this happens is by repeated penetrative interaction between the observing system and what it observes. The initiative for this interaction can only come from the observing system when it is consciously looking for a new information.[14] The accepted view is that over time recognition of factual changes in knowledge systems will erode long held opinions and new patterns of acceptance will appear. The same basic phenomenon will probably apply with even greater force in value systems. Testing them will not be based upon facts and counterfacts, but on convictions and counter-convictions. These often have even stronger basic circularities based upon hierarchical notions of what is true or false and what should or should not be done. As a result, we find that new value systems are built next to older ones, which are challenged rather than subject to erosion from within or from boundaries being broken at the margins, as is the case of knowledge systems.

From this short discussion of some notions impinging on the structural dimension of image formation processes, I conclude that in image formation as part of governing interactions, structural components might be even more important for governance purposes than at the intentional level. We know relatively more about the direct influence of images in governing interactions than about their systemic counterpart.

> Because of the self-referentiality and basic circularity of observation systems, knowledge and value systems can only be changed by penetrating and repeatedly challenging them.

Images and societal diversity, dynamics and complexity

A central assumption of this book is that the diversity, dynamics and complexity of contemporary societies can be reflected in governance. Therefore, it is important that these features also find their way in governing images and image formation processes.

Images and diversity

When examining diversity in image formation we investigate how those who govern and those who are governed are able to make their own images explicit, how by observing and comparing their images with those of others and their specific images, they integrate these in governing images when engaging in governing interactions. This has been phrased as 'management of meaning'.[15] Explorations in linguistics, cultural anthropology and the cognitive sciences have recognised a fundamental heterogeneity from the individual actor to larger cultural contexts such as temporary areas of consensus to be recreated in particular circumstances'.[16] We all continuously devise our own definitions of situations and form our own ideas about reality, these definitions form the basis for selecting, ordering and interpreting the diversity of our experiences. Management of meaning aims at establishing a link between, on the one hand, 'meaning' as making sense of a world as diverse in images as there is personal subjective knowledge, and on the other hand, activities within groups and organisations within societal sectors and societies at large. By managing meaning, actors involved in governing interactions will be able to cope with the diversity of the meanings of others in those inter- actions, and the claims this puts on them, being object of and subject to these interactions.

   Governing actors also construct shared or public images, informing each other about the ways in which information exchange influences their images. Images are constantly established, adapted and consolidated in governing interactions. Much, necessarily, remains in the background and is implicit, but certain aspects of the diversity of images in governing interactions will become shared with others. Hannerz speaks about 'flows' of collective socially organised meanings, culture as shared images in society. These 'flows' can also be applied to the sharing of the diversity of governing images. In cumulative and interactive processes people deal with other people's meanings, and by the interdependence of the social and the cultural, flows of culture are enacted and distributed. There are meanings and meaningful forms to which responses have to be made, and as these responses occur, or even in anticipation of them the diversity of culture expresses itself. Actors within interactions with other actors are constantly inventing culture or maintaining it, reflecting on it, experi- menting with it, remembering it or forgetting it, arguing about it, and passing it on.[17]

> Governing actors explicate, select, order and interpret the diversity of images by observing and comparing them with those of others in governing interactions. They integrate these as 'flows' of shared responses to existing images of governing issues.

Images and dynamics

The central question regarding images and dynamics is whether the obser- vations and the storage of images are flexible enough to represent social- political dynamics. Image formation in relation to dynamics concerns, in particular, tensions arising due to clashes of meaning at the inter-actor level, inconsistencies in the cultural context of governing interactions, or between the two levels of those interactions. Tensions and related strug- gles such as those between free and unfree flows of meaning form a large part of the dynamics of governing interactions and the image-formation taking place within them.[18] In developing a theory of cultural dynamics, Archer argues that we need to look at the interplay between ideas and interests or between 'people' and 'parts', and refrain from collapsing or conflating one into the other. She distinguishes between 'cultural system integration', referring to relations between components of culture (i.e. parts) from 'socio-cultural integration', which looks at the relation between cultural agents (i.e. people). She analyses cultural dynamics on the basis of mutual influencing between the cultural system and socio-cultural interaction.[19] Actors can exploit relative problem-free or problem-ridden clusters of beliefs, theories and ideas. On the cultural level this can be expressed in terms of sequences culminating in cultural elaboration or of negative feed-back loops that result in cultural reproduction.[20] These theoretical notions are in line with my endeavour to conceptualise the dynamics of image formation processes in terms of the tensions between the different levels of governing interactions.

In the flexibility of governing images the dynamics of governance culture can be expressed.

Images and complexity

How can complex relations between elements of governing situations be represented and ordered in governing images? Image formation is always a reduction of complexity; how, then, do we prevent such reduction from becoming unacceptably simplistic in the context of image formation? Often such reductions take place through latent mechanisms, but if we want this to happen in a more formulated manner, the image formation process itself must be governed. Thinking about the role of complexity in image formation should not start at the actor's level, but at the structural aspects of this process, because an actor won't make a great effort to look for essential aspects of complexity. This is contrary to diversity, where the basic phenomenon is the uniqueness of individual actors to give meaning to, and make sense of, the world they live in on whatever scale or place or in whatever time span. Complexity – according to Luhmann – is in the world and the only thing we can do is make the best of it, or in my terms: reduce it to a sensible and, in matters of governing, responsible manner (see Chapter 12).

But how does this apply on the level of governing actors: how do they cope with complexity? DiMaggio argues that the memory stores culture in relatively unorganised ways. The question then becomes one of how actors organise the general cultural information he or she possesses. Research points to two quite different processes or cognitive modes. The first can be referred to as automatic, the second as deliberative cognition. In the first, schemata play an important role: knowledge structures that lend a rather precise insight in the way culture shapes and biases human thought. The second mode shows that people can override such programmed modes of thought to think critically and reflectively.[21] In image formation we are always searching for ways and means to organise our mental schemes as close as possible to social and political reality.

> Because of the complexity of modern societies, governing images will always be incomplete. Only interactive governance will be able by comparing different methods of reducing it to conquer this basic limitation.

The (social-political) public sphere

Governing actors with individual or group images interact and communicate with each other, based on their respective ideas on governing issues. These communicative interactions do not take place in a vacuum, but usually are structured. Some of them are highly organised and formalised such as those between governments and interest groups; others are much less formal as with discussions between groups and associations with a civil society character. All of these communications and meaning-creating interactions on public or governing issues can be deemed as taking place within the 'public sphere'. The public sphere can be seen as the domain or arena in which societal images on governing issues are formed, discussed and tested. Indeed, that public as well as private actors participate in this communication, it might be called the social-political public sphere. This section begins with a discussion about some aspects of communication, followed by a look at the (social-political) public sphere and the role of the media in it.

Communication

In image formation processes and structures, as in governing interactions, communication is a central concept. Theoretically, 'interpretative' as well as 'mechanistic' views on communication can play a role.[22] In the interpretative view elements such as language, meaning, interpretation, sharing, and ambiguity play a role; in the more deterministic view elements such as channels, networks, flow, measurement, and cognition are the concepts in use. In conceptualising governance, communication can be seen as a mixture of these theoretical orientations. In the recursive process of administering attention between the actor and structure component of governing interactions, emphasis will shift between them. There is a trend in communication thinking towards a convergence, of seeing communication primarily as an informative process first effecting what we know or think, and only after this how we feel or behave. Along with McQuail, I favour a view of communication as a complex network of interactive relationships whose understanding is a necessary condition of 'successful' communication.[23]

The public sphere and image formation

Although in liberal democratic societies there is no lack of opinion formation on social-political problems and opportunities, actual, interactive, participation in these processes is another matter. Images of social-political issues occur in relatively arbitrary processes, strongly influenced by specialised political and social forces, in which the media also play a role. Systematically organised image formation processes on (major) social-political problems and opportunities are much more scarce. This is unfortunate because in many cases such an (early) image formation process would signify an open public effort to bring fundamental issues to the surface, without the necessity for consequent social-political action. An active social-political public sphere is a basic condition for such an endeavour. The notion of the public sphere, as originally conceptualised by Habermas, has become an important component of social and political theory. For image formation in the governance perspective the availability of a 'forum' that is accessible to as many people as possible, where a large variety of social experiences can be expressed and exchanged, is of the utmost importance, as is the confrontation of these diverse opinions and views on a rational basis, so that insight can be gained into political alternatives.[24] Like Habermas I feel that the media play an important role in offering the widest possible range of interpretive frames for these discussions. To understand the working principles of the public sphere we must focus on the interactions between the actor and the structural level. We should not only look at institutional arrangements within the public sphere, but also at the top-down-bottom-up movements within it. The public sphere can be considered as a highly complex, dynamic and especially diverse field with constantly shifting boundaries between public and private, being the outcome of social-political forces. This view requires a broad discussion of the issues raised about the growing 'mediation' of the public sphere.

(New) communication media not only establish or facilitate forms of interactions, they also create new forms of interactions, on the actor as well as on the structural level, and mediate the tensions between the two.

The most important change for communication in the public sphere is that exchange of information and symbolic content has become less and less dependent on spatio-temporal settings as mediated communication. This might mean the need for a new definition of what we consider the public sphere and its interactions.[25] This allows for a distinction between three types of communicative interaction: face-to-face (non-mediated), mediated, and mediated quasi-interaction. Participants in mediated communication do not share the same spatio-temporal setting. They use a medium such as a telephone or a letter to communicate. This limits the number and sorts of cues face-to-face interactions allow. Quasi-interactive forms of communication use mass media (books, newspapers, TV and the Internet), which have no specified participants and dialogues. This communication is only quasi-interactive, because it is predominantly one-way. However, it still ought to be regarded as structured interaction, in which information is disseminated. This distinction is important because communication in governing has increasingly followed the quasi-mediated forms, with the (mass) media in a dominant role. However, recent developments in communication by internet may bring back more mediated forms, enabling governors to communicate directly with their constituents and vice-versa.

All these different forms of communication, their conditions, possibilities and changes, form the essence of the public sphere. Understanding it becomes more and more a subtle process, requiring familiarity not only with its institutional nexus, but also with relevant discourses in the media and political involvement in it.[26]

> Only in a public sphere characterised by direct communication and dialogue can representative images about societal diversity, dynamics and complexity be established, serving as frameworks for the choice of effective governing instruments and legitimate governing action.

The role of the (mass) media

The mass media play an important, if not the most important, role in the public sphere as the major arena in which image formation is played out in modern governance. This role can be seen as a communication process involving the viewpoints of a provider and a recipient. At the provider's side are media such as newspapers, radio and TV stations, and the internet, with their commercialisation, localisation and globalisation tendencies and their influence on image formation in governance. Moreover, role conceptions of professional communicators (journalists, spin-doctors) and the autonomy of, or constraints in, media-land define and influence the social-political public sphere and its boundaries. At the provider side of this process, professional communicators fulfil the actor level role of this type of interaction. The technological and commercial developments of the media are their structural constraining or enabling conditions. Neither the dominance of the mainstream media can be ignored nor their homogeneous or monolithic character.[27] On the recipient's side are readers and listeners with ideas about their roles as participants in this communication process.

Modalities of communication play a crucial role in developing a public sphere concept in which the relations between communication senders and receivers form the basis of image formation for governing. The term 'quasi', introduced earlier, indicates that in the relation between the 'producers' of communication and their 'recipients' the concept of interaction can still be applied but only with certain restrictions. In cybernetic terms this centres around the question of feedback: does feedback take place at all, and if so how? Communication theory stipulates that on both sides of communication processes is the assumption of an active component – although this may be latent and thus the feedback or reciprocity may be implicit.[28] This means that with the use of mass media, active communication in principle can take place, but does not in reality. Factors on both sides of the mass communication process can bridge this gap between intention and realisation. One, rather sophisticated, analysis of this shortcoming states that there are passive as well as active elements on both sides in the interaction.[29] The communicator is active in the selection and the mode of presentation of information. He or she is passive due to taking the effects of the communication and the influence of all the conditional factors for granted. The recipient is passive in selecting information presented to him/her and in handling the information supply in a habitual manner. He or she can be active in developing selection criteria and integrating information presented. This approach can be seen as the effect of an interactive media process between media messages on the one hand and recipient expectations on the other.[30]

Media theory provides two ideal types in the discussion on this issue: the 'pluralist' and the 'domination' perspective.[31] The latter has the following characteristics: media control resides in the hands of an elite or a ruling class; ownership is highly centralised and controlled by a relatively small coterie of interests; the selective view of the world present in the media is controlled from above, thus they represent and reinforce the dominant interests in society. The selection results in a limited range of 'undifferentiated' viewpoints, where the alternatives are filtered; the critical capacity of the public at large is reduced; and thus conformity to the established social order reigns.

The pluralist ideal model stresses more or less the opposite. Media power is institutionally constrained and open to competing political, social and cultural interests; the media system is open to change and democratically controlled; media output is seen as a cultural good free of coercion and censorship thus representing a range of diverse and competing views.

In practice the existing media structures in liberal democracies exhibit a mixture of both, with the pluralist model as the 'ideal', while certainly some interests will exert more influence than others, either economically, politically or culturally, as the dominant model predicts. In a pluralist perspective the ever-present tendencies towards such traits of dominance have to be resisted, either through strengthening competition, increased regulation, by media policies and by journalist and editorial codes of conduct.

In these days when there is much talk of revolutionary changes, the new information technologies and their impact on the media certainly are a source of dynamics. Technology has always had a major influence on mass communication: print, radio, TV and now ICT (information and communication technology). The social and economic acceptance and use of these new media seems to be overwhelming, the consequences for governing are not yet clear. Optimists expect that this influence will be revolutionary in terms of the opportunities for interactive communication; others remain somewhat more sceptical at this point. However, it is clear that at the level of inter-personal and inter-organisational communication changes of scale are already taking place. Structurally, the globalisation tendencies of this 'revolution' are of great importance, with all the usual (partly speculative) inferences about certain causes and certain effects: what came first and with what kinds of short and/or long term effects. The boundaries between actual and virtual reality are becoming hazy and 'cyberspace' will provide all kinds of new governance problems and opportunities, such as matters of privacy (first-order governing), but also institutional design (second-order governing), and meta questions of values, principles and norms of governance.

Although in principle the media are located within civil society, there are quite clearly overlaps with the other two sectors in society, the market and the state. Mass media are usually owned by private companies, although non-profit foundations are also found. As such the rules of the market, including competition and profit making, or at least not loosing money permanently, apply to and influence the media. The other inter-connection is media's influence on market parties. Companies are sensitive to what is published about them, and many have media strategies as one of their standard areas of operation. The same – or even more so – can be said about public authorities. The sensitivity of public bodies and officials, in particular political ones, to the power of mass media in shaping opinion is commonplace. The influence of media agencies and media strategies is increasing: spin-doctors are the latest additions. This is definitely a case of inter-penetration, the consequences of which – at least hypothetically – add to the complexity of governance. Furthermore, in the opposite direction, the state increasingly can be seen to penetrate the media sector. There we find regulating measures to assure diversity, but also the seemingly diminishing tendencies of parties to 'own' their own mass media and use them as essential parts of their aspirations for governance: critical while in opposition, or as support agencies when in office.

> The less direct interactions between governors and governed are (and hence the communication between them) depends on (mass) media, the more important the mediating, instead of the quasi-mediating, role of these media becomes for image formation in governance.

Conclusion

In this chapter I have outlined the contours of the first of three elements of governing: images, instruments and action. All three are important analytical and actual components of governing and governance. Governing images may be the most important of the three from an interactive governance point of view: not only does interactive societal governance depend on – at least partially – shared images, the way they are formed is in itself interactive governance. However, images-in-governing are not stable and clear-cut pictures. Governing images can have stable and well-founded aspects to them, but they are also made up of presumptions, hidden values and false knowledge. That is why in this chapter attention was first paid to some of the major components of governing images. One must also be aware of actor and structural components and the relation between these in interactions where governing images are formed. The way governors and governed think is embedded in broader patterns of fact and value systems, which are difficult to reveal. Revelation occurs only when those participating in governing question their own perceptions and engage in self-reflection or reflexive thinking, and by doing so are able to challenge existing and dominant views on governance. This is the binding element between the intentional and the structural level of interactions. Both these levels in the governance perspective are needed to gain a real understanding of the formation and qualities of governing images.

The only way to find out the often implicit qualities of images used in governing is to test them in interaction, as happens in the social-political public sphere. This testing is of particular importance when we take the diversity, dynamics and complexity of modern societal governance issues seriously, issues which are by themselves not easy to understand. More than one governing actor is, almost by definition, needed to get governing pictures 'right', or at least (partly) shared. In modern societies, it would be exceptional for all knowledge or insights needed to solve societal problems or create societal opportunities to rest with one actor, private or public. This is not to say that governing action always needs to be the responsibility of more than one actor such as in co-arrangements between them. This subject will be discussed later in the book. What I want to argue here is that all social-political images for major societal challenges usually can only be properly tested publicly in interaction. And this is what the social-political public sphere is about: the communication forum where implicit images are made explicit and explicit images are tested for their relevance for issues at hand.

The intentional component of this communication is expressed in actual debates, such as: who is participating and who is left out; how persuasive do arguments remain in exchanges taking place; are participants able and willing to learn, or willing to learn how to learn? The structural view looks at the contexts that enhance or restrict image formation for governance: how open are channels of communication; who 'owns' these channels, and can suppression of knowledge or other insights be expected; what does penetration of state, market and civil society mean for an open and active public sphere? The notion of an open and active social-political public sphere is an ideal one, which in reality, would clearly present limitations in actual image formation for governance. Possibilities and limitations on the intentional as well as the structural level of interactions in the social-political public sphere will have to be taken seriously, if we want to get the picture right and focus on the qualities of the images used in modern governance. That is what I have tried to argue in this chapter.

Notes

1 Boulding, 1956, esp. Chapter 1.

2 Fornaess, 1995, esp. Chapters 3 and 4.

3 Van Eeden, 2001, esp. Chapter 4.

4 Van Eeden, 2001, pp. 72–74.

5 Smith, 1988, esp. Chapter 1.

6 Berting and Villain-Gandossi, 1994; Berting et al., 1997.

7 Radaelli, 1995.

8 Sabatier and Jenkins-Smith, 1993.

9 This section is adapted from Jentoft et al., 1999.

10 Bateson, 1972; Argyris, 1992.

11 Rist, 1994, p. 202.

12 Argyris, 1992, p. 10.

13 Berting, in press.

14 Boulding, 1956, esp. Chapter 1.

15 Smircich and Morgan, 1982.

16 Gastelaars and Hagelstein, 1996.

17 Hannerz, 1992, Chapter 1.

18 idem, Chapter 4.

19 Archer, 1988.

20 idem, p. xii.

21 DiMaggio, 1997.

22 McQuail, 1994.

23 McQuail, 1984, pp. 236–237.

24 Habermas, 1989.

25 Crowley and Mitchell, 1994, Chapter 1.

26 Dahlgren, 1991, p. 19.

27 idem, p. 9.

28 Burkart, 1998, p. 62.

29 Früh and Schönbach, 1992.

30 Burkart, 1998, p. 241.

31 Curran, 1991; Humphreys, 1996.

4

GOVERNING INSTRUMENTATION

Images, instruments and action are highly connected, and instrumentation can be considered the linking pin between the other two governing components. Selecting an instrument is close to forming an image; using an instrument is close to governing action. This link-pin role in itself is an argument for conceptualising governing instruments not as separate tools from a tool-kit, although the metaphor is a felicitous one, but as devices in a context, as crafts applied to jobs at hand within the context of craft cultures and craft institutions.[1] In the literature the question of the 'metaphorical' character of the use of the concept 'instrument' is on the agenda, as well as its connotation with a 'mechanistic worldview'.[2] Certainly, governing instruments are not the neutral media the toolkit metaphor suggests. To the contrary, there is always battle and conflict around their design, choice and application.

Using an instrument in governing practice can usually be recognised without much effort, the resources from which to draw instruments, are more difficult to assign. The variety of instruments used in governance is almost unlimited, and will vary from 'soft' ones such as information and advice to 'hard' ones such as taxes and regulations. Not all actors can apply all instruments, this depends on their governing position, and their willingness or ability to apply instruments they potentially can bring into action from the resources they possess. Actors in interactions judge and interpret the use of instruments in the context of the resource base at stake.

Societies and their governors, public, semi-public or private have developed an enormous array of instruments to influence societal interactions. Some of these have a wide application, such as general rules, involving almost everybody in governance, others are quite specific governing interactions, and directed at one individual or enterprise, a grant or a licence for example. Some have a highly formal quality as laws, treaties, appointments and decorations, others have a much more informal character: oral agreements, paying a visit, or making a speech are examples here. Some are accepted in one part of society and not in others: sending a gift is quite acceptable in the private sector, but not so in the public one. This reservoir of instruments is such that some may pass into disuse, and some may be replaced by new ones. All governing instruments have their own supporters with vested or developing interests in them, as well as opponents who are willing to emphasise their shortcomings and resist their application. Instruments may become goals in themselves, making it even more necessary to discuss them in relation to the governing interactions they are part of.

A governor needs an instrument or set of instruments to move from one state of affairs to another. This applies to public as well as to private governing. In public governing, because of the binding character of instruments and because of the nature of the sanctions attached to them (sometimes even of a physical nature), employing them is traditionally couched in all kinds of formal restrictions. This practice has spilled over to other societal institutions, so in the private sector the application of governing instruments can be surrounded with formal guarantees of all kinds, sometimes with a mixed public-private character. Most often a particular instrument and the way it is used can easily be recognised as being public or private, however sometimes this distinction becomes blurred. For example, professional rules and codes are sometimes private arrangements, and sometimes they are backed up by public support and get a mixed status (see Chapter 6). There are also 'new' instruments, like the covenant (an informal and specific agreement between public and private actors) and certification (an independent proof of capability or quality) developed at the borderline between public and private calling for discussion about their role and status.

In this chapter I will focus on the intentional level of interactions in selecting and using governing instruments, although the structural characteristics of these interactions remain in sight. I call these structural aspects of instruments resources. All governing instruments derive from the broader societal base from which they are selected: information from a knowledge base, subsidies from a financial base, and regulations from a juridical base. The distribution, availability and access to governing instruments from these societal resource bases are important subjects of governing, and thus of interest in governance.

The chapter starts with a general discussion on how instruments and their resources can be conceptualised as governing interactions. This is followed by a review of three instruments generally used in societal governing, information, organisation and rules, and their relation to the three sorts of societal interactions I distinguish, interferences, interplays and interventions. The chapter ends with some observations about the link between governing instruments and the diversity, dynamics and complexity of modern societies.

Instrumentation as interaction

The usual approach in the literature on instruments is to ask questions of a typological nature, of the kinds of instruments and effects to be expected. The circumstances or contexts in which instruments are applied have recently been receiving attention. In the governance approach such contexts are considered relevant, as can be witnessed in the analysis of instruments in relation to images and actions. This approach means disagreements about what a particular instrument or what a particular action pattern or image might be can be avoided. For example argumentation in a governing interaction can be called an instrument, but one could also say that argumentation is instead a form of image formation, or even an action.[3]

Making a distinction between choice and use aspects in instrumentation comes close to a process model of policy-making, of which instruments are an element. These models differentiate phases of decision steps, such as preparation, formalisation and evaluation, and each of these stages has something specific to say about the way they influence instruments. Though my use of the terms selection and use is somewhat akin to this, I prefer dealing with them not as stages in a process, but as forms of interactions, the central concept chosen for this book. So we discover special types of governing interactions around the selection of instruments, and we find such interactions directed at their use and implementation. Conceptually, the choice and use of instruments occurs at the intentional level of governing interactions. The resources they are drawn from are relevant at their structural level. Governors will start looking for an appropriate instrument in a governing situation among those they, generally speaking, can dispose of from an available resource: a regulation from the juridical source, a subsidy from the financial base, a plan or an information campaign from a knowledge resource. They will organise the interactions needed to select one or more of these accordingly. There is always a relation between the wish to choose a certain instrument and its availability at the resource level. If there is no legal basis, choosing a particular administrative measure will be difficult; likewise, if there is no knowledge, the choice for information or planning as governing tools will be difficult. If this is the case, the governor, public or private, can move to another governing level: the governing effort can be directed at the creation of room at the resource level (second order governance), enabling the use of a particular instrument (first order governance). For example, the governor can spend energy in increasing income as a resource, or bring a general law about as a legal resource base. But the governor can also go a step further, putting effort into the creation of a normative base for strengthening a particular resource, or favouring the use of certain (sets of) instruments (meta governance). Debates about a 'regulating' or an 'enabling' state point in this direction (see Chapter 8) and – as will be understandable – choices such as these require different kinds of governing interactions. In the step from first to second order governance, and in the step from first or second order to meta governance, the governing horizon becomes broader, as does the scope of those involved in the interactions connected with these steps. This highlights the intricate and important relation between the selection or choice of governing instruments and the resource base they can be extracted from.

Often, preferences for instruments are due to habit and insufficient knowledge about, or experience with other ones. Inventing a 'new' governing tool will be the exception, deploying one or more from an existing set is the rule, although at the boundary between public and private we find experimenting with new instruments, of operationalising new patterns of interaction between state and society. This lack of knowledge of existing instruments, and lack of fantasy in bringing new governing devices into operation, does not only refer to basic political or ethical questions and problems with instruments, but also involves practical aspects, for example the effects of instruments in their implementation or side-effects they may display. For a long time the general conviction in public circles was that once an instrument, such as a law, had been passed by a legislative body, the major work had been done. Implementation would follow as a matter of fact. However, it has become increasingly clear that the implementation of laws and other public instruments is usually more difficult than assumed, and surrounded by all kinds of uncertainties. In implementing instruments matters are at stake other than those an instrument is aimed at, other actors come into play, and other sources of resistance have to be overcome, i.e., other types of governing interactions unfold than those typical for choosing an instrument.

Ceteris paribus, comparable issues will present themselves around the choice and implementation of instruments as governing elements in the private sector. In light of their large number of social-political governing tasks, the state has developed a wide array of instruments to influence citizen's behaviour.[4] In comparison those of the private sector are more limited, although even private organisations have many behaviour influencing tools at their disposal, but these serve mainly self-governing purposes. Public bodies have a much broader radius, as a result the public array of instruments has become so varied.

One can also ask what kind of interaction a governor seeks to create, or in what kind of interaction he or she wants to participate, and what instrument fits this choice. Here, selection criteria for such interactions are of time, risk and uncertainty, the choice of a general or specific form of interacting, of problem or opportunity orientations with varying diversity, dynamics and complexity dimensions attached to them. When a governor wants to be certain of a specific effect in a governing interaction, choosing a more deterministic instrument is appropriate. In such a case he will be well advised to select an instrument where the relation between goal and the desired effect is linear and direct, for example, a strict regulation.[5] More probabilistic instruments fit with other governing interactions, for example when a governor is more involved in goal seeking than in goal setting, and is uncertain about what the effects of an applied instrument might be, then information, advice or a subsidy might be the better instrumental choice. The more formal the governing interaction inherent in the choice of an instrument, and the more sanctions attached to it, the better interactive governing behaviour can be predicted, because of the procedural guarantees built-in in the instrumentation process. This is the prevailing course of action in law-making as a governing inter-action. The choice for a covenant as instrument implies quite a different, less certain, pattern of governing interactions. The principle of 'bounded rationality' may apply here: on the basis of information available, the presence of alternatives and weighing of these alternatives, addressees will follow a rule or accept an incentive. Within the constraint of bounded rationality the effects of an instrument might be predicted.[6] The relation between the availability and choice of an instrument and its interaction effects, (or vice-versa), will be discussed in more detail in the next section of this chapter.

When thinking about choosing an instrument or a combination of them for a particular sort of interaction, governors need to know on which instrumental resources to draw. What kinds of resources are available? Can such resources be refilled at will? Is a resource unique or can it be replaced by another one? How central is a resource in a society, and how is it distributed society wise? These questions are more easily put than answered. The search for answers on these aspects of the resource base of social-political instruments is in line with the growing interest in the 'contingent' aspects or 'contextual' approach to policy instruments.[7] Theoretically it is interesting to start the exploration of resources by exam-ining which instruments can be drawn from a broad societal perspective. If a governor wants to make use of a legal instrument for his or her governing effort what does the legal infrastructure look like that explains why a certain type of law can or cannot be chosen and what kinds of legal, – or maybe socio-political – legal properties can account for such a choice or non-choice? Or if a public or private governor opts for a com-municative instrument for the kind of interaction he or she has in mind, what kinds of societal characteristics promote or hinder the choice and application of such instruments? Large bodies of specialised literature exist on qualities of instruments, but not much is known about the quali-ties of the resources in which they are embedded, or the societal context in which an instrument will work one way, and in another context in another way, or not work at all. In the next section I will begin to answer some of these questions by relating three kinds of governing instruments to the three types of societal interactions.

Governing actors can choose from existing instruments for the short term, create new ones from an existing resource base for the medium term, or they can spend their governing energy developing new instrumental resource bases for the long term.

Instruments and varieties of interactions

To start systematising the use of instruments in societal and governing interactions and their contexts, I shall use the three major forms of interactions ascertained, interferences, interplays and interventions. In those three forms of societal interactions the distribution of instruments available, and the use of them, is unevenly spread. In interferences instruments with a less formal character will dominate; in interplays we will find semi-formalised instruments being applied, and in interventions instruments will be of the most formalised character. This is not to say that in interventionist interactions we will not find informal at all, *ceteris paribus* for the other forms of interactions, but they are not the most characteristic for them. We also might turn the argument around and assume that the use of a particular instrument or set of them, characterises different forms of interactions; an element of their definition, as it were. For the sake of clarity – amidst the use of other instruments – for interferences information is the most characteristic instrument; for interplays organisation assumes priority, while interventions require foremost the application of rules. These three instruments, widely applied in governance, but unequally distributed across the three modes of societal interactions, will be discussed in the following sections.

> For goal-setting governing interactions more formalised instruments fit; for goal-seeking governing interactions less formalised instruments will do.

Information and interferences

The exchange of information and the transmission of meaning is, according to Katz and Kahn, the essence of every interaction. But there are limits to this: lower limits when interactions are under-utilised as communication channels, as well as upper limits when over-utilisation threatens to overload them. Governing interactions are, as are all social systems, limited communication networks. Information as a governing instrument presupposes selectivity – avoiding noise, and specificity – avoiding loss of meaning.[8] This is of particular importance for inferential societal interactions, because of the fluidity of their communication circuits. In interferential interactions, because of their informal nature, it is essential that participants know what others are doing. Because of the relative unimportance of organisation and rules in interferences, the process of providing and receiving information is the key to the progression of these interactions. In principle, governing an interferential interaction is guiding the exchange, interpretation and internalisation of information between those interacting. This is not as simple or as neutral as it may look: in interferential interactions not only is the behaviour of the internal actors uncertain, unpredictability is itself part of the environment. Governing interactions thus have an important role in reducing this uncertainty, in making interactions more predictable. Feedback, in its positive and negative forms, is the basic mechanism for influencing such communication and information processes. For interferential interactions complex feedback processes are needed where information on preferences, priorities and the governing decisions about them are communicated and disseminated.[9]

As such, we might say that governing in interferential interactions both: enhances the certainty of the behaviour of those participating in them by regular feedback; and reduces external unpredictability by governing filtering processes common for self-organising entities. This implies, that a minimum of organisation and rules follows information as the major governing instrument of interferential interactions.

There are many things happening at the structural level of information as a governing instrument: there is even talk of an information 'age', an information 'revolution' or an information 'society'. Notwithstanding the undoubtedly rapid advances in information technology and the accompanying rhetoric about its promises, the question of how fundamental these developments are for modern societies as a whole, and consequently also for governing interactions, is still unanswered. While the concept of an information society is gaining influence, its content is not as clear as one would think at a first glance.[10] First there is the view that its importance can be seen in particular in the work it creates; a second opinion stresses the exponential growth in information flows; and a third characterisation is given in terms of technology. Societal interferences will most likely be influenced by all three notions of the information society: in terms of work patterns, in terms of increasing flows of information, and, in a – at least partly – 'computerised society', as a condition of the other two.

Interplays and interventions, the two other major categories of interactions have instruments other than information at their disposal that are more important to their functioning. Interferential interactions, because of their dependence on information as a governing tool, will probably be most affected by an information society, in whatever form this develops. Thus, the information society creates interesting and important governance challenges for information as a governing instrument at the intentional and at the structural level of governing interactions, especially interferences. For the information society, considered as a process, this can already be seen in the discussion about its regulation or self-regulation. At the provider's end censorship, access and responsibility are relevant and at the recipient's end aspects such as the right to receive or not to receive are debated. Naturally the channels themselves are also subject to private and public (governing) attention: substance, coding and decoding, noise, service, control and ownership.[11] From a governance perspective the protection of privacy of, and data for, actors in governing interaction deserves special attention.[12] All these aspects will influence governing interactions, particularly interferential ones, because of their dependence on information as their major governing tool.

> In interferences the volatile nature of information allows for rapid feedback to cope with internal uncertainty and external unpredictability.

Organisation and interplays

Ours is an 'organizational society'.[13] The capacity to organise systematically is considered one of the major resources in the development of modern societies. This organising capacity actualised in governing interactions can also be seen as a major governing instrument or tool. What organisations are or might be is easier put than answered. As with so many concepts used in social theorising, there are almost as many answers as scholars interested in giving them. In his widely used book *Images of Organization*, Morgan distinguishes eight of these images, each highlighting one aspect or school of thought analysing them.[14] Morgan's basic message is: organisations are what you want to see in them; in governing terms we might say, what you see them do. Because of the many-sidedness of the organisational phenomenon, one can pick and choose the aspects one wants to highlight. I will do this by relating organisations to governing interactions as interplays. To recap: interplays are a semi-formalised form of societal interactions with a mainly 'horizontal' character. What follows is a discussion about the intentional perspective of interplays, and of organisation as their major governing instrument, followed by some observations about their structural context.

Organisational forms with a 'horizontal' nature fit quite well into an operationalisation of interplay forms of societal interactions. Some decades ago scholarly interest in this area was mainly directed at inter-organisational relations; currently the focus is on looking at networks of organisations, somewhat different phenomena, but with comparable elements. There is an overwhelming amount of literature available on both: how they come into existence, how they operate, and how they may end. Both modalities, may be considered the most widely used forms of societal interplays. Inter-organisational relations are usually limited to a few entities; networks can be larger, but will also have a limited number of partners. Essential in their functioning is the tension between autonomy and interdependence. Interplays occur when organised actors realise that for the basic primary process(es) they are performing – and this may vary from the production of a commodity to delivering a social service – they share dependencies with others over a longer period of time. Concurrently they realise this insight has to be accompanied by a willingness to sacrifice part of the autonomy of the organisation itself, now deployed towards the common arrangement, of whatever type. This may happen on the input side (supplies needed), on the throughput side (common experiences), on the output side (shared markets or publics) and even on the feedback side (common evaluative concerns). Interdependencies such as these are translated into organisational forms of interplay interactions. This can be the case within the three societal domains of state, market and civil society, but increasingly we find them also between these domains (see Chapter 7). While organisation is the major instrument for governing interplays, it should not be seen as an exclusive governing device. Rules, to be discussed in the following sub-section, also play a role in the different varieties of societal interplays. Interplays can be interpreted as being governed by two sets of rules, interaction rules and arena rules. Interaction rules specify aspects such as access and forms of contact, with exclusivity, selection and exit possibilities as examples, whereas arena rules regulate aspects such as reality (identity and product), pay-off (status, evaluation criteria) and positions (competence).[15]

Recently developed ideas from 'New Institutionalism' are a useful source for looking at organising from a structural societal resource point of view (see also Chapter 11). With different emphases, the central argument in new institutional analysis is that many aspects or qualities of organisations can be explained by the institutional arrangements they are part of. Societal fields or sectors are such institutional arrangements, and their influence on organisations may be great, resulting in 'isomorphism', the tendency for likeness: banks, as part of a banking sector will tend to look organisationally alike, hospitals will tend to look the same organisation-wise after a while, and government departments will display isomorphism because parts of the public sector tend to have the same traits.[16] For governance theorising this might mean that interplay forms of societal interactions in the same sector will tend to show the same organisational characteristics. Also, at the boundaries of sectors, public-private partnerships end up showing the same characteristics: successful examples will be followed and failures discarded. This kind of inference can be made when we assume that the institutional frameworks such instruments are developed within share similar features. We can even broaden the structural conditions of societal interplays to societies in general. A classical example of this broad perspective is Stinchcombe's view on the 'organisational capacity of a society'. This capacity has as good as been adopted as conventional wisdom, varying with degrees of modernisation: 'wealthier societies, more literate societies, more urban societies, societies using more energy per capita, all carry on more of their life in special-purpose organisations while poor, or illiterate, or rural, or technically backward societies use more functionally diffuse social structures'.[17]

A governance aspect not to be overlooked is the role of organisations, and thus of inter-organisations and network organisations, in the distribution and access to societal resources. The emphasis in studies dealing with this structural aspect of organisations is often on their contribution to the rationalisation of productive and administrative societal resources, although the negative sides of this development receive greater attention: '… organisations are singled out as the source of many of the ills besetting contemporary society',[18] and as Wolin put it: 'all organizations are inevitably political in character, or conversely what is most politically significant in the modern world is contained in organizational life'.[19] It goes without saying that these theories will not have direct application in the search for societal factors opposing or enabling the creation of governing interactions, or in particular interplays. They indicate that a concept as 'a societal capacity to generate new organisational initiatives' can be used not only to help analysing structural conditions for such initiatives, but also to assist in phrasing hypotheses about their chances of success or failure as a governing instrument.

> In interplays organisational capacity is the answer to the tension between autonomy of the partners on the one hand, and the commonality of the partnership in the other.

Rules and interventions

Interventions are societal interactions with a highly organised and formal nature. They can be found in all sectors of societies, but the more generally constraining ones are under the competence of public authorities. This is because the process of preparation, formalisation and implementation of public instruments with an interventionist character is bound by all kinds of guarantees. This does not mean that interventions are not common in the market and civil society, they are, but they are less formalised and sanctions are usually less severe. As will be seen in Chapter 6 there are many forms of formalised self-governance, such as in professional fields where definite forms of interventionist instruments are available. Labour relations also engage many interventionist instruments. Civil society, where interventionist interactions are least common, also presents us with examples, such as in sport where they play an important governing role, sometimes with strong sanctions attached to them. However, this is qualitatively and quantitatively limited compared to the interventionist nature of much governing in the public sector. Therefore in this discussion the emphasis will be on interventionist instruments with a public nature, and in particular on rules and regulations.

Rules are everywhere and rule proliferation is even considered a major problem of modern governance. Fortunately most people, as private persons or as citizens, have only limited knowledge and little engagement in rules in general. This in turn may contribute to structural incoherence and even contradictions in their use for governance purposes.[20] Rules are prescribed guides for types of conduct and classes of action and an authoritative definition of them is as follows: 'a followable prescription that indicates what behaviour is obligated, preferred, or prohibited in certain contexts'.[21] Rules vary from informal, symbolic and even implicit ones such as good manners or etiquette, to formalised sets of decrees or regulations as in administrative, commercial or penal laws. Because rules, although they may be very general, are always directed at specific behaviours or actions, efforts have been made to classify them according to their specific role or purpose.[22] This is especially true of international arena type rules, and questions such as about the relation between rules and their moral quality, about why actors (such as states) comply with rules, and how rules come into existence, have been the subject of theoretical activity.[23]

Much can be learned from this work for governing purposes, and can with relatively little effort be adapted for specific areas of social-political interventions. As with the distinction between an intentional and a structural level of (interventionist) governing interactions and the relation between the two levels, the analysis of rules and sets of rules can be approached either from an actor perspective, from a structural one, or from the relation between the two. The more organised and formalised rules are, the more one can speak of rule systems, and the more it makes sense to approach them from a structural angle.[24] This is not to say that the way actors relate to interventionist rules is unimportant, but that approaching them analytically from the structural angle gives more insight in their specific qualities. Each societal sector has its own characteristic of rule making and rule application, which comes close to or can be defined as forms of institutionalisation. As we shall see in Chapter 10 even institutions are defined in terms of rules. Rules specify all kinds of aspects of interactions: who interacts with whom, for what purpose, how to enter an interaction or how to leave, how they might be changed, how complaints against them can be filed and processed, and how they will be evaluated. For interventionist interactions, especially when sanctions are attached, rules 'will define rights and obligations, including possible rules of command and obedience, governing specified categories of actors or roles vis à vis one another'.[25] Here – again – we can see how the interaction perspective is helpful, because all the elements as given in this definition (and in a later definition) can be observed for their interaction qualities at the intentional level, the structural level and in the relation between the two. Analysis can consider each of these different aspects of interventionist rules in isolation, and its use as a tool of synthesis will show structural-systemic qualities belonging to them, such as rule proliferation and rule density. Finally, the way in which rules constrain or enable actors in governing interventions, can be seen in all the diversity, dynamics and complexity of modern governance.

Apart from public instruments such as planning, finance and information, it is laws, decrees and regulations that, as varieties of public rules, are dominant and influential types of public interventionist instruments. But dominant does not always mean unproblematic. The ordinary citizen or member of an organisation will only encounter public rules in the final instance, when a permit is needed, when an offence has been committed, or tax has to be paid. Underlying such relatively simple rules – often of an implementation kind – a whole world of judicial work is hidden, covering all sectors of society and often in detail. Two structural aspects of rules as interventions are considered problematic. One is rule intensity within modern society, which means that judicial interventions become so widespread that no one has an overview of them anymore, and in many ways their effects become contradictory: what one rule regulates, is – at least partially – undone by another. Second is societal 'juridification'. This means that there is a tendency to regulate societal conflicts by juridical means. This has a self-perpetuating nature, not only complicating societal interactions, but also giving disproportionate weight to the juridical system in comparison to others. Problematic aspects of law-giving and rule-making receive more and more attention, and in spite of efforts to resolve these problems, results aren't impressive. In Chapter 8 some of these (problematic) issues will again be raised in discussion about the relation between interventions on the intentional level of governing interactions, and their structural component as hierarchical governance.

> The systemic nature of rule making in governing interventions contributes to the principle of 'diminishing returns' when applying them.

Instruments and societal dynamics, diversity and complexity

In advancing my ideas on governance in association with societal developments, the next step will be to conceive relations between governing instruments and the three central societal features, dynamics, diversity and complexity.

> Different instruments are likely to illustrate different qualities in coping with societal features: for dynamics flexibility is needed; diversity asks for accuracy; while for coping with complexity a combination of instruments seems necessary.

Instruments and dynamics

Dynamics has been defined in terms of tensions, such as between the wish to conserve an existing situation or interaction or to change it. Dynamics is also related to the often non-linear character of societal change. For governance instrumentation this means that instruments should be employed that can handle societal dynamics as expressed in tense and non-linear transformations. A signifier would be the potential capacity of instruments to manage such dynamic tendencies in displaying cybernetic qualities, i.e., instruments fitted with positive and negative feedback, feed-forward or feed-while processes (see also Chapter 12). Governing by feed-while means influencing developments as directly and quickly as possible, more or less with stand-by tools. Feed-while instruments of an organisational nature can, within limits, deal with dynamic processes.[26] Governing by feed-forward dictates that instruments should be able to cope with dynamical situations likely to take place in the future and assessable in advance. Many public instruments with long-term effects such as laws and planning are not expected to be effective in highly dynamic governing situations. Not only does their preparation take time, the probability is that once they are implemented something unexpected will happen, meaning additional measures will have to be taken, and so on. Also, insights into the reflexivity of social systems and individuals show that those to whom instruments are addressed will in due time learn how to evade, avoid and resist them. This in turn means that those applying the instrument will react to such reflexive behaviour, giving the whole process a certain dynamics of its own.[27]

The application of feed-back oriented instruments seems to be the most appropriate to cope with dynamics of governing situations. Flexible instruments that can be (relatively easily) adapted to unknown developments or unexpected events are the most appropriate in (highly) dynamic governing situations. Juridical instruments usually are not ideally suited here, but some, flexible ones like covenants and other instruments with a 'co'-interactive character will do a better job in dynamic governing situations.

Instruments and diversity

Diversity in modern society is not easy to cope with from an instrumental governing point of view. There is always a tension between treating citizens as equally as possible in governing, while also approaching them in as focussed a manner as possible. Although the first option is usually considered to be most appropriate on constitutional grounds, the second one has strong proponents as well due to pressures from special (interest) groups, lobbying for special measures for their members. In an instrumental governing perspective there certainly are advantages in diversified governing interactions for specific purposes, and they are often assumed to be more effective. However, forms of specialised and diversified social-political interactions and the instruments used in them can easily (a) become ends in themselves, (b) have a spiralling effect because other groups will ask for special treatments as well as reaction, and (c) stray from the constitutional principle: all equal before the law.[28]

From an instrumental governing angle three options are open. One is the more traditional approach where, based upon general principles enshrined in laws or other generic instruments, application of these rules is diversified for practical purposes. Administrative law is the best example of this. For areas where principles and practices are relatively simple and stable, dealing with diversity by fine-tuning, seems to be quite effective and legitimate. However there are limits to this way of coping with diversity: how far do you go, what do you do when situations change, how do you guarantee equality in the long run. A second option might be appropriate. This is to decentralise, or in European terms apply the subsidiarity principle: govern at the lowest level possible. There are many arguments in favour of this approach. The assumption that the closer to those effected by governing measures the more efficient and legitimate their application will be, seems to hold in principle. Furthermore this option is not only applicable to geographic lowest levels but also to sector-wise lowest levels. There are again limits to its applicability: the tension of ensuring 'equal treatment in equal situations' is quite obviously an important one; retaining an overview is another. A third option is to shift the emphasis in governance from the political to the social, in other words minimise the public element in governing, and rely on the self-governing capacity of societies, communities, groups or sectors. Instrumentally, deregulation and privatisation, management tools like performance indicators, or more generally, 'steering at a distance' have an association with promoting a self-governing capacity. Two disadvantages of this third option figure widely in the literature: how to deal with 'opportunistic' behaviour and how to deal with 'negative externalities'. To use this third option and to at the same time combat its unwanted effects, it is clear that a combination or mix of governing instruments is needed (see further Chapter 6).

Instruments and complexity

Of the three governing challenges, instrumentally considered complexity appears the most simple to deal with, yet it escapes most types of common sense solutions. Why simple? Complexity is such a basic feature of any approach to governance issues, that consequently it is entering the domain of 'images' rather than of 'instruments'. For a time it was thought that computers could do the job, overcoming limitations imposed by numbers, computing complex issues very quickly. They help in some cases, but in most important governance issues computers are incompatible with societal problem-solving. If we accept that dealing with complexity, as Simon has shown, is rather a question of intelligent composing and decomposing, according to the principle of 'nearly composability', we have to look for evidence of instruments being helpful: deducted instruments, as it were. This search can go in three directions: (a) 'trial and error' processes to become aware of neglected or overemphasised relations; (b) methodologies to reduce complexity in a 'proper' manner; (c) organisational instruments for pooling whatever is necessary: authority, knowledge, experience, creativity.

Instruments available for a 'trial and errors' approach are mainly procedural. Rules, procedures or agreements can be implemented following complex governing situations. Whenever it becomes clear that aspects are neglected or overemphasised in a governing situation a procedural step can be taken. Modelling is another deductive way of looking for methodologies that help to reduce complexity. A methodological example for governance might be called interactive modelling. These are methods that bring together a number of stakeholders who define in an interactive way what the dimensions and interrelations of a complex governing situation are, and what the effects might be of certain governing measures. This process is supported by a computer model, following interactively all the steps taken and clarifying the consequences of these steps.[29] Third, the most commonly practised instrument for dealing with complexity are co-ordination mechanisms such as matrix-organisation, project management, and its most recent addition, networks (see further Chapters 5 and 7). Finally, I want to emphasise that all these options are only partially doing the job. As said before, complexity is more a question of image and image formation than of an instrumental nature: complexity being primarily in the eye of the beholder.

Conclusion

In this chapter the selection and use of instruments – the intentional level of governing interactions – has been measured against the background of the resources they can be drawn from; the structural component of governing. Governing instruments are neither chosen or applied at random: many factors leading towards success or failure have and will have to be taken into consideration. Also, attention was paid to special instrumental qualities, and situations in which they may become apparent. All societies have at their disposal, the three main instruments of rules, organisation and information and some of these aspects have been discussed in detail. The embedding of instruments, either singular or related, is an important factor to be considered. Due to historical legacies instruments retain certain cultures: legal and administrative traditions are clear examples of this. As with all resources, their availability, accessability and cumulated knowledge of how to operate them, is what counts. Structural factors such as distribution of social, economic and technical capacities within a society can be decisive in the potentiality of having certain (categories of) instruments available and ready for use or not. Some say that information (technology) has such potentiality, and it cannot be denied that its availability and use for purposes of governance is not equally distributed in different parts of the world.

There is also the intentional and structural relation with the image and action component of governing. Image formation will often precede instrumental choice or may run parallel to it. Those involved in a governing challenge, either public or private, will bend to preferred options for the choice of particular instruments. Images with a short-term vision will lead towards the choice of easy-to-select, existing instruments. This in turn will play a role in the relation between the implementation of an instrument and the action component of governing. If support for an instrument is not overwhelming, its formulation might create space for varieties in implementation. Considerations such as these underline the relation between the three governing elements, images, instruments and action. At the intentional level of governing interactions the choice and use of instruments can often be seen as an arena in which aspects of both other elements are brought to bear, possibly influencing the result of these interactions heavily.

At the structural level I refer to resources as the embedding of instruments and as potentialities to draw from. The distribution of and access to such resources are major governance issues by themselves, which in the literature receive insufficient and only scattered attention. The discussion on the instrumental element of governance has to be broadened to include these structural dimensions. In the next chapter I speak about social-political capital, which has definite connotations with what in this chapter I consider resources. These remarks reiterate the fact that instrumentation has an important role coupling the other two elements, at both the intentional and the structural level of governing interactions. Normative and meta notions on governing instruments and their relation with governing images and actions will be taken up in Chapter 11.

Notes

1 Hood, 1983.

2 Ringeling,1983; Peters, Nispen van, 1998.

3 Ringeling, 1983.

4 Hood, 1983; Scharpf et al., 1976; Bressers and Klok, 1987; Bruijn de and Heuvelhof ten, 1991.

5 Schuppert, 2000, p. 138.

6 Bressers, Klok, 1987.

7 For examples: Peters and Nispen van, 1998.

8 Katz, Kahn, 1966, Chapter 9.

9 Deutsch, 1963.

10 Duff, 2000; Bellamy, Taylor, 1998.

11 Longstaff, 1999.

12 Raab, 1993, 1999.

13 Presthus, 1962.

14 Morgan, 1986.

15 Klijn, 1996.

16 Powell and DiMaggio, 1991, Chapter 3.

17 Stinchcombe, 1965, p. 146.

18 Scott, 1992, p. 4; Reed, 1992; Geus de, 1989.

19 Quoted by Geus de, 1989, p. 167.

20 Burns, Flam, 1987, pp. 374 ff.

21 Shimanoff, 1980, p. 57.

22 Arend, 1999.

23 Beck, et al., 1996.

24 Burns, Flam, 1987.

25 idem, p. 13.

26 Delden van, Kooiman, 1983.

27 Veld In't, et al., 1991.

28 Hood, 1976.

29 McGlade, 1999.

5

GOVERNING ACTION

In order for a social-political instrument, regardless of design or application, to work, the action element of governing interactions relies upon convincing and socially penetrating images and sufficient social-political will or support. Scharpf calls this *Durchsetzung*,[1] and I phrased this earlier as 'will power'.[2] A minister, a mayor, a trade union leader, a hospital superintendent, an industrial manager or a citizen as a social activist will try to influence a governing interaction in a specific direction. However, action is also a societal quality. The image of an 'active society' is a strong one, and well documented by Etzioni in his seminal book of that title. The active self is as a rule not an individual, but instead a number of persons who collaboratively activate their social grouping and thus alter their collective life and individual selves. There is much potential societal energy to be harnessed. To be active is to be aware, committed, and potent.[3]

In accordance with my general concept I see action of individual actors and entities in governing interactions as embedded in broader contexts within which these actions unfold. These actions themselves will have an impact on these contexts. 'In the literature there is a tendency towards overcoming the dichotomy of voluntarism and determinism in action theories, and, to interpret both action and structure as non-opposed but interdependent variables of a unique process. Although accounts vary, action and structure are now considered "as inextricably grounded in practical interaction"'.[4]

This chapter will demonstrate that governing action occurs at the intentional level of social-political interactions, while simultaneously societal circumstances limit or enhance such actions. I will begin with individual and collective action and introduce the concept of social capital, followed by the relation between the two levels in governing action in three operational areas: leadership and stratification as an expression of societal interferences; social mobilisation and social capital as expressions of interplays; and co-ordination and bureaucracy as expressions of societal interventions.

Action: actor and structure orientations

How do social-political entities such as individuals, public or private organisations, interest groups, social movements or other forms of collective action become activated in governing interactions? Although in the literature individual or collective forms of action dominate discussion, here, individually or collectively oriented approaches will be analysed, because I want the interactive notion of social-political action, on whatever level, to be the focus. Literature on social-political action predominantly deals with collective action through participation in political activities, the action of interest groups, protest movements and other social groups: action in micro or meso governing circuits, within macro contexts. Where does such action come from? Who acts and who reacts? What is action and what is reaction in the process of governing?

In democratically governed social-political systems, political governing often can be said to assume a more reactive character, while initiatives for action are often located in the social sphere. Political governing often lags behind societal actions, not only because of bureaucratic inertia, but also due to the majority principle in collective decision-making. Governing actors within civil society or the market can act much quicker, and can invest all their energies in a distinct governing question, providing they command enough support for them. Therefore much political governing can be seen as a reaction to actions of other societal actors. However, one has to be careful here: in diverse, dynamic and complex societies, or parts thereof, it is often not easy to ascertain whose action calls for whose reaction. Governing action and reaction are best seen as continuous and recurrent processes, where in a given circumstance one governing entity takes the initiative and in a following circumstance another does: governing as patterns of chains of action-reaction.

The often 'chaotic' nature of societal processes means that small incidents can have major consequences (the butterfly effect), and even non-action may develop – dynamically – into a crisis. Because of the complexity of modern societies where so many things are inter-related, it is more apt to speak of complexes of societal action than of collective action. And as modern societies are quite diverse, one has be careful in differentiating between types of action, from individual or small group activity to mass demonstrations, either spontaneous or well-organised. Thus, the traditional distinction between individual and collective action in modern governance is a hazardous one. Some recent theorising on social action attempts to overcome limitations inherent in earlier theory. Melucci notices three changes in the study of social action connected to three evolutions in the social sciences: (a) the development of macro-theories linking collective action to a systems analysis of 'post-industrial' or 'post-material' society; (b) the enormous growth in organisational theory and research, that conceives of organisations as being a field of resources, with an autonomous capacity of mediating between 'objective' constraints and actual organisational output; and (c) the development of cognitive theories connecting action to the capacity of actors to construct their own 'scripts' of reality, to influence each other, and to negotiate the meaning of their experience.[5]

> Interacting governing actors will choose individual action strategies in dynamic governing issues, collective action strategies in diverse governing issues and strategies of a mixed character in complex governing issues.

Social-political capital

The conditions in which social-political action are embedded can be focused upon if we concentrate on the structural aspects of governing action. Earlier this aspect was referred to as action potential, it is action that can be resorted to at a particular place and time.[6] Action potential could arguably be replaced by the concept of 'social capital' to express the structural level of governing action. To fit the governance approach, I will call it social-political capital, although its main analytical purpose is similar to what in some parts of the literature is known as social capital. Social capital as a research subject has been 'rediscovered', indeed Putnam's study on the relation between social capital and democracy has greatly popularised its analytical use as a normative concept.[7] Increasingly, it has been used to explain phenomena as varied as family support and social control,[8] and community capacity and social trust, to name but two.[9]

For my purpose, I will refer to two original sources, Bourdieu and Coleman, who are seen as 'godfathers' of social capital theorising.[10] In quite different ways both consider social capital a structural quality. Essentially, this structural interpretation of social capital involves seeing it as a societal resource that individuals and groups can draw upon and mobilise, depending on their particular situations. Both authors consider differential availability and access to such resources a significant topic, and I see it as a major issue in governance.

In Bourdieu's conceptualisation social capital is an actual and potential resource. This 'credit' is constructed and institutionalised by long term and durable relations through membership of groups and networks, in which members can access and receive the backing of the collectively owned capital, a credit in all senses of the word. The value of social capital depends on the connections that can be mobilised and the volume each of these connections possesses in its own right. Social capital can never be completely separated from the other kinds of capital Bourdieu distinguishes: economic, cultural and symbolic.[11] Elsewhere he acknowledges that social capital 'can take a variety of forms [and] is indispensable to explain the structure and dynamics of differentiated societies'. From examples Bourdieu is using it is quite clear that he sees social capital as closely connected to political capital and having 'the capacity to yield considerable profits and privileges ... by operating a "patrimonialization" of collective resources'.[12]

Coleman looks at social capital as an aspect of social structure facilitating individuals and groups to take certain actions. Social capital is partly fungible: a specific form of it may be useful in one situation, but not in another; it can be created, it has to be maintained and it may get lost. Its conceptual value is that it identifies resources that actors or actor groups can use to realise their interests, and also allows for resources to be combined 'to produce different system-level behaviour or, in other cases, different outcomes for individuals'.[13] Obligations and expectations, information potential, norms and effective sanctions, but also authority relations and appropriable social organisation and intentional organisation can be seen as 'direct investment in social capital'.[14]

For Bourdieu, social capital is a theoretical concept used to constitute individual identities and strategies, while Coleman employs it as an instrument in the rational calculation of self-interested agents. However, both consider social capital to be a structural resource with differential access and uneven distribution. This can be expressed in terms of inter-relations at different levels of societal aggregation.[15] This makes it possible to conceptualise social-political capital as sets of interactions, within a broad societal context that has historical antecedents and broad demonstrable stratification patterns, such as societal sectors or 'social fields' as Bourdieu calls them. Looked at in this way, social-political capital is a rich concept to use as a three-levelled analytical tool to conceptualise the structural component of governing action.

> Access to social (-political) capital for governing actors depends on characteristics of social sectors or fields.

Different types of governing action and their potential

The previous conceptual considerations have to be taken into account when looking at what action might mean as an element of governing. Of note is the notion that governing activities and social capital as a societal resource should be seen as being closely related. Such a comprehensive action concept can be developed, based upon my ideas of governance as patterns of societal interaction, in societies that are characterised by diversity, dynamics and complexity. To make these ideas more tangible three examples are presented below that illustrate how the governance perspective helps in advancing such an elaboration. The examples also represent action situations at different levels of aggregation of governance: leadership is typically governing action at the level of an individual actor (micro); social movements are analysed at the (sub) societal level (meso), and co-ordination is supplied as an example of action situated at the (inter)national level of governing (macro).

Leadership

There can hardly be any doubt that leaders as activators are of great importance in governance. Social and political leaders promote new courses of action or make changes palatable, thus creating (new) bases for societal governance. The scope of leadership studies has broadened to include the study of leadership in organisations, informal next to formal kinds of leadership, and leadership contexts.

The study of leadership went through several stages.[16] An assumption that leaders differ from followers led to the study of traits, in which all kinds of personal qualities were measured. The results were considered inconclusive, and other, more situational variables were looked for.[17] A further stage led to the behaviour of leaders being studied. Again: some steps were set, but few 'hard' conclusions were drawn. More recently, leader–follower relations were looked at: exchange processes, interpersonal relations and legitimation figured in this approach. Comparative research on leadership shows the importance of cultural differences across governing situations, and some studies indicate that findings often say more about the observer's values than about the behaviour of the leaders observed.

Theory development around leader-follower processes merits special attention here, because emphasis is placed on the interactional aspect – even on the dynamics of leadership. Three major inputs can be found in leader–follower studies: social power, exchange and motivation.[18] The power variant proposes that leader–follower interactions are based on resources the leader possesses. The interaction is founded on follower's perceptions of their need for these resources and the way the leader uses these perceptions in his or her interactions. The exchange version of leadership studies emphasises the (often implicit) long-term transactions between leaders and followers and the reciprocal nature of those interactions: the more success, the more credit and vice versa. The motivational school assigns a prominent role to reinforcement (feedback) in interactions. These perspectives on leadership all can contribute in advancing the action concept in governing and governance. The following three examples will show this. Motivational leadership theory can help explain the why and how of leadership in fluid collaborative governing interactions with an interferential character. Exchange aspects of leadership can be situated in interplay governing, such as within social movements. The social power variant provides insight into aspects of political leadership, or to governing interactions with an interventionist character. Other theoretical views on leadership might provide understanding of other governing situations. Adding the three societal dimensions, the following relations can be considered:

- motivation in *interference* interactions dealing with diversity and dynamics;
- exchange in *interplay* interactions dealing with dynamics and complexity;
- social power in *interventionist* interactions dealing with complexity and dynamics.

First leadership in governing *interferences* and the type of leadership supposed to suit this form of governance will be examined: collaborative efforts to solve local community problems are an example of this. Huxham and Vangen see these collaborative interactions as weakly organised, fluid in membership and as quite dynamic – fitting well my concept of interferences. In collaborative interactions that occur on a semi-voluntary basis, with hardly anything fixed, most aspects can be influenced by leaders, even leadership itself. Leadership is realised by affecting structures, processes and participants, but also through controlling and managing the agenda, by mobilising member organisations and by enthusing and empowering those who contribute to collaborative aims.[19] To put it bluntly, qualities attributed to leaders are a more powerful explanatory factor than the qualities of the interactions themselves. The diversity aspects and to some extent the dynamics of these collaborative interactions can be influenced by leadership activities.

Second, governing of *interplays*, horizontal, and semi-formalised forms of societal interactions, can be examined. The role of leadership in social mobilisation through social movements (see also next section) can be instructive. In governing such mobilisation leaders have to establish a connection between goal setting and motivational activities of followers. Incentives include positional rewards in exchange for support and loyalty; but sanctions such as the withholding of resources can be applied. Leaders of social mobilisation (movements) have to be careful that exchanges are seen as equitable and that their dynamic balance is not distorted. Governing of such dynamics is not simply one way, but consists of complex networks in which influence circulates.[20] Broadly speaking, leadership in interplays is particularly related to the dynamic balancing and handling of complex circuits of incentives and loyalty.

The third type is leadership of interactions as *interventions*, for which political leadership is illuminating. This is an area of theory where the role of the individual leader involves being quite outspoken. Classic thinkers, such as Machiavelli and more recently Weber, have set the tone for analysing such leadership. The influence of (great) political leaders is to be seen in terms of interactions, and how one-sided these might appear at first glance. In modern governance with its social-political complexity, political leaders work within formalised frameworks. They operate within the confines of systems, where their scope for action depends upon their skill in shaping complexity to their advantage, by turning constraints into opportunities. Political leadership is activation of resources from a social-political 'field', as conceptualised by Bourdieu, or by (re) combining expressions of social capital. By doing so, political leaders act as brokers in the midst of changing structural conditions and thus they give interventionist interactions a dynamic potential. Political leadership actualises this potential by creating opportunities for coping with the complexity of institutional conditions for a particular purpose.

In closing, a few words about the structural features of leadership itself. Social-political capital was presented as the general concept for the structural level of governing action, and within its context a sub-type can be specified, of elite structure or stratification, denoting more precisely the constraining or enabling conditions for all social-political leadership, i.e. leadership as an action element of governing is embedded in broader stratified elite structures. Classical and recent theories can help in relating leadership to this structural background.[21] All these approaches try variously to explain the inevitability of elites, their nature, structure and circulation.[22] For governance a spectrum with three positions is helpful, unified, interlocking and autonomous elites. A unified elite is relatively integrated, concentrated and not easily accessible; its cohesion is built on functional co-ordination and frequent social interaction. Interlocking elites consist of the (top) representatives of the major societal institutions. Finally, there are autonomous elites. Their structure is constantly shifting, it is dispersed among societal institutions, the level of conflict between them can be high on specific issues, and there is also a considerable amount of convergence in social-political perspectives, which is sustained by frequent personal exchanges between them and by varying degrees of openness.[23] All three forms of elite stratification seem to fit quite well within Bourdieu's view on social capital, and my use of social-political capital. One could quite easily establish hypothetical relations between these types of elites, sorts of governing interactions and modes of governance. For example, a unified elite may fit structurally well with hierarchical governance and with political leadership; an interlocking one with co-modes of governance and varying forms of social mobilisation; and finally autonomous elites can identify themselves with self-governance and more incidental collaborations such as at local and community level.

Different types of governing interactions require different types of leadership in modern governance. These are embedded in varieties of societal stratification or elite structures.

Social movements

The action capacity of social movements as a form of social mobilisation for governing purposes will be analysed because mobilisation also appears in interests groups and political parties. All three are varieties of participation in governance processes, as social-political activism on the part of citizens organised in different ways and thus belonging to the core of civil society (see also Chapter 10). These actions have been called a 'repertory' of activism, and this repertory is considered to be growing and becoming more varied.[24] Recent studies show furthermore that organised forms of social-political action change and the dividing lines between them become diffuse. So the distinction between social movements and interest groups becomes vague, and political parties tend to imitate movement features.[25] We even find the metaphor of a 'market of activism', where parties try to capture their share of issues, attention and participation.[26] I limit myself to social movements as a means of mobilisation for governing purposes. Some observations probably can be generalised *ceteris paribus* to the whole market of social-political activism. And this market can also be seen as a translation of varying manifestations of social capital.

In the actor orientation on social movements, theories try to explain why people become social-politically active in them. In this outlook social movements are populated by individuals who share aims and a collective identity by engaging in common action.[27] However, participation in social movements is far from commonplace, and even large movements mobilise only relatively small proportions of the population. Acting according to one's principles is never easy, and this is what social movements are about. So the question remains why do people put so much effort in them on a voluntary basis? Focusing on the individual, it is likely their motives for participation differ, that the ways they contribute to collective action differ, and that concerted energy may be more than the sum of individual activities.

Nor is the collective character of social action self-evident. The way that social discontent is transformed into organised action has always been a key issue in social movement literature. Participation in a social movement is a good example of what so called rationality-based collective-action theory has to offer. In fact it states that from a rational actor's viewpoint, there is little reason to engage in collective action.[28] Social movements fight for collective goods (human rights, clean environment, democratic government) and/or against collective bads (nuclear energy, ethnic conflicts, authoritarian regimes). The supply of collective goods and the termination of collective evils, however, are characterised by their jointness. That is, once a good is made available or a bad eliminated, all the members of the collectivity applied can enjoy the benefits, regardless of whether they participated in the collective action needed to secure it. Still, history shows time and again that individuals do participate in collective action, sometimes even at very high personal costs, and populate social movements. The (collective) rational actor paradigm is unable to solve this dilemma, and thus can only partially answer the question of why some people participate in social movements, whereas others do not.

In the study of social movements in a structural perspective two schools of thought can be distinguished. The first (also seen in time), the so called *resource mobilisation theory* is strong in the US; the second, under the heading of *new social movement theory* has predominantly a European base. Resource mobilisation theory develops the idea that potential for conflicts exists in all societies. Actualising this potential largely depends upon the proper usage of resources and selective incentives for action.[29] A conceptual vocabulary including political entrepreneurs, social movement organisations and even social movement industry was adopted. It focuses on a micro-level of analysis, postulating connections between individual properties and protest insurgency, claiming that the most cultivated actors possess the necessary resources to act as leaders and organisers of social movements. Social actors pursue their interests, especially those actors excluded from established channels of influence.[30] The decision to join a social movement is treated as just that – a rationally calculated one, distinguishing risks and rewards.[31] This approach has its limitations, it cannot provide the foundations for a self-sufficient theory of social movements; it says little about the emergence and definition of stakes involved in the struggle of social movements; it operates with overly simplistic models of rational behaviour; it tends to overestimate the importance of formal organisation for collective mobilisation, and in a comparative perspective, primarily reconstructs the dynamics of social movements in particular societies.[32]

The new social movement theory approach is rooted in European traditions of social theory and political philosophy.[33] It searches for a logic of collective action based in politics, ideology, and culture, and looks to other sources of movement identity such as in ethnicity, gender and sexuality. Some theorists in this school seek to update and revise conventional Marxist assumptions, while others try to displace and transcend those. There are many variations within this approach to movements, however a number of themes can be identified. In the first place many scholars in this school of thought underscore symbolic action in civil society or the cultural sphere as a major arena for collective action, alongside instrumental action in the state or political sphere. Second, the importance of processes protecting autonomy and self-determination, instead of strategies for maximising influence and power are emphasised. Third, some theorists underscore the role of (post-materialist) values in this form of collective action, as opposed to conflicts over material resources. Fourth, the – often fragile – process of constructing collective identities and identifying group interests is in focus, instead of assuming that conflict groups and their interests are structurally determined. And finally, a variety of submerged, latent, and temporary networks often under-girding collective action are recognised, rather than seeing centralised organisational forms as prerequisites for successful mobilisation. However, it should be noted that various theorists in this approach apply different emphases to these themes. New social movement theory has also been subjected to criticism.[34] There is significant doubt whether contemporary social movements are specifically a product of post-industrial society: do these contemporary movements represent anything unique, except for the issue of identity? It can be argued that 'new' ones are just recent additions to the general repertoire of social movements, and that changes in these repertoires don't necessitate new theories.[35] Ultimately, the main contributions of this 'European' perspective are its emphasis on identity, culture, and the role of the civic society aspects of social movements.

Stratification demonstrates how leadership might structurally be distributed in modern societies, and pluralism shows the same for the distribution of organised action potential as part of social-political capital. This is certainly in line with Bourdieu's application of the concept, and to some extent it is also in line with Coleman's opinion (see above). But what about pluralism, can it play the role I assign to it? As with many concepts in social science discourse there are many ways of looking at pluralism. So there are pluralist, reformed and neo-pluralist theories,[36] there are liberal, communal and radical theories,[37] and combinations of these.[38] Although not unproblematic with its normative, descriptive and analytical qualities, pluralism remains an important tool in theorising about governing interactions and on the topic of how power or influence in those interactions are divided society-wise.

The essence of a pluralist view on society is that no single group, organisation or class can dominate its governance.[39] The dispersal of societal sources of power and influence, and thus of action potential, are at the root of pluralist views on the structure of societies. The competition and tensions between these sources give societies their dynamic quality. The continuous upward and downward movement not only of interests groups and political organisations, but also of professions, industries and even classes expresses this dynamic. Social-political capital as the resource base from which social movements and other groups draw, depends heavily on these dynamics and thus partly on the pluralist nature of society. As Olsen points out, it is possible to distinguish a mobilisation version of pluralism focusing on voluntary associations organising social-political interactions, and a mediating version of pluralism, particularly concerned with interest mediating as a form of political influence.[40]

> At the intentional level of mobilised governing action distinctions between parties, movements and interests are becoming vague and at its structural level voluntary pluralism can be considered the major feature of modern societies.

Co-ordination

Co-ordination is similar to leadership and social mobilisation and is of great importance to governance, but is not always given the place it deserves. Leadership was considered in relation to the diversity of modern societies, mobilisation to its dynamics, and co-ordination is posited in governance thinking because of societal complexity. Co-ordinated action is a good way of coping with societal complexity. However, this is easier said than done, because 'everybody likes to co-ordinate, nobody wants to be co-ordinated'. I will first discuss co-ordination at the actor level of governing interactions, followed by a few observations on the structural component, which will be conceptualised as the bureaucratic context for co-ordinating governing interactions.

Co-ordination mechanisms are frequently used within and between organisations. Of concern in dealing with complex issues is the co-ordination of relevant organisational entities in governing interactions: units, organisations, even states. These interactions determine to a large extent the outcomes of activities in handling the complex issues these organisations or systems are involved in. Systems theory, especially as according to Simon, has taught us that usually in social systems not everything is equally strongly interrelated with everything else. This makes for de-composability of complex issues and co-ordination is one way of doing this, although complexity – as will be seen later – is to a large extent in the eye of the beholder, as is co-ordination (see Chapter 12).

The origins and necessity of co-ordination lie in the processes of division of labour, functional differentiation and specialisation, of the separation of making decisions and implementing them. Pulling things together is needed as a complement to these processes in all larger organisations or systems and at all levels of governing: interrelations between organisations[41]; regional[42]; in international governance.[43] Although differentiated and specialised, organisational actors remain dependent on each other. This interdependence provides the rational for co-ordination. It is a process of (re)integrating separated but interdependent actors who somehow need to adapt to each other, while there is always a degree of antagonism among them, based on the different and specialised tasks they perform within an organisation or between them. As interdependence varies, so does the need for co-ordination. Usually in governance issues co-ordination is required, but not as a standard formula. In line with Simon, interdependence in complex situations varies, as does the need to co-ordinate: 'If co-ordination is a response to interdependence . . . then the amount and form of co-ordinating capacity should be related to the needs that arise in particular circumstances'.[44] High interdependence demands strong co-ordination; lower degrees of interdependence weaker co-ordination. Weaker forms of co-ordination are information exchange and consultation and stronger forms are setting parameters or establishing priorities.[45] Developments surrounding organisations will often dictate the level of co-ordination. From the perspective of this book it is particularly the complexity of the outside world, and the translation of this in internal responses, which drives organisations towards the need to co-ordinate their internal activities, particularly when these are highly differentiated and specialised. Co-ordination is not the same as collaboration or co-operation (see Chapter 7), co-ordination is more formalised, and is applied within an institutionalised framework.

Rogers and Whetten see three advantages for organisations co-ordinating their internal activities: (1) as a means of raising the quality of the services (or products) it delivers; (2) as a way to avoid duplication and improve efficiency; (3) to cope with limited resources by sharing them.[46] In terms of the co-ordination of governing interactions this means – negatively formulated – that insufficient co-ordination of differentiated governing processes make for sub-optimal, ineffective and costly governance outcomes. For organisations with a public role co-ordinating demands are even more crucial, dealing as they usually do with multi-faceted and multi-disciplinary subjects and services, requiring not only internal co-ordination of specialised units, but often, external co-ordination of social actors.

Factors complicating co-ordination are easy to find. Co-ordination always means some loss of autonomy and a certain degree of uncertainty for those participating in it because seldom can it be seen in advance who is going to win or lose from co-ordinating activities. Co-ordination takes time, energy and other resources, and without a clear idea of goals and results expected, the return of investments made is not at all certain. In the literature many factors influencing co-ordination as an action mechanism are discussed. Dijkzeul, in his study on co-ordination within the UN summarises these in nine points, several of which concern coping with complexity.[47] He considers the processing of information by reducing on the one hand the scope of data needed and on the other hand increasing the capacity to handle it, one of the key dimensions of co-ordination. This is an interesting example of the action component of governing being the one in which image formation (data) and choice of instruments (processing) come together.

Many aspects of co-ordination involve dilemmas, ordinarily not easily conceptualised. However, in the governance perspective they can be looked at as issues dealing with the action component of governing inter-actions, related to the image and instrumental component, and then handled accordingly. For instance what kinds and intensity of inter-dependences are recognised by those involved in a governing issue? Phrased in terms of dealing with complexity: what (key) interrelations within a problem or opportunity situation are to be found, and where are boundaries to be defined (-'image' condition)? How far does this co-ordination have to go to assure that the whole performs better than the sum of the parts,[48] what kinds of mechanisms should be used and can sanctions be applied ('instrumental' condition)? What kinds of activities by what sorts of actors interacting in what sort of governing situations are to be co-ordinated and which levels of co-ordination should be involved ('action' condition)? Questions such as these can be raised about co-ordination at the actor level of governing interactions. In principle the governance approach offers the framework to answer them.

It is appropriate to consider bureaucracy to be the structural context for co-ordinating activities dealing with complex social-political govern-ance issues. To handle complex societal problems of opportunities one needs not only knowledge from different sectors and disciplines, but also organisational capacity to select, reduce and order this knowledge and all things related to it. This in principle is what bureaucracy is about, and for a public variant of this, interventionist types of interactions based upon controllable and accountable procedures are needed. For this reason the growth of the bureaucratic mode of hierarchical organisation in the public as well as in the private sector is one of the major social trends of our time. It has called forth critical attention, in particular of negative bureaucratic traits. These have been well documented, even giving rise to hostility against bureaucratic power as an alleged fourth branch of government, a threat even to democratic governance.

The Weberian 'ideal' model of hierarchical, legal-rational bureaucracy is still the dominant social-political construction dealing with complex social and political issues in modern societies. While we will see later (Chapter 9) that co-modes of governance, next to hierarchical ones, are on the ascent, this is not to say that interventionist governing interactions for handling complex societal problems and opportunities by bureaucratically organised entities are superfluous or outdated. As a study on program management in the UN shows, there isn't a realistic alternative for the co-ordination of complex and sensitive international societal issues, that isn't based on co-ordination within a bureaucratically organised administrative setting.[49] The main principles, of hierarchy, continuity, impersonality, expertise, and the strict separation between the bureaucratic apparatus and its governing body, as defined by Weber, are still greatly in evidence. Theoretical refinements, amendments and additions to Weber's original model, have greatly enriched our knowledge of the way large scale administrative systems operate, such that limits have also become apparent.

These insights are useful for conceptualising the structural context of co-ordination as an important form of governing interaction in coping with the complexity of large scale societal problems and opportunities. This is not to say that as with so many governance questions, dilemmas of co-ordination and their bureaucratic context are easily solved, just that a more appropriate governance strategy would be to bring these dilemmas and choices out into the open, rather than to avoid them. Governing complex issues by means of co-ordinated interventions requires controlled and responsible bureaucratic organisations for which the paradox holds true that: 'The indispensability of skilled administrators makes modern bureaucracy autonomous, but professionalisation makes it a subservient tool', or to express it in power terms: 'Bureaucracies are ... all-powerful and at the same time incapable of determining how its power should be used'.[50]

> Co-ordination is a major governing mechanism at the intentional level of governing interventions in handling complex societal issues; whatever its shortcomings bureaucracy serves as a relatively controllable hierarchical structure for those co-ordinating interactions.

Conclusion

In this chapter I have discussed a number of features, which taken together, conceptualise the action or will component of governing. Action can be seen as the element in which the two components of governing – image and instrument – come together. Because of this, governing action can become coherent and effective. Actors in social-political governing arenas can be individual governors, public as well as private, and large scale organisational entities such as bureaucracies can also be active in governance issues. What is important is that they master sufficient 'will-power' to put into action an instrument they have chosen to govern with, on the basis of an image they have formed for a governing initiative. Such an activity can never be seen in isolation from an action context, conceptualised here as social-political capital: an action resource from which an actual governing activity can draw from. Social-political capital can be found on all levels of societal aggregation, from the local community to the UN. In this chapter three themes have been differentiated in which social-political action at the intentional level of governing interactions and social-political capital at its structural level can be operationalised. These three are linked to three major governance challenges facing today's societies: of using their diversity, dynamics and complexity for governance purposes. A second link established concerns the three kinds of interactions we find in societies, interferences, interplays and interventions. A third step has been to link these features and patterns of interactions to three examples of action and action potential. In the sphere of interferences, different types of leadership can be considered to handle societal diversity. In the same vein societal interplays are connected with social movements, and comparable groups and organisations, and these can be considered as sources of activation, within the boundaries of social-political capital for channelling societal dynamics. Finally, co-ordination is an important way of dealing with complex societal issues, involving the realisation of complex governing interventions within the constraints of bureaucratic structures. As a result, what action as an element of governing might look like conceptually, has been discussed.

Notes

1 Scharpf, 1973.
2 Kooiman, 1988; Campbell, 1999.
3 Etzioni, 1968.
4 Crespi, 1992, p. 133; see also Archer, 1990.
5 Melucci, 1992, pp. 241–242.
6 Kooiman, 1988.
7 Putnam, 1993.
8 Portes, 1998.
9 Morgan and Shinn, 1999.
10 Foley and Edwards, 1999; Portes, 1998.
11 Bourdieu, 1986, pp. 248–252.
12 Bourdieu and Wacquant, 1992, p. 119.
13 Coleman, 1990, p. 305.
14 idem, p. 307.
15 Edwards and Foley, 1998; Foley and Edwards, 1999.
16 Chemers, 1997.
17 Stogdill in Bass, 1990.
18 Conger and Kanungo, 1998, pp. 43–45.
19 Huxham and Vangen, 2000.
20 Huxham, 2000a.
21 Grusky, 1994.
22 Evans, 1995.
23 Olsen, 1993, pp. 157–159.
24 Kaase, Marsh, 1979.
25 Costain, 1992.
26 Richardson, 1995.
27 Klandermans, 1997, pp. 3–8.
28 Olson, 1965.
29 Diani and Eyerman, 1992.
30 Tilly, 1978.
31 Oberschall, 1993.
32 Kitscheld, 1991, p. 330.
33 Buechler, 1995.
34 Pichardo, 1997.
35 Notably, Tilly, 1978.
36 Smith, 1990.
37 Andrain and Apter, 1995.
38 Smith, 1995.
39 idem, p. 209.
40 Olsen, 1993, pp. 148–150.
41 Rogers and Whetten, 1982.
42 Chisholm, 1989.
43 Metcalfe, 1994.
44 idem, p. 279.
45 idem, pp. 280–282.
46 Rogers and Whetten, 1982.
47 Dijkzeul, 1997.
48 Metcalfe, 1994, p. 278.
49 Dijkzeul, 1997.
50 Bendix (1945) as cited in Merton et al., 1952, p. 129.

PART III

MODES OF GOVERNANCE

6

SELF-GOVERNANCE

Introduction

Self-governance is an important mode of societal governance.[1] Self-governance refers to the capacity of social entities to govern themselves autonomously. However, what 'self-governance' is and what its contribution to societal governance is and could be in modern society is not (yet) fully understood. Without sustaining a capacity for self-governance, societal governance becomes an impossible task, as the history of many totalitarian regimes has shown: the fate of the former East European 'People's Republics' is a clear example. However, societies cannot rely on self-governing as the only mode of governance. Even the staunchest supporters of liberal societies see a (limited) governing role for the state, and in practice fully self-governing societies do not exist. However, there are societies in which self-governance plays an important role.

Self-governance exists, and to a much greater extent than is often realised. There always will be initiatives for new forms of societal interactions, usually involving strong self governing tendencies. Innovations such as the new communication 'revolution' is a source for all kinds of new societal interactions. Many of these interactions 'govern themselves' until certain effects become apparent that require some kind of formal regulation.

Self-governance, as one of the three modes of societal governance, is the capacity of societal entities to provide the necessary means to develop and maintain their own identity, and thus show a relatively high degree of social-political autonomy. Societies differ in the way self-governance is practised. Interest in self-governance as a mode of societal governance is in line with trends of withdrawing public interventions by means of deregulation or privatisation. However, much of what is sold as deregulation or advertised as self-regulation is better seen as forms of re-regulation or altering traditional forms of public control into 'steering at a distance'.[2] From this perspective it seems doubtful these governing tendencies can seriously be labelled self-governance.

This chapter looks at self-governance from different angles. In the first part, four approaches to self-governance are presented, two from German origin and two based upon concepts developed in this book. This is followed by two examples from the literature, one on the professions and one on governing natural resources. Both give more specific insights into self-governing activities in modern societies and how they can be conceptualised. The chapter ends with an elaboration of some ideas on self-governance, based on experiences in a societal sector.

Some theoretical positions

Self-governance as autopoiesis

A good start for thinking about self-governance is the concept of *autopoiesis*, literally meaning self-production. *Autopoiesis*, as developed by the biologists Maturana and Varela, is a concept developed to better understand 'living systems', not as the reproduction of parts, such as lungs or nerves, but as systems of interactions of components, as living wholes. Through internal, coherent interactions, *autopoietic* systems reproduce their own identity, without being dependent on the environment for this reproduction, except for the supply of energy and other material needs. By definition an *autopoietic* system is autonomous.

This theory of living *autopoietic* systems was not only attractive for 'general system theorists', but also for social scientists, who saw all kinds of opportunities for creative analogies.[3] Although Varela and Maturana themselves were careful about the application of their ideas to social systems, this did not prevent *autopoiesis* becoming quite a popular concept in many areas of the social sciences.[4] The most important representative of this line of thinking, Niklas Luhmann, built a whole theory of social systems around it, also using the concept of self-referentiality, connected to *autopoiesis*. Communications, not actors, are the essence of the self-referentiality of social systems, because communication can exist and reproduce itself, independent of actors. By means of communication, systems 'decide' self-referentially what is relevant to them, what conveys meaning to them, and what does not.[5] How then to govern *autopoietic* social systems, as economics or law, from the outside? In the functional differentiation of modern societies, the political system is no more than a societal sub-system like any other, according to Luhmann. It has its own functional code, making it sensitive to signals from outside, enabling it to act as an *autopoietic* system by itself. This special code for the political system is *power*: by communicating power it is able to incorporate other societal subsystems in its communication. However, being a subsystem like any other, the political system has no special – hierarchical – position in relation to other societal subsystems. For the political system this equality is problematic, because it is required to take decisions binding society as a whole. The political system can exempt itself by defining itself as 'the state', and in so doing creating a special governing role, at least for itself, according to Luhmann. The consequence of this *autopoietic* thinking about *Politische Steuerung* is a pessimistic view of the possibilities of governance in modern societies. Some of Luhmann's followers, although accepting the basic *autopoietic* principle, are trying to relax the strictness of his message. An example of this is Teubner's theory of reflexive law, which I will discuss shortly.[6]

Like all social systems (systems of) governing interactions will demonstrate
self-governing (*autopoietic*) attributes because of a strive for self-identity; the
stronger these attributes are, the more difficult to govern them from the outside.

Self-governance as actor constellations

The actor-oriented approach to self-governance that has Renate Mayntz
and Frits Scharpf as key proponents is partly a reaction against
Luhmann's pessimistic view in the German debate on *Politische
Steuerung*.[7] The essence of their argument is that there is nothing systemic
to difficulties in *Politische Steuerung* but that these are the consequence of
special features in actor-related self-governing situations. The dynamics
of modern societies are an important explaining factor in such situations.
To underline the actor as opposed to the system approach, the contexts in
which governing actors operate are conceptualised as constellations, hence
the term actor-in-constellation used in this approach to self-governance.
For actors they use the term corporate actors, who represent organisations
or interests in these constellations.[8]

In the actor-in-constellation perspective on self-governance analysis
focuses on the dynamic processes that occur in the mutual stimulation
between identifiable actors in reinforcing, non-linear behavioural patterns. The effects of these dynamic processes can be seen in terms of their
growing autonomy and towards dispositions of self-governance. The
actor oriented school concerns itself only with self-governing tendencies
exhibited by societal sectors that are intervention resistant. The degree to
which such self-governing tendencies can be observed depends, in their
view, on a number of independent and varying factors, found on the side
of the sectors themselves, as objects of external influence, as well as on the
part of authorities wishing to intervene.

On the side of sectors in the governing interaction the 'primary process'
of a sector is of importance. The difficulty or ease with which services or
products can be replaced is an issue: the more difficult their substitution,
the higher will be tendencies for self-governance, and vice versa. Resisting
or supporting governing intentions is also a matter of contingency: are
these intentions congruent with those of the subjects they are aimed at or
not? If there is a discrepancy between them, the larger the discrepancy, the
more difficult will external governance be achieved. Organisational capacity of social sectors is probably the most important variable in the way
they are internally governed. Mayntz hypothesises that with the institutional consolidation of societal sectors, especially with the emergence of
multi-level structures including governing entities of a higher order

(umbrella organisations, and peak associations), their ability to self-govern increases. The scope of their organisational capacity is important. On the one hand a large organisational capacity might aid external interventions, but it also might be a barrier towards such interventions. Self-governance does not necessarily diminish political governability, it can enhance it. The effective organisation of sector interests can be used as a veto power to block solutions to societal problems. It can also mean that consensus between corporate actors can be reached and decisions taken to solve a particular societal problem, exactly because there is a high level of self-governing capacity in a sector. A simple inversion, then, of the general thesis that highly organised subjects will resist governing attempts more adamantly, would be as wrong as the thesis itself.

On the side of intervening political-administrative authorities several factors can be mentioned that are relevant to the relative success or failure in governing societal sectors. A political condition requires that governing needs be articulated, because if a governing activity is initiated by pressure from an interest group, autonomic tendencies will be promoted. The same occurs when the state lacks legitimacy to intervene in a sector; there is an availability of governing instruments and the question is of whether these instruments can be implemented. If a sector is highly dependent on public finances and the knowledge required to intervene in them, the use of governing instruments may be effective in curbing self-governing tendencies. This last element, required knowledge, is also mentioned by systems theorists. When corporate actors, both the governing and the governed, coalesce, governance becomes complicated. This happens when private corporate actors combine forces with fragmented political-administrative authorities to pursue their own interests. At such points actor constellations may arise in the form of networks, in which state and corporate actors participate, often with cross-alliances between them. In these networks, the distinction between governing object and subject becomes practically impossible to define. In such situations, these networks become basically self-governing units *par excellence*. However, not all policy sectors are characterised by more or less well-organised subsystems. Compared to the relatively tightly coupled neo-corporatist structures, the consensus and decision-making capacity of policy fields characterised by open and fragmented 'issue networks' are less developed, although even there some large organisations may assert themselves as corporate actors.[9] In the view then of Mayntz and her colleagues the question of the (un-) governability of a societal subject is an empirical one. The actor-in-constellation theory of self-governance reasons that the indisputable governability problems of complex and dynamic modern societies has less to do with the basic *autopoietic* character of social subsystems, than with (1) their dynamics resulting in self-governing capacities; (2) the organisational and other abilities of organised policy fields to resist political governance; and (3) the political will and administrative competencies to intervene and govern. Under specific conditions the very capacity of societal actors to act in an organised way can hamper as well as facilitate governance in solving problems originating from societal dynamics and complexity.

> Wherever (corporate) governing actors, representing different societal domains, are able to organise networks in which they combine resources from those domains for common purposes, these networks will show strong self-governing tendencies.

Self-governance as patterns of interaction

As introduced in Chapter 2 (to be continued in Chapter 13) I believe the most spontaneous forms of societal interactions are interferences. Interferences can be found everywhere in societies. They are interactions taking place within and around 'primary' societal activities such as welfare, care and education, but also with the production and distribution of commercial goods and services. The issue under discussion now is the relation, or the embeddedness, between interferences and self-governance. Thus self-governance as a mode of governing interactions are embedded in the sphere of societal interferences. We find self-governance most often in the civil society domain, somewhat less in the market, and least frequently within the state. Although interferences have a somewhat fluid and relatively unorganised character, even the market and the state cannot do without them as a mechanism for ordering informal personal traffic between actors in these domains. What must be demonstrated, is how self-governing as a major mode of governance fits with this broader category of interferences. Can something more specific be said about this embedding in analytical terms?

To do this, we return to the general interaction concept, with its intentional and structural aspect and the relation between these two. The intentional level of these interactions is the reservoir from which self-governing activities are drawn. If there is a wish on the part of those involved in these spontaneous and relatively little organised forms of interactions to continue them, they will start experimenting with and designing governing arrangements for them. These can take the form, of informal agreements, self-applying rules, and also semi-formalised codes of conduct. The essence of these arrangements is their voluntarism and consent, and as such they are the *nucleus* of self-governance, looked at from a structural point of view. However, the relation between these agreements, rules and codes, to arrangements of a more structural nature, is a subtle one. At the organisational level it has been shown that to run a national voluntary organisation of some size with many local chapters, traditional 'top down' management concepts are ineffective. Rather, models built to exploit interferences and interplays, do a much better job in the self-governance of such organisations.[10] This could be due to the nature of civil society, the domain such organisations belong to. It is in the domain of civil society where interferences dominate, where potentialities have been internalised and limits to self-governance set. To use a term we will encounter later, when speaking about institutions, there is the *mimesis* effect: organisations learn from each other how to govern themselves, and these patterns become generalised and even institutionalised (see Chapter 10).

For social-political governance, empirically, every level of interrelation between interferential interactions and or self-governance structures are of interest: from self-governing roles, organisations, sectors, societies, to a self-governing 'world community'. At all these levels one can look at the ways structural embedding of interferences unfold, or conversely how structures of self-governance trickle down into more widespread inter-ferences. This, as has been discussed, may have happened within the state. In the past decade we have seen a changing role conception of (higher) civil servants: from 'public administrators' to 'public entrepre-neurs' (intentional aspect). This is influenced by the general introduction of market mechanisms to the state (structural aspect). Therefore, struc-tural developments including 'inter-penetration' of market traits in the public domain have an effect on the role conceptions of actors on the intentional level of their interactions, and these in turn may have an effect on the overall management of the state.[11] Also, in the market place exam-ples of self-governance developed on the basis of interferential societal interactions can be found, of loosely organised interactions between multinational firms and environmental organisations resulting in the formulation of voluntary codes of conduct in areas of environmental awareness.[12] However, the incidental nature of the introduction of such codes shows that inter-penetration has not yet taken place on the struc-tural level, in contrast with the state where management-type interactions have materialised at the intentional as well as the structural level of governing interactions, and in the relation between these levels (see further Chapter 13).

> Only by taking the basic aspects of societal interferences seriously can the self-governing societal capacity be fully appreciated and structurally used for governing purposes.

Self-governance and images of the field

All three perspectives on self-governance discussed above vary on the difficulties in governing subjects as social sectors, but they agree on one point, that for governing of whatever kind, a clear picture what is 'going on out there' is a must. The *autopoietic*, systems school emphasises self-referential image formation for governing because they believe communication is the most vital if not the only way to govern. For the actor-in-constellations view on self-governance lack of knowledge, in particular about the 'Eigen' dynamics of subjects to be governed, is, among other things, seen as an important element in problems with *Politische Steuerung*. In the interactive governance approach the too simplistic reduction of the constantly moving, diverse and complex character of governing challenges in image formation is seen as a basic trap for governance, next to inappropriate instruments and lack of will to act.[13] For both Teubner and the governance approach, and incorporating *autopoietic* characteristics, an adequate image for governing is a similar necessity. Teubner, because of his basic belief in the self-referential and self-governing nature of all social systems, doesn't include governance based upon communication of 'equal' partners.[14] In the governance approach image formation is only one element of governing, and not necessarily one sharing parity. Both approaches look for autonomous, interferential social-political processes and the self-governance capacities inherent in them. Where the governance approach describes governing as the influencing by and through interactions, Teubner believes that reflexive law activates the institutional design of self-regulating social institutions. Teubner and governance theory similarly emphasise the great importance of 'image formation' by empirical research of concrete social-political self-governing situations, an emphasis that is shared by the actor-in-constellation school. Social-political governance argues this from the diversity, dynamics and complexity of modern-societal opportunities and problems, Teubner from the basic self-referential nature of social systems, and the actor-in-constellations approach takes the network features of these self-governing constellations as a starting point. All three search for self-governing capacities in modern societies for governance purposes, but with different basic or central hypothesis of self-governance in the background.

Governance theorising emphasises the interactions within societal fields, starting with their interferences, that is to say the direct interactions involved in the primary processes taking place within them. It is the actors, structures and interrelations between them that are the primary focus of this approach, in this case the self-governing interactions embedded within those interferences. Charting the diversity, dynamics and complexity of a field or sector, makes the picture of its self-governing traditions and capacities more visible and realistic. The analysis of self-governing interactions is regarded as an instrument for tracing the diversity, complexity and dynamics of a certain field. In doing so, one needs to focus on this first level of interactions, the level of interferences, that is, the level of the spontaneous and relatively unorganised and informal movements within a field. Interplays and interventions should not be neglected but there is always a tendency to overrate their influence because of their relative visibility, as opposed to interferences, which usually do not get sufficient attention. Those representing the field and their governing often think more in terms of instruments and action than of images. To give self-governance its due place in the overall governance of modern societies, images of the field, especially of its primary processes, should have their proper place.

> The self-governing capacity of a societal field will easily become skewed towards the images and interests of the actors representing the field, rather than of those directly involved in the interferences of its primary processes.

Two applications of self-governance

To give a more precise picture of actual self-governing qualities or capacities of societal sub-sectors that have been subject to scholarly attention, two examples will be elaborated upon. In the first example the issue of self-governance is discussed in the context of the professions as a societal sector. The professions have for a long time been subjects of scholarly attention and much systematic knowledge has been gathered about them in comparison to other societal sectors. This will be followed by an example in which issues relating to the self-governance of a particular type of use of natural resources, the so called 'commons', will be presented.

Self-governance of the professions

Who or what governs the way professionals do their work? How autonomous or heteronomous are professions in modern societies? These questions abound in the literature. Are professions able to control entry to and exit from them? What about competitive practices, market organisation and remuneration,[15] or elements such as accountability, codes of ethics, enforcement/discipline and accreditation?[16] In terms of self-governance, are rules and other instruments governing the professions within their own areas of competence or do others, outside the professions, have an influence on them, and if so, to what degree? In the literature this aspect of the professions is phrased respectively as their 'autonomy' or 'hetero-nomy'. Views on this differ, as do experiences. On the one hand there are authors who see the professions as mainly self-regulating; they focus mainly on Anglo-American situations, where powerful professional bodies indeed formulate and enact their own rules to the exclusion of outsiders. The legal and medical professions are the primary examples of this approach.[17] Others position themselves at the other end of this autonomy-hetoronomy scale and perceived professions as being almost exclusively state controlled.[18] These authors discuss continental European experiences, where states traditionally have a much tighter grip on professions. Others still look at the way professions are governed in a mixed mode,[19] in which, it is argued, professionals, the state, and the market all exert an influence on the way professions are governed.

A working definition of professions that includes a number of issues raised in the literature is as follows:

> they are largely non-manual, based upon specialised training enti-tling entry to them. They tend to monopolise their services as well as their freedom of control by outsiders. Based upon their closed nature, their alleged competence and professional ethics they claim special material rewards and higher social prestige.[20]

As can be deducted from this working definition, the professions can be structurally located at the crossroads of market, civil society and the state. The influence of all three societal domains can be traced within the professions, and thus their self-governing qualities and capacities can be usefully explored in relation to these three societal domains. *Profession-market* relations can be seen as a process in which producers of special services seek to constitute and control a market by their expertise.[21] Scarce resources of specialised knowledge and skills are translated into social and economic rewards by creating and sustaining a monopoly for services delivered. This is expressed in a monopoly of expertise in the market. A monopoly of status is also acquired; professions generally strive for market closure by pursuing monopolistic or quasi-monopolistic privi-leges. By playing down the utilitarian aspects of their services, they enhance the moral, ritual and cultural aspects of their work *(relation with civil society)*. This dual characteristic is essential for the self-governing nature of the professions. *State-profession* relations have strong historical roots, from the advent to the demise of the guilds and on. These relations also vary greatly between American and continental European traditions and are closely connected with state-society relations in general and over time: 'Professions are important to the state … but the degree of importance varies according to the profession and to the role of the state … in a particular nation at a particular time'.[22] Domination between interests has periodically shifted due to such instances as the establishment of authority, strategic interests, forms of collective action, and most recently cost-evasion or sharing. These mutual influences have both limited and enhanced the self-governing capacity of the professions, depending on specific balances between them. For the *civil society* aspect of the professions cultural aspects have already been discussed. In this role the emphasis is on the knowledge created together with their counterparts at universities, in specialised or mass media. For the 'new' social professions the relation with the voluntary sector is an important one. Another civil society relation of note involves professions and users of their services: due to both the growing emancipation of citizens and the increasing organising capacity of the non-profit sector itself, the professions are taking this relation more seriously. However it is debatable to what extent the users are able to influence the self-governing quality of the professions.

Freedom of control, in the literature known as closure, sits well with the earlier discussion on the *autopoietic* quality of societal sectors. However, connections between the professions and the state can also be interpreted as actor constellations with shared ideas on their self-governing behaviour. And interrelations between professions, the state, market and civil society can also be conceptualised as interaction patterns with an intentional and a structural level. At the structural level it has been argued that with varying emphases in time, place and type of profession, state and market influences have increased: '[F]ormerly self-run professional groups [the guilds] have slowly been losing the ability to control the workplace, to control the market for their services, and to control their relation to the state'.[23] This development may not be unique to the professions but may also apply to other societal sectors.[24] At the intentional/ actor level these long term changes may conclude differently as more freedom may be available to individuals or small groups for interacting with others. Constraints on their interactions, because of the necessity for internal coherence within the professions, has been replaced by professional role definitions, allowing greater scope for individual or small group initiatives. Therefore, *ceteris paribus* structurally self-governance of the professions has decreased because of growing external influences, and self-governing at the actor level has increased because of a growing freedom in conceiving and defining professional role interpretations.

Self-governing capacities of societal sectors (such as professions) will vary according to social-political cultural (governance) traditions.

Self-governance of the Commons

In literature on the 'commons', that is to say a natural resource exploited by a number of users together, self-governing has been a focus of attention from different theoretical perspectives.[25] In the parable of the 'Tragedy of the Commons' Hardin suggested either privatisation or state regulation as alternative solutions for the (in his eyes) inevitable over-exploitation of commons by their users.[26] A whole body of literature developed in reaction to this, stressing other governance modes inbetween state and market, with 'self' as well as with 'co' variants (see also next chapter). I will use one approach concerning self-governance of the commons, by Elinor Ostrom. She is at the centre of a whole body of literature trying to conceptualise, analyse and design institutions able to effectively and sustainably self-govern natural resources by those who use them. In the analysis of institutions capable of handling this form of self-governance, or in her terms 'institutional options for solving commons dilemmas' Ostrom uses elements of the 'Tragedy of the Commons', game theory and theories of collective action.[27] In her game, users of a commons will negotiate on the carrying capacity of their collectively used natural resource, resulting in an agreement in which the users equally share in the yield of the resource and in its enforcement costs. Working with games as these, may, in her view, lead towards new thinking about institutions capable of self-governance of the commons.

Such forms of collective action with a long-enduring character, dealing effectively with free-riding and other forms of opportunistic behaviour, are not as rare as one might think, and she has studied several of them in forestry, grazing areas and irrigation systems in different parts of the world. She assumes rational behaviour of those using a common resource, their individual choices being affected by four variables: expected benefits, costs, internal norms, and discount rates. Her approach also includes a model of institutional choice, again with a number of variables: information about shared norms and other opportunities, information about benefits and proposed rules, and information about costs of transforming, monitoring and enforcing alternative rules. The individual user of a commons, participating in this collective choice institution for self-governance, can support the continuation of rules in place or support change of them. According to Ostrom to understand the capacity for developing and sustaining collective action for self-governing commons, there are three theoretical puzzles that have to be solved: supplying new institutions; making credible commitments and mutual monitoring.[28] However, she admits that new institutional theories are not well equipped to finding solutions for these puzzles. In Ostrom's approach to self-governance rules play a central role, 'nested' rules at different levels. These kinds of rules come quite close to the three 'orders' of governing and governance to be discussed later in this book. First, there are *operational* rules relating to day-to-day choices made by users of a commons. Then there are *collective choice* rules aimed at defining policies for managing the commons. Third, there are *constitutional choice* rules that 'formulate governance adjudication and modification'.[29] Rules such as these do not give a general explanation for the sustainability and robustness of self-governance of the commons, however they help explain which rules in specific situations might contribute to the enduring nature of their self-governing capacity.[30] Although criticism can be found about Ostrom's model,[31] her contribution to a systematic theorising, analysis and design of viable self-governing institutions is a considerable one, worth continuing attention.[32]

> Under the assumption of rationality of governing actors at the intentional level of governing interactions, self-governing frameworks (institutions) can be designed for them at the structural level of those interactions.

Self-governance in societal fields

Societal governance in modern societies is a mix of different governance modes. Therefore governance mode by itself is a partial one, completed with other types. This applies to self-governance as well as to co- and hierarchical modes of governance. As was evident in the example above, a basic issue in governance of the professions is exactly this mix, in that example between self- and hierarchical governance. The question now is of which perspective this relation between or mix of different modes of governance should be applied. Does one consider rules and regulations and other hierarchical governing instruments as the main way of governance, and other categories such as self-governing – to put it somewhat bluntly – as a marginal society category? Or does one see self-governance as a societal capacity, having governing qualities of its own, and deserving a place of its own in a governance mix? This is an important point, not because the latter view would be typically 'liberal' and the former typically 'socialist', but because the discussion on modes of governance so easily becomes an instrumental one, where one type of instrument is exchanged for another, as in the discussion on self-regulation or de-regulation. What is required is a fundamental debate on the capacities and qualities of the different governance modes, what the boundaries of such capacities and qualities are, and the way these capacities and qualities can be deployed for broader societal governance purposes. Before going into these more fundamental aspects of the various modes of governance later in the book (Chapter 12 and Part V) the relation between self-governance and concepts such as de-, re- and self- regulation will be examined.

Deregulation, self-regulation and self-governance

In the last few decades many governments have started to shed many rules and regulations, to simplify them, and to do something about the accumulation of them. What concepts such as deregulation, self-regulation, re-regulation or conditioned self-regulation mean, what their relations are, and what relative benefits each offers is far from clear. Self-regulation is seen as an accompaniment of deregulation. However, the automatism of less governmental regulation and more self-regulation is not as natural as it might seem. Debate on the issue reveals a balancing act: deregulation is a withdrawing of the public sector; this withdrawal automatically implies an increasing degree of self-regulation on the part of those concerned. The supposition and, at the same time, effect of this point of view is that self-regulation is seen as an instrument in the hands of the state: it is an instrument that the state can, if it chooses to, bestow. The implication is that the market or other sectors of society do not govern themselves unless the government allows them to do so. Self-regulation becomes a form of interventionist governing – albeit a weak one. In other words: self-regulation as one of the tools in the toolbox of government. This is an opinion adhered to in legal circles, however in public administration there is a tendency to see self-regulation as a phenomenon in its own right, separate from government. Where self-regulation for administrative scientists is a possibility to break through the, in their view, obsolete central rule paradigm, self-regulation for legislative scholars is an instrument that can enhance the legitimacy of public action. In this perspective self-regulation is not so much the strengthening of the self-steering capacity of society, but the search for new instruments of government policy. A retreating government does not intend by it to lose part of its domain, but rather to create conditions, follow and adjust their interactions with societal sectors, instead of intervening directly. A deregulating government remains the body responsible for the effects of its own deregulating and thus for the self-regulating operations of societal fields. This short discussion demonstrates that even though the words used are the same, their background and meaning are quite different. They are two, quite different, approaches to the way dilemmas of modern governance can be conceptualised.[33]

This reflection on deregulation and self-regulation demands conceptualisation and a clarification of their relation to self-governance. Self-organising, self-steering or self governing are, in the governance perspective, not capacities or qualities created by governments, they are instead societal phenomena, existing elements of social reality that governments and others need to take into account. Self-governing as the formulation and implementation of rules by societal actors themselves, as in the example of the governing of the commons, should be considered as a mode of self-governance as a matter of definition or even principle.

Recognition, stimulation and possibly adjustment to such forms of self-governance can be considered as part of a mix of governing alternatives. Equating self-governing with self-regulation as described above narrows the discussion on what self-governance in modern societies might mean, as a consequence an opportunity is missed to explore and find out what self-governing qualities of societal sectors or other societal entities are, next to or in place of the more official forms of self-regulation. However it is the different approach rather than the different wording that is essential here: either 'self-governance' is considered an officially granted 'favour' or it is an inherent societal quality with or without official approval.

In the self-regulation option the task is of improving failing hierarchical modes of governance by replacing one form of governing for another type, hoping that it might do better. In the governance perspective self-governance is considered a societal quality to be employed more widely and systematically, and by doing so the governing failures as mentioned might be avoided or approached from another angle. This is what concerns all three theoretical notions on self-governance, the *autopoietic*, the actor constellations and the interactive governance approach: the strong doubts about the effectiveness of large-scale direct intervention by governments. Mayntz and her colleagues look for such alternatives in networks, the *autopoietic* school in better communication and the interactive governance perspective in better mixes of modes of governance. As an alternative for the dominance of hierarchical governance, all three approaches to self-governance conceptualise their own way of dealing with the complexities, diversity and dynamics of modern society.

Self-governance is an inherent capacity of societal entities at the actor level of governing interactions, and not to be mixed up with de- or re-regulation; at a structural level external influence can be exerted to enable or control such capacities.

Conclusion

The debate on and around *Steuerung* can, according to Von Beyme, be considered an expression of a growing modesty in the thinking about the capacity of the state to influence societal structures and processes.[34] This is also a major element in the governance perspective. As such, the search is for other modes of governance that can fill a potential gap if the state cannot fulfil its governing pretensions, or it could be a search for the governing capacities of other societal institutions, next to the state, in their own right. In this chapter the concept of self-governance has been explored according to the latter perspective. The governance approach to self-governance has been juxtaposed onto two others, the *autopoietic* and the actor-in-constellations schools. Both are of German origin and have been debated and contrasted for many years.

The *autopoietic* school reminds us that all social systems have a tendency for closing themselves off from their environment, and of developing and maintaining their identities based upon self-referential processes. This closure tendency is an important one, because it leads this school towards a pessimistic view on societal governance. Public governance on systemic grounds is limited. Social systems 'understand' and integrate external influences only if they can understand and accept them as part of their own internal codes. Although the insights from the *autopoietic* school are arguably too one-sided and limited, its contribution to theorising self-governance emphasising the striving for autonomy in all social systems, and the self-governing capacities based thereupon is important and should be taken seriously.

The actor-in-constellations approach to self-governance looks for self-governing tendencies in modern societies as combinations of observable and varying factors. Some of these can be deducted from historical processes of the dynamics of societal differentiation, promoting auto-nomic tendencies such as of societal sectors. Other elements such as socie-tal dependency on the product or service delivered by a sector and its organisational capacities may enhance such tendencies. Other aspects of difficulties in governing modern societies find their origin in the govern-ors side of the equation. The state is often not willing or able to curb autonomy-creating tendencies in modern societies. In particular when private corporate actors representing a sector join forces with their public counterparts actor constellations or networks can develop that are very hard to influence from the outside. The self-governing capacities of such networks can be used for governance purposes when broader interests coalesce with these networks; when broader societal governance endeav-ours are at logger-heads with these interests resistance can be tough and hard to beat.

In the social-political perspective on governance self-governance is seen as a particular mode of governance with its own particular qualities. Self-governance is considered a governance mode embedded in the inter-ferential interaction processes around primary societal processes. Self-governance is a societal quality of its own, because these primary interactions have a special capacity for dealing with societal diversity and dynamics (less so with complexity). Direct insight in these interactions is needed for governance purposes, acknowledging the special nature of these interactions, and their governance.

Whereas the systems school puts particular emphasis on limitations with a structural nature, action-oriented theorists concentrate on the developmental or dynamic aspects of such capacities, while the interaction approach stresses structural as well as intentional aspects of the capacity of social systems to govern themselves. Basic to an understanding of self-governing in all three approaches – and in some respects a common element between them – is the realisation that the differentiation process so characteristic for modern societies fundamentally influences the way these societies are and can be governed. The systems school has a more radical epistemological stance because it considers the autopoietic or self-referential tendencies and thus closed character of societal sub-systems to be 'the' characteristic of all social systems. This *autopoiesis* expresses itself in its almost complete reliance on societal self-governing and its 'pessimistic' outlook on public and co-governing.

The action-oriented school predominantly conceptualises self-governance as related to the 'Eigen' dynamics of societal subsectors, operationalising this in social and political variables such as actor constellations (or networks), interest aggregation, organisational structures etc. On self-governing and its role in social-political governance the action school has a more subtle position. *Eigen* dynamics can be looked upon and can work as a contribution or a limitation for governance depending on all kinds of situational factors, which are not 'givens' but variables to be influenced in the context of a balance between differentiating and integrating developments.

The interaction approach combines actor as well as structural elements in analysing self-governance, and emphasises the relation between the two. The centrality of its use of diversity, dynamics and complexity as structural components of modern societies introduces systems-related ideas. But with its emphasis on the interactional aspects of governing on all levels of societal aggregation, it also creates room for intentional activities of social-political actors and entities to influence factors that hinder or promote the self-governing capacity of their own or other societal (sub) systems. On the optimistic or pessimistic scale of social-political governance it probably is the most optimistic of the three: self-governance is with us (and is increasingly with us), but there is no reason to be fearful. On the contrary, self-governance of social subsystems is a prerequisite for effective social-political governance.

Self-governance is only one mode of governance, one which has received insufficient practical and scholarly attention. In this chapter I attempted to give self-governance its due place in the context of social-political governance, and some of its conceptual contours have been sketched for this purpose. However, its real capacities can only become systematically apparent in relation to the other two modes, and with the different governing orders. This will be the subject of later discussion.

Notes

1 This chapter is based upon Kooiman, Vliet van, 2000 and makes use of Merlin, 1997.
2 Kickert, 1993b; Hollander den, 1995.
3 Veld In't et al., 1991; Kickert, 1993; Teubner, 1993; Willke, 1992, 1993.
4 For two recent introductions in English, see Dunsire, 1996; Brans and Rossbach, 1997.
5 Luhmann, 1974, 1984.
6 Teubner, 1993.
7 Mayntz, 1993b, 1993c, 1997; Mayntz and Scharpf, 1995.
8 Mayntz, 1993c.
9 idem, 1993c.
10 Meijs, 1997.
11 Gerding, 1991.
12 Kolk, et al., 1999.
13 This section is based upon Merlin, 1997.
14 Teubner, 1993.
15 Moran and Wood, quoted in Buchner-Jeziorska and Evetts, 1997, p. 61.
16 Orzack in idem, p. 61.
17 Johnson, 1972.
18 Torstendahl and Burrage, 1990.
19 Freidson, 1994; Abbott, 1988.
20 Kocka, quoted in Burrage, et al., 1990, p. 205.
21 Larson, 1977.
22 Krause, 1996, p. 23.
23 idem, p. 280.
24 MacDonald, 1995, pp. 119 ff.
25 For a recent overview, van der Schans, 2001.
26 Hardin, 1968.
27 Ostrom, 1990.
28 idem, p. 45.
29 idem, pp. 52–53.
30 idem, pp. 88 ff.
31 Schans van der, 2001, pp. 101–102.
32 Ostrom, 1992; Ostrom et al., 1994; Keohane and Ostrom, 1995.
33 Eijlander, et al., 1993.
34 Beyme von, 1995.

7

'CO-' GOVERNANCE

By conceptualising 'co-governance' all kinds of co-concepts as used in the literature can be discussed. The implications of what co-governance as a special mode of governance may mean in the broader perspective can also be looked at. For many observers the co mode of governance is itself what governance is about, or even a specific type of co, such as networks are more or less equated with governance.[1] For this book this is too narrow an approach to co-governance, although networks, as will be seen in this chapter, certainly are an important co-governance phenomenon. But there are other concepts and experiences that deserve equal attention. These co-arrangements offer an opportunity to conceptualise co-governance in a broader sense and with more conceptual weight.

My first aim is to discuss a number of concepts integral to all forms of 'co-governance' albeit with different degrees of emphasis. There is an abundance of literature utilising concepts such as collaboration, co-operation and co-ordination at different levels of societal organisation, varying from inter-individual collaboration to co-ordination at the level of markets, networks and hierarchies as general social mechanisms. The first part of this chapter will be devoted to a short definition of collaboration and co-operation. Although co-ordination, is certainly about 'co', I don't see it as a central one in co-modes of governance, or to say it differently as a co-way of governing interaction. With co-modes of governance the essential element is that the interacting parties have something 'in common' to pursue together, that in some way autonomy and identity are at stake. Co-ordination, in my opinion, does not fit this definition. Co-ordination is arguably a mechanism in which parties adjust their behaviour without their identities or autonomy being directly involved. In this way the idea that 'market parties co-ordinate their behaviour' by the 'price mechanism' or by an 'invisible hand' is correct. They do this autonomously without giving up anything of their identity; on the contrary, they may intensify their identity by doing so. However, because I do think, that co-ordination is an important element in governance, I discussed it as part of the action component of governing (see Chapter 5).

For the purpose of advancing my ideas on co-governance we also have to find out what kinds of collaboration or co-operation we find in the practice of co-governing. This is achieved with a short analytical description of five different types of co-arrangements found in the governing world at present. Together they give a picture of what forms of co-governing, as a relatively new mode of governance, look like. This is only the beginning of a more systematic exploration of the importance of co-governance for the broader governance *problematique* of modern societies.

Co-governance as a mode of governance deserves special attention because from the point of view developed in this book co-governance in its varying appearances may be an answer, a reaction to or an expression of what I see as a major societal development, the tendency toward growing societal interdependence and inter-penetration. These are assumed to be related to the (growing) diversity, dynamics and complexity of modern societies and the governance issues these tendencies bring about (see further Part V). Co-governance means utilising organised forms of inter-actions for governing purposes. In social-political governing, these are key forms of 'horizontal' governing: actors communicate, collaborate or co-operate without a central or dominating governing actor as can be witnessed in the more general cetegory of societal interplays. It is especially these forms of governing that in my conceptualisation are considered to be well-equipped modes of governance in diverse, dynamic and complex situations, but certainly not exclusively so. Societal forms of co-governing are embedded within these interplay forms of societal inter-actions. This will be the subject of the last part of the chapter.

Collaboration and co-operation

Collaboration and Co-operation may seem to be two words for the same thing, but it is important to differentiate the two. Collaboration is the less formal of the two and co-operation the more formal. However the distinction is also somewhat pragmatic, because it allows me to introduce two quite distinct scholarly approaches to 'co'. The terms collaboration and co-operation allow me to do this. Concerning collaboration, ideas on 'co' are presented from both an action research tradition that paid attention to empirical detail and practical experience, and the second a political-economic tradition, strong in deductive analytical reasoning. Both are important contributions to our insight in 'co' behaviour, 'co' processes, and 'co' structures, and both offer a basis for further thinking and conceptualising 'co' phenomena in modern governance.

Collaboration

Collaborating is difficult, nevertheless it happens all the time, because it is considered to be a valuable way of tackling social-political challenges, for instance at the community level between public and private partners.[2] Doing things together in an organisation, and in particular inter-organisationally, is what we mean by social-political collaboration. Such collaborations are interesting because they are a microcosm of the broader social-political world with all its complexity, dynamics and diversity. They are not only part of this world, but in a way also represent the social political world in their efforts of governing together, instead of doing things alone.

The *diversity* of the governing world is represented in differences in aims and inputs, in language and culture, and in perceived power. The diversity of aims aspired to by those co-interacting is not only to be found across the table in the various interests of those collaborating within the confines of an agreed-upon mission or strategy. Those participating often also have hidden agendas, which may be of a private nature, but also driven by organisational aspirations. The variety of inputs obvious or hidden is certainly an important aspect of all collaborations, creating the possibility of synergetic effects. Perhaps without a certain diversity of means brought into a collective effort, there is not much sense in collaborating at all. In regard of civil servants, members of voluntary organisations, professionals and even businessmen collaborating, it is logical that the diversity in individual history, knowledge and experience will themselves be the source of 'collaborative advantage'. However, different customs and even language coupled with unique backgrounds may also present a stumbling block in the way things work out in a collaboration. Further, diversity in power is a recognised issue in collaboration: too much difference is usually considered a problem and is often a cause of anxiety among participants; on the other hand, too much equality in power may hamper the instigation of initiatives or developing leadership.

Collaborations also can be seen as being *complex* in membership and in tasks. It is not uncommon for collaborations to exist between individual members, members representing an organisation, members representing an umbrella of organisations or even a collaboration itself. So what is membership and what does representation mean? Who is accountable to whom for what the collaboration stands for? Often, tasks require varying forms of interactions between members in diverging roles and overlapping functions, depending on layers of working relations and mandates accorded to members. All this results in ambiguity, which shouldn't always be considered a negative quality of collaborations. Such vagueness may create space for members to contribute in varying ways, and involve themselves to an extent that otherwise might have been impossible.

Finally, there are tensions and changes within collaborations giving them their specific *dynamics*, they are seldom static. Internal as well as external influences add to such tensions, and affect membership and even purpose of a collaboration. Membership in collaboration often changes rapidly: organisations may come and go as well as their representatives. Often, personal commitments varying in time due to other obligations, are of greater importance than official membership. Such changes can have severe consequences for subtle balances reached, and even have an effect on what the collective effort is about, even in terms of goals pursued. Here

Huxham speaks of 'domain shifts': a cyclical relation of participants defining the focus of a collaboration, and focus defining may mean new participants.

Collaboration is a higly diverse, volatile and complex form of co-governing arrangement. It represents, in a direct way, societal diversity, dynamics and complexity in governance, and by doing so illustrates many co-governance issues.

Co-operation

Influential in conceptualising co-operation are the efforts by game theorists to develop theories of co-operation in situations of a prisoners' dilemma. A classic is Axelrod's *The evolution of Co-operation* in which the success and failure of co-operation under conditions of pursuing self-interest by co-operating actors are analysed.[3] Several behavioural rules can be deduced from these co-operation games, however being somewhat limited in their application, applying to only two players, they would be the exception rather than the rule in social-political governance. Game theories of co-operation between states in international relations have been widely used and tested, with results also potentially applicable in other governance arenas. An example of this is what is called 'achieving co-operation under anarchy'.[4] Anarchy refers here to situations lacking common authority, but not denying structured interactions. Three dimensions help to understand the propensity of actors to co-operate in such situations: mutual interest, the shadow of the future and the number of actors. The analysis of benefits to be reaped shows that a short-sighted pursuit of self-interest in such situations can be disastrous. Both sides can potentially benefit from co-operation – if they know how to achieve it.[5] Concern about the future helps to promote: co-operation long term horizons, regularity of stakes, reliability of information about the other's action and quick feedback about changes in the other's actions. The number of actors is also an issue, the main one being the possibility of defection: the larger the number of interacting actors in this 'anarchy', the greater the chance of defection.

The effect of a heterogeneity of actors co-operating in solving collective-action problem situations also have been studied systematically.[6] Three dimensions of heterogeneity have been distinguished: in capabilities, in preferences and in the heterogeneity of information and beliefs. Results of analysis are ambiguous: heterogeneity of actors can facilitate or hinder co-operation, depending on the type of heterogeneity and the context. The concentration of capabilities in a few actors may facilitate co-operation between them, but only if these actors benefit significantly from such co-operation. Heterogeneity of preferences can lead to gains from exchange, resulting in more co-operation. Conversely, heterogeneous private information can be a great hindrance to negotiated agreements. It also seems that the nature of institutions affects heterogeneity, and vice versa.

> Governing actors will co-operate under conditions involving mutual interests, limited numbers, and common concern about the future, and will provide the necessary institutions, in the shape of self-enforcing agreements based upon principles of reciprocity.

Varieties of 'co-modes'

In this section a number of major manifestations of co-governance are introduced. As stands to reason, they each express different 'co' aspects, and the way they are conceptualised depends on the disciplines dealing with them. 'Co' regimes are a subject almost exclusively looked at in International Political Economy; networks are the subject of research in Sociology, Political Science and Public Administration and public-private partnerships in Public Management and Local Government Studies. Co-management is within the territory of Marine Studies and Political-Economy, while communicative governance has been studied from a Political Science standpoint. There is hardly any cross-reference between the discussions on these five co- subjects, nor much cross-fertilisation between them. For analytical purposes the two versions of 'co' interpreted as collaboration and co-operation, can in principle be applied to all five forms of 'co' being discussed. The same can be said of the two methodologies presented in those examples. These five co-modes are structural arrangements within which governing actors collaborate or co-operate.

Communicative governance

New patterns of governance are addressed to stimulate learning processes, leading to co-operative behaviour and mutual adjustment, in order that responsibility for managing change is shared by all or most involved actors.[7] One such alternative form is communicative governance. In this type of governance a form of rationality is assumed, that considers social actors to be 'reasonable citizens'. This call upon the 'reasonable citizen' corresponds with Habermas' concept of communicative rationality, often appropriate for complex problem-solving as a substitute for instrumental, functional or strategic forms of rationality. The concept of communicative rationality is based on the idea that in interaction (temporary) actors can reach inter-subjective understanding. The authority is the 'good argument', related to empirical as well as to normative judgements. Although communicative rationality in the reality of governing is not easy to realise, it seems there are ways of practising it: 'increasing social complexity improves the chances of a calculus rooted in self-interest, leading actors into communicative rationality'.[8] Increasing social complexity means increasing interdependence and increasing potential for positive-sum solutions not obvious at first sight, but negotiable.

The prime reason for communicative governance is that for actors in the real world, faced with complex, long term and ambiguous social-political problems, joint decision-making is more adequate than traditional co-ordination by bureaucracy or the market. Communicative rationality is 'translated' into governance, especially by public participation, and guarding the public nature of the process enhances the legitimacy of its outcomes. Communicative rationality in practice is pursued, not by making the dialogue 'power-neutral', but by widening the process of governing. Results of communicative governing are expected to be defensible from the point of view of public interest and not solely to satisfy the needs of the most powerful actors. The involvement of interested actors is also expected to engender support for and commitment to mutually agreed objectives. They must be 'condemned to co-operate', and as a result communicative rationality can overcome pure political and economic reasoning.

Research on communicative governance suggests that this form of governing is feasable. However, it is obvious that communicative governance is not suitable for problem-solving when interests involved are sharply contradictory: then it will only lead to a delay of decision-making. Furthermore, interdependencies between interested actors may be expressed through harmful and obstructive objectives being pursued to the detriment of others. When rewards for obstructive behaviour are substantial, the search for consensus will be time-consuming. However, exchange of information leads to greater understanding about problems and solutions and about one's own and others' interests, improving chances for consensus. And finally analysis suggests not only the involvement of direct interests, but also to encompass broader support for issues at hand. If 'interested third parties' only play a marginal role in communicative governance projects, prospects for a broad acceptance of its results can be expected to be low.

Communicative governance suits governing situations where those involved in governing interplays are willing to reach inter-subjective understanding for co-governing purposes.

Public-Private Partnerships (PPPs)

Public-private partnership (PPP) as a form of co-governance has been of great interest for some years.[9] Explanations given for their development cite pragmatism as well as ideology, or combinations of these.[10] The appreciation of governing in partnership cannot be separated from changing views on the way public and private interact. In the 1970s relationships between state and market were alienated and estranged, resulting, from the 1980s on, in a desire for certain issues to be dealt with effectively by public and private parties jointly, rather than separately. In the 1990s, due to both an effort to enhance the legitimacy of public actions and because of a greater involvement of citizens and citizen groups, state and civil society began interacting more systematically. Such interactions between public and private, expressed in concrete forms of public-private collaboration or co-operation, are often referred to as PPPs. Their advent and growth as a form of co-governance can be seen as 'an increase of the recognition by government and the private sector of the necessity to channel, or even exploit, mutual interdependencies by means of co-operation'.[11]

A relatively narrow but concrete form of PPP occurs when there is a financial-economic motive for public-private co-operation. In such a PPP private capital is invested in (semi-) public projects or programmes. In such cases the private sector may benefit from the removal of various social, legal or administrative bottlenecks. Much broader are managerial-strategic motives for PPP. By entering into them, governments can make use of market know-how, expertise, cost-awareness and other qualities present in the private sector. On the business side one finds strategic motives such as establishing longer-term relations with the government for competitive reasons, and to gain insight in the operation of public administration. PPP also can be part of a strategy of corporate communication or social responsibility. For the voluntary sector PPPs as a form of interaction with the government can be seen as a relatively normal phenomenon. Many are active in fields that are also covered by public agencies and for them a prime motive will be to enhance their scope of activity, find legitimation for their activities and also find financial support to develop and sustain their work.

For the (successful) functioning of PPP, the following conditions should be met. Trust is important when entering into a co-operative relation such as a PPP, it brings about mutual respect and adaptation, so oiling the wheels in the complex co-operation of a PPP. Common objectives, the distinction of inputs, risks and returns, as well as the division of responsibilities and authorities, should be fairly expressed. PPP, as a process, is subject to dynamics, e.g. with regard to participants, power structures and rules of the game. It is therefore important that a dispute regulation is embodied in a PPP agreement, which also defines conditions for changing and, possibly, terminating the relationship. From the government's perspective, accountability is a key issue in PPP. From the point of view of business partners, public bodies must take their commercial orientation into account.

Many countries the world over have been the breeding ground for the political, managerial and legal trials of a great variety of PPPs. Understanding the success and failure factors at the actor level of these co-governing forms of social-political interaction is growing, but less is known about the structural conditions under which they may come into being, flourish or die. The increasing realisation of mutual interdependence in public and private circles has been an important factor in the changing climate into one more favourable to PPP. How enduring this realisation is, and how experiences with PPP will be influential in increased structural changes in the relation between the state, market and – where the voluntary sector is involved – civil society is still a moot question.

> PPPs suit governing situations where public-private parties co-operate in governing interplays to reach a win-win outcome, by exploiting mutually available resources.

Co-management

In the governance of natural resources such as forest, lakes, and coastal areas there is a tradition in managing these resources, next to self-governing by users (see the previous chapter), in a co-governing way.[12] Co-management, by definition, means that government agencies and users share responsibility for the well-being of the resource, such as preventing depletion or illness. Co-management tries to steer a middle course between government regulation and community-initiated regulation, as it requires users to organise themselves formally. Organisation is participatory rather than hierarchical, it is decentralised rather than centralised, and in my analysis typical interplay forms of interaction take place among the actors. Conseqently co-management differs from regulation by government agencies, and also from corporatist arrangements, although the line may be thin here. Co-management is more than consultation, it involves a say in formal public decision-making, and the authority to make and implement regulations on its own. It is expected that by involving users of the resource directly in its governance, the knowledge on which this is based is more adequate than would otherwise be possible. This might in turn lead to more adequate governing measures, taking into account particularities of local ecological and social governing situations. It is also expected that governing measures taken in this way, will mean that users involved: 'willingly accept the regulations as appropriate and consistent with their persisting values' and world views'.[13] And finally it is expected that if users accept governing measures as legitimate, they are more willing to comply with them.

This set of expectations is the basic reasoning for those promoting co-management as a form of governance, especially for managing natural resources. Although participation of users in governing the resource they live from and share is argued from the 'intrinsic complexity of the task at hand',[14] there may be differences of interest among them and between them and other users of the resource, or between them and society at large. As such, interest is growing in looking for institutional frameworks that go beyond inclusion only of users in co-management schemes, of putting co-management in the perspective of a broader representation of interests. Therefore, co-management as a specific form of natural resource management is not only a technical issue but also a political one. The general idea behind pleas for co-management is to make users co-responsible for the sustainability of the natural resources they exploit. However, 'market parties cannot be expected by themselves to set a process of modernisation of ecological processes by themselves. The state is needed to initiate, stimulate, inform, formalise and now and then enforce'.[15] This sharing of responsibilities between users and the state is exactly what co-governance is about.

> Co-management suits governing situations where in governing interplays the inclusion of knowledge of users (images) leads to more legitimate measures (instruments) and raising the compliance to these measures (action).

Networks

'Networks' is one of the catchwords of the day, deployed for broad sketches using the concept for an overall theory of society (Castells) to very detailed, precise and quantitative analyses of particular types of multiple interactions in all societal domains.[16] In network theory explanations given for the rise and existence of networks are as a rule of a functional interdependent nature: needs for resources, combatting common environmental uncertainties, strategic considerations etc. Interactions in networks are mainly of a horizontal nature, although minor hierarchical elements also can develop in networks, for example by linking-pin organisations.[17] Next to networks of firms, non-profit organisations or public agencies within their own societal domain, are network developments between the societal domains, the market, civil society and the state, as specimens of co-governing these are of special importance in the governance perspective. Networks between state and market have been a source of intellectual curiosity and discussion for quite some time. Network arrangements for policy purposes characterised them for a long time, but recently attention to their management has increased. Among network studies are approaches with an emphasis on the actor or organisation level; these are supplemented with studies looking at actor-structure qualities and one also can find studies theorising their structural components. In these studies all kinds of labels or metaphors typify them: pressure pluralism/competitive pluralism, state corporatism, group sub-government, corporate pluralism, iron triangles, sector or meso-corporatism, issue networks, policy communities, negotiated economy and others could be added.[18]

Approaches to networks that explicitly conceptualise them as modes of governance, expressing 'new' government-society interactions, merit special attention. Several lines of thinking can be noticed, of which three examples will be given: one from the UK; one from the Netherlands; and one from Germany. In a UK analysis network development as a new governance mode is closely linked to ideas about 'hollowing-out of the state', the argument being that, especially under the influence of New Public Management, the state has become 'a collection of inter-organisational networks made up of governmental and societal actors with no sovereign actor able to steer or regulate'.[19] In this perspective governance becomes more or less equalised with networks as a third governing structure next to bureaucracy and the market.

The Dutch approach to managing networks, is linked to questions of governance.[20] This network perspective is a reaction to the rationalist central rule approach and to the multi-actor perspective on governance. The central rule approach emphasises relations between a central ruler and target groups. These relations are authoritative, and recommendations for governance involve co-ordination and centralisation. In the multi-actor perspective again we find dimensions as relations between a central ruler and local actors, but governance emphasis goes in the opposite direction, and recommendations involve a retreat from central rule in favour of local actors. This Dutch network perspective emphasises interdependent interactions between actors, in which information resources and goals are exchanged.

Finally we have an example from Germany, that also considers networks singularly as a mode of governance, and in some ways this is the most radical network view. Although different authors give different accents, the common theme among them is that societal developments on the one hand, and a shifting role of the state on the other, have located network formation on the borderline between state and society to a new and specific governance mode.[21] A participatory drive from societal groups and interests resulting in strong promotional or blockage forces, coupled with governments confronted with growing demands and diminishing *Steuerungs*-capacities, have made for 'a major shift ... in societal governance from hierarchical control to horizontal co-ordination', [22] and networks play a crucial role in this co-ordination. This form of co-ordination is not without problems, because co-operation between actors within networks cannot be assured. Scharpf, building on insights from bargaining theory, and Marin drawing on exchange theory, have tried to make it plausible that such negative effects of networks can be overcome.[23]

There can be hardly any doubt that the emergence of mixed networks of public and private actors is an important complement to or change of more traditional governance structures. How fundamental one considers these occurrences to be, is partly a matter of theoretical orientation, partly of personal judgement and taste. In the governance perspective mixed networks between public and private parties are seen as an expression of interdependencies at the intentional level of governing interactions within the context of inter-penetration tendencies between societal sectors, including the public sector at the structural level of these interactions (see further Chapter 13). There is little doubt that networks are a major form of governance dealing with societal complexity: in their plurality they express societal diversity, and they can also be seen as a partial answer to the dynamics of modern societies, capable of handling tensions related to these dynamics.[24] Networks as mixes of public and private actors have potential as a governance device, they also give rise to a number of 'constitutional' questions. These are not to be neglected in their life cycle.

> Networks as forms of co-governance suit governing situations where a relatively open form of (public-private) interplay can be organised to represent a variety of interests.

Regimes

Regimes can be said to have been designed to manage the multiple interconnectedness of modern international relations.[25] In a leading definition, regimes are seen as 'a set of implicit or explicit principles, norms, rules and decision-making procedures around which actors' expectations converge in a given area of international relations.[26] Several authors have noted that the four elements of this definition are not on the same level: norms and values underlie rules and procedures. Rules and procedures may change over time, but must remain consistent with the norms underpinning – and defining the characteristics of – the regime. Changes in rules and procedures mean changes within regimes, changes in norms and values imply a change of regime. Why create, why join a regime? A stock answer is: to solve puzzles posed by common problems or by technology. But recognition of a common problem is not a necessary condition for joining a regime; joining may be encouraged by the attractiveness of proposed solutions, even if the problem itself is of little concern to the actor.[27] So what do regimes provide for their members? First, they establish stable expectations of each other's behaviour, permitting the development of working relationships; and second they provide information and yardsticks/standards of – not necessarily proper – behaviour.

How does one recognise successful regimes? Crucial elements are their coherence, effectiveness (compliance) and durability. It appears that regime performance should not be overestimated. Despite professed intentions, regimes are in practice anything but constant, nor are they continuous over time. They are easily upset by changes in balance of bargaining power or changes in perception of national interest. What is actively promoted as an orderly regime may not work well, while elsewhere unstoppable regime-like structures may arise in silence. New understanding of regimes facilitates this. Bühl sees a web of regimes closing in on the globe. The density of some regimes is such that an *Alleingang* becomes an impossibility.[28] A regime can be called 'strong' when it is highly institutionalised, high-trust, and enhances the identity of its members. If principles become less coherent, or if actual practice is increasingly inconsistent with them, a regime will weaken.[29] However, even strong regimes may fall apart when powerful challenges or exogenous shocks change the beliefs and/or allegiance of members.

Formal regimes may be regarded as the tip of the iceberg, what lies beneath is a formal–informal amalgam governing an issue area, constraining or expanding the scope for individual action, and sanctioning non-compliance. Regimes and actors, in turn, are nested in structures that can also be termed (sub-)regimes and (sub-)networks, which constrain or expand the terms in which 'upper-structure' regimes can evolve. For example, (implied) sanctions for non-compliance may find their way into accepted norms and practices of international law.

Much of what has been said above points to the power of value judgements. Normative questions are involved: is equilibrium desirable? Is order positive? Attention to structures of security, finance, welfare, knowledge and power is crucial to correct easily overlooked value biases. Due to their position inbetween permanent structure and general policy planning, regimes are much like technocratic management systems and therefore difficult to control democratically. But though they are often (at least nominally) based on consensus-building, they are not politically neutral. Regimes are politics, exactly because they are based on values. Therefore the development of a meta-regime consisting of rules and criteria necessary for creating regimes that are accountable to those affected could be a useful and fruitful objective (see also Chapter 11).

Regimes are in the eye of the beholder. It is acceptable to posit regimes conceptually even if they cannot easily be demonstrated. Regimes are conceptualised as institutions, as systems of governance, and as express-ing 'both the parameters and the perimeters of international govern-ance'.[30] Typically a demand for governance arises in issue areas where interdependence among states creates both conflicts and incentives for co-operation.[31] The above quotes underline the importance of regimes as a form of co-governance in the international arena. They also hint at gener-alising insights from this literature to arenas outside the scope of inter-national relations.

> Regimes as a form of co-governance suit governing situations where parties adhere to a set of agreed upon action rules.

Synthesis

An analytical description of five different governing arrangements has thus far been presented. Comparing these five 'co' forms, together form-ing what I consider to be the *nucleus* of the co mode of governance, was done using the interaction concept as a synthetic tool. A short discussion about the intentional level of these five co governing arrangements follows, followed by some conclusions about the structural aspect of them. Finally, I will speculate on some wider issues related to these various forms of co-governance.

Co-governance at the intentional level of governing interactions

When discussing co-governing interactions, I have in mind that these interactions 'fit' within the general sphere of societal interplays, displaying the main features of interplays, but for governing purposes. Interplays I see as all those semi-formalised 'horizontal' societal interactions in which actors or entities participate more or less equally; these interactions are relatively flexibly organised and aim at a comparatively concrete, but negotiable purpose. Basically all five modes of co-governance previously discussed fit this category of societal interplays, albeit with different modalities of organisational flexibility and specificity of common govern-ing purpose. To simplify the exposition, discussion will be limited to the first three examples presented, communicative governance, PPP and co-management. The latter two, networks and regimes, will appear as examples for integrating some ideas on the structural level of those co-governing interactions.

Two sources can help shed light on the intentional level of co-governing interactions. First they can be considered from the point of view of inter-actions, with its attention to actors and processes (see Chapter 2). Second, we can search for special qualifications they have in terms of elements of governing, i.e. their contribution to image formation, instrumentation or activating co-governing interactions. From both sources examples will be given exploring integrated findings on the intentional level of co-governance. In a process perspective we examine aspects such as motives (inputs) and consequences (output) of co-operative governing interactions. In PPPs motives for co-operation can be short term and pre-cise when both parties want to share resources for the realisation of a con-crete project. However a PPP can also have a long-term and not such precise a character, when collaborating parties plan to pool capacities for strategic purposes. Motives for a co-arrangement can also be of a mixed character with short and long term goals, explicit and implicit purposes and obvious and hidden agendas, as often will be the case in social-political governance. Notwithstanding these differences, a general motive for entering a 'co' governing construction of this nature is the search for synergetic effects, where outcomes not easily or not at all can be reached acting alone. This may also include 'positive' side effects, when for exam-ple a strategic alliance also forms the basis for short-term benefits, but also can have 'negative' side effects when a too formalised organisational framework prevents reacting to unforeseen problems or unexpected opportunities. However, the motivation to set up a communicative governing framework, can itself be due to foresight of unexpected events and developments taking place. Communicative governing has demon-strated its value in areas where the need to work together is recognised, but the objective or the expected result is as yet unclear. Learning-by-doing is not only the *modus operandi* in communicative governance, but might be considered one of the purposes as well.

Co-management schemes are put in place, again, for other reasons. As indicated, there is not only a string of reasoning behind them, each being a (sub) motive in itself, but the combination of them makes for co-management. Thinking in terms of managing means already a multi-purpose arrangement, a striving for integrated outcomes. Summarising these findings on the process facets of co-governing interactions, we can say that for each of them special motives can be deduced, and kinds of outcomes expected.

In an actor perspective, overseeing these three forms of co-governance, the findings seem to support the idea of analysing the intentional level of interactions as 'actors-in-situations': Such situations can generate, define, and determine the course of an interaction process. Actors in inter-actor-situations have the capacity to control some of the variation in their own actions....[32] This is precisely what the presentation of these three actors in co-governing-situations show, the possibility to extend and refine insights in co-governance from their conceptual richness and detailed practical experiences.

The synthesis can also be enriched from the second source referred to: the three governing elements distinguished. This can simply be summarised, because the above argumentation holds: communicative governance can be considered co-governing with an emphasis on image formation, learning-by-doing; PPP can be seen as primarily instrumental, of pooling resources; and co-management I see as a co-governing scheme aimed at activation, of creating action space for legitimate governance.

Co-governance at the structural level of governing interactions

I will first say something about an issue that I alluded to earlier, but have not as yet explicitly put on my conceptual agenda: the concept structure has so far been used in three somewhat related ways, without making the relation between them clear. In Chapter 2, and again in this chapter, structure as the social, economic or other, circumstance was discussed, enabling or limiting the intentional level of interactions. Also, in Part II of the book, structure was used as an indication of contexts for the three elements needed for governing: factual and evaluative systems for images, resources for instruments, and social-political capital for the action component of governing. Furthermore, in this part of the book, I designated the three modes of governance themselves, self co- and hierarchical, as being of a structural nature. Starting with the use of structure, the relation between them is relatively simple: we can see the structural components of the three governing elements as specifications of the general structures of societal interactions. In other words, fact and value systems, resources and social-political capital can be considered to be the structural component of all governing interactions, with images, instrumentation and activation at their intentional level.

The conceptual relation between structure and intention as discussed in Chapter 2, can also be extended to the modes of governance. Here one might think of the way in which certain structural-cultural circumstances may enable or hinder practising certain types of co governing arrangements, such as the five presented in this chapter. In some countries 'co' has traditionally occupied, next to self and hierarchical governance, a rather prominent place. This might enhance the opportunity for experimenting with new co-modalities, for instance communicative governance in the Netherlands, or co-management in Norway. Comparative analysis can reveal how structural and cultural factors enable or control the actual use of such co-arrangements. This also may apply to the reversed movement: how experiments with new forms of governance, such as 'co', may seep through structural constraints and lead to new (structural) mixes of the three governance modes, such as the experience with networks as a form of co governance. As demonstrated, at least three schools of thought can be found about the role and place of networks as co-governing arrangements. And it is notable that these three points of view, originate from European countries, the UK, the Netherlands and Germany, with quite different governance traditions. Thus it may be understandable that within these traditions different questions about networks as co forms of governing are being raised. Regimes, and the way these fit traditional patterns of international relations may also be a source for the same kinds of questions asked and issues raised. However, my knowledge on regimes, and the literature I consulted on them, means I cannot say further than that it is my impression that the major discussions on regimes focus in particular on their structural nature, rather than on their intentional level. Concluding these short observations on the structure of co-governance I am quite convinced it is a rich subject for systematic contemplation, especially when the relation with the intentional level of governing interactions is also taken into consideration.

This theme – of the relation between these two levels of governing interactions – will return time and again, but in particular in the last part of the book, when I discuss the concepts of interdependence and inter-penetration. Systematic attention will be given to the why and how of assumed interdependencies in solving (major) societal problems or creating (major) societal opportunities in modern governance, within broad, structural, developments, which I call inter-penetration. For co-governance this translates into whether we can find forces of a structural/cultural nature stimulating or hindering 'co' in becoming an independent mode of governance, next to self, and hierarchical governance. This might be the case when (structural) inter-penetrations, such as between state, market and civil society, make the boundaries between them somewhat permeable. These overlaps at the societal level also may become the source for experimenting with new forms of co-governance at the intentional level of governing interactions. 'Co' as a middle way between self-governance and hierarchical may be particularly open to shifts in the balance between the three governance modes. However, we must also recognise that such shifts and the way these find their expression in new forms of governance are not always easy to ascertain, because some features of self-governance may come close to 'co' forms, and in co-governance hierarchical aspects are not lacking completely. Also opinions can differ on where to locate a relatively new phenomenon such as co-management: one might emphasise the self-governing aspects of it, or instead it may be considered an offspring of neo-corporatism, and thus a variant of hierarchical governance.

Another structural issue of importance pertains to cultural conditions for promoting or hindering the advent of 'co'. Two contrasting hypotheses can be developed. One states that conditions for the development of co-governance are structurally more favourable in countries where there is a tradition in consensual governance. However, one might also hypothesise that countries with a more polarised tradition in social-political governance have a particular need for alternative ways of dealing with problems or opportunities of modern societies, and consequently there will be a greater need to develop new modes of co-governance. Recent literature suggests the second option is more probable, as networks in the UK (more polarised governance) are considered to be *the* new mode of governance,[33] while in the Netherlands (more consensual governance) interest is not so much in networks as a new mode of governance, but in their management.[34] A second indication in the same direction arguably is that in Sweden[35] and the Netherlands, both countries with a consensual tradition, PPPs occur relatively infrequently and have a narrow project character, whereas in the UK, Australia and the USA (more polarised governance) PPP's have a higher frequency and a broader programme orientation.[36] Whatever their specifics, these examples suggest that structural conditions may influence the emergence of co-arrangements as discussed in this chapter, and probably also the other way around. Much more research is needed to make conceptual relations more substantive, and empirically little has been proven.

Co-arrangements between public and private actors permeate the boundaries between the societal domains of state, market and civil society, thus creating more opportunities for experimenting with varying forms of interplays.

Conclusion

In this chapter the contours of co-governance as one of the three governance modes have been sketched. In the first part of the chapter I spoke about 'doing things together', as to be found in the reality of governance, sometimes referred to as collaboration, sometimes as co-operation. How they are referred to is of no consequence, what matters is the way in which different scholars or schools of thought highlight particular aspects of 'co', while ignoring others. In that respect the two approaches mentioned both merit attention, as they represent a variety of ways of observing more or less the same object, and it is amazing to see how contrasting the insights derived from the methods used are. Personally I am satisfied more with the action-research than with the political-economic version of 'co', both of course have their separate contribution to make to the study of 'co' in modern governance: one more from an inductive angle, the other from a deductive one. Combining the two into an overall framework for advancing the study of 'co' may remain wishful thinking, and certainly is far beyond the scope of this book.

The second part of the chapter presented several examples of co-governing that together form the co-governance mode. The intentional level of these governing interactions, as well as their structural component and the relation between the two levels revealed the differentiated ways the co-mode can be substantiated. All three aspects gave rise to specific matters requiring that they be looked at separately, and compared as a collective. What is striking about them is that in one way or another they seem to be answers to the sort of questions raised in a general sense in this book, enabling established relations between them and other parts of the conceptualisation to begin, such as differentiating them according to elements of governing, relating them to different 'structuration' theories, and to concepts such as interdependence and inter-penetration.

Whatever contributions to, and ambiguities about, forms of 'co' are brought forward, the relevance of co-governance as a separate governance mode will grow, the more interdependencies and inter-penetrations in modern societies are recognised as of practical and thus of theoretical importance. However, as I formulated it in the concluding chapter of *Modern Governance*, for new forms of social-political governance to emerge, a number of 'objective' and 'subjective' conditions have to be fulfilled. Traditional methods and structures must have failed, organisational and interest-mediation patterns not (yet) well-established, issues raised should be of great concern to those directly involved, and potential 'win-win' outcomes to be expected. Those objective conditions should be supported by more 'subjective' ones such as a certain amount of mutual trust, willingness to take (common) responsibility and the presence of a certain degree of political involvement and social support.[37]

Notes

1 Rhodes, 1997.

2 This section is partly based upon Huxham, 1996, 2000a and b. For another fruitful way of conceptualising and testing co-operation as a co-governance mode, see Greca, 2000.

3 Axelrod, 1984.

4 Oye, 1986.

5 Axelrod and Keohane, 1986.

6 Keohane and Ostrom, 1995.

7 This section is based on Vliet van, 1992, 1993.

8 Dryzek, 1987, quoted by Vliet van, 1993, p. 103.

9 This section is partly based on Kouwenhoven, 1991, 1993. For a recent overview of PPP, See Osborne, 2000.

10 McQuaid, 2000.

11 Kouwenhoven, 1993, p. 123.

12 This section is based on Schans van der, 2001 who offers a broad overview of the recent discussions on this concept; and Dubbink, 1999.

13 Jentoft, 1989, p. 139.

14 Jentoft and McCay, 1995, p. 228.

15 Dubbink, 1999, pp. 157–158.

16 Castells, 1996.

17 Jansen, 1995, pp. 103 ff.

18 Jordan and Schubert, 1992.

19 Rhodes, 1997, p. 57.

20 Kickert et al., 1997.

21 Marin, 1990; Marin and Mayntz, 1991; Kenis and Schneider, 1991; Mayntz, 1993a; Messner, 1997; Scharpf, 1997; Börzel, 1998.

22 Kenis and Schneider, 1991, p. 15.

23 Marin, 1990; Scharpf, 1993.

24 Marsh, 1998.

25 This section is based on Warner, 1996.

26 Krasner, 1982, p. 186.

27 Gupta et al., 1995.

28 Bühl, 1995.

29 Krasner, 1982.

30 Kratchowill and Ruggie, 1986, p. 759, quoted by Hasenclever et al., 1997, p. 1.

31 Young, 1994, p. 15, as quoted by Hasenclever et al., 1997, p. 2.

32 See Chapter 2, Intentional level of interactions section.

33 Kickert et al., 1997.

34 Rhodes, 1997.

35 Collin and Hansson, 2000.

36 Osborne, 2000.

37 Kooiman, 1993, p. 251.

8

HIERARCHICAL GOVERNANCE

If from the exposition on modes of governance so far, it might have appeared as if governing has basically changed, this impression is (probably) wrong. The rationalised, bureaucratic or hierarchical state so well described and modelled by Max Weber, is still around us, and very much alive. At its margins – and maybe even at the centre here and there – cracks are appearing and critical voices about its performance are becoming more vocal. Whether the state is 'withering away', 'hollowing out', *Entzaubert* ('lost its magic') or even *La fin de l'État?* ('ended'), as some observers advance, remains more a point of view than anything else. The hierarchical model of societal governance may have lost some of its classical glory, but in many areas of social-political life it is still a major governing actor to reckon with, and thus it should be given its due place in analysing societal governance. It would be neglectful then, not to take this model of societal governance seriously, either state-wise or in other societal domains.

Equating hierarchy with bureaucracy, and even more so with public bureaucracy, as is often done, is too easy, and means losing the opportunity to use these concepts for different purposes.[1] For instance, the organisation of the Roman Catholic Church is always called a hierarchical one, not due to its bureaucratic traits, but because of the hierarchical structure of the clergy. I treat bureaucracy as a structural level of certain governing actions (see Chapter 5), and hierarchy as a far broader concept. In fact I consider it the structural component of governing interventions. For systematic thinking about hierarchy as an important form of 'rational social action' we can go back to Dahl and Lindblom's classic *Politics, Economic and Welfare* (1963). For them hierarchy is, next to polyarchy, the price system and bargaining, one of four major processes for calculation and control, involving leaders and non-leaders. 'Hierarchy is the process in which leaders control non-leaders'.[2] Hierarchy is not seen as a pure unilateral control and is considered to be a continuum, conceptualised in terms of its contribution to rational social action, as well as its costs.[3] This way of looking at hierarchy fits quite well within the approach of this book.

I have entitled this chapter 'hierarchy', to underline the fact that the types of governing interactions discussed display a 'top-down' character: those governing are, or see themselves, as in some way superimposed above those governed. There are many ways to express this relation, but hierarchy comes closest to the essence of the ordering of such governing interactions. Although the term hierarchy may suggest a uni-directional mode of governance, we deal here with governing interactions, be it of a special type. Hierarchical governance as a structural arrangement, should be seen as embedded in a broader category of societal interactions, in this case interventions. These, of all forms of societal interactions, are the most 'vertical' and formalised ones. Governing entities influence the behaviour of other actors participating in these interactions, even involuntarily and often with sanctions attached. Such interventions are common to all spheres of societal life, as well as to the hierarchical way of governing interactions. Because of their general binding character and the sort of sanctions available, public interventions (and the state as its hierarchical expression) have received more attention in theory as well as in practice, than those in other societal spheres. These undoubtedly have an importance of their own, but in the context of this chapter, the public form of interventions and hierarchy will receive most attention (see further Chapter 13).

To start the discussion, I will first deal with the two concepts steering and control, which can be considered as giving body to this governance mode. Steering and control are ways of conceptualising intervention processes, and as such express and cover many societal governing interactions of a top-down nature. This discussion will be followed by focusing on the state as the interventionist institution *par excellence*. As will be shown, we may better speak of a changing role than of a shrinking role of the state in societal governance. This will be illustrated by drawing attention to some changes in state activity: from command to regulation, from procuring to enabling and from benevolence to activation. The chapter ends by focusing on three major forms of interventionist interactions, and the changes they are subject to. To underline that we have to see these interventions 'in context', as expressing the hierarchical governance mode they represent, the 'arena' will be referred to in discussing them, the legal arena and the policy arena.

Steering and control

Steering

Steering is a powerful metaphor for (public) governing in the traditional sense. In Plato we find evidence of this image for the *polis*, the city or the state as a ship. And even at that time it had lost its course in his opinion: 'speaking about a captain a bit deaf and short-sighted, limited in seamanship; a crew quarrelling about how to navigate the ship not having learned the art of navigation ... trying to get hold of the helm'.[4] Recently, the idea of steering as a governance concept has lost favour, despite it, only a few decades ago, being one of the promising ideas in cybernetic-systems theorising, with its high expectations of the governability of societies. Although 'steering the ship of state' has apparently lost its attraction in scholarly political and administrative circles, steering is still daily governing practice, particularly when coping with societal dynamics. In current literature, it is assumed that such governing situations don't exist any more, and thus this sort of theorising is outdated. This is a short-sighted view. There are still many areas of societal governance where the steering metaphor is still apt at capturing what is going on and describing practical ways of dealing with societal dynamics (see further Chapter 12).

The key element of steering, whatever version one might apply – from a rather mechanistic to a highly voluntary one – is direction. Steering is arguably a global and non-mechanistic form of 'directed' governing. Direction dictates that governors, in interaction with those governed, have a general idea of where they want to go: a global image of a future state they prefer above the existing one. This direction in steering as a governing activity may be goal oriented, but it is better to speak of goal-seeking than goal-setting. Since steering is a way of intervening, it looks uni-directional and top-down, such as expressed in goal-setting. However, as with all governing activities, steering is an interactive occupation, for which goal-seeking seems preferable to goal-setting. Plato was well aware of this. The ideal state is, in his opinion, like a well-built ship, when steering the right course depends on the interaction between captain and crew: 'But how do reason and the senses combine to ensure the safety of a ship, in fair weather or foul? Isn't it because captain and crew interpret sense-data by reason, as embodied in the expertise captains have, that they keep themselves and the whole ship safe?'[5] And in socio-cybernetic theorising, the steering governor is not conceptualised in terms of exerting power, but 'as the boss ... who guards over interactions'.[6]

Control

Traditionally, control in the public sector is considered a matter of political accountability and/or a matter of political-bureaucratic relations. In the Weberian tradition both were 'insured' by proper legal/constitutional and bureaucratic rules. While this 'insurance' as norm is not in doubt, serious questions have been raised about the practice of such rules.[7] Modern public organisations are highly complex and diverse 'cobwebs'. Controlling them from within or from without demands abilities to 'mirror' these traits, in other words the controller has to be as complex and diverse as the cobweb to be controlled. The more complex tasks to be carried out are, the more difficult it is to control them. In modern (public) governance top-down control is still an important mode of controlling complex activities, but other arrangements providing checks and balances, and even bottom up control, are wide spread to cope with complexity. Control of diversity within the public sector is not only expressed in the variety of institutions with specific control functions (audit offices, courts, management controls), but also by the plurality of instruments available to and used by these offices. Not only is trying to master diversity in the ways mentioned a characteristic of modern (public) governance, many of these controlling efforts are at odds with each other, in substance, scope, time and sanctions attached to them.

Within the market sector, the hierarchical mode of governance also exists, and is phrased in the relevant literature either as control or as power and control. In their typology of governing mechanisms Campbell et al. distinguish all kinds of hierarchical interactions in the market, such as vertical and horizontal integration, conglomerates and job-control union contracts. Each of these governing mechanisms has its own rules and procedures for compliance, with combinations of coercion and consent. Exercising power and control is, according to these authors, a critical impetus for change in markets, in particular in the struggle for new governance structures and institutionalising new power relations.[8] In the same vein Fligstein argues that control processes within markets reflect internal and across-firm power struggles. Concepts of control and the understanding of how a market works, allowing actors in it to interpret their world and to act in control situations. He also discusses a hierarchy or status ordering of firms in a given market. In stable markets the identities and status hierarchy are well known, as is a great deal of agreement on conceptions of control and the strategies implied in them.[9]

Of steering and control as major expressions of hierarchical governance, steering is the more 'political' of the two; control is more 'administrative' in nature. Steering has more dynamic features, while control is geared further towards governing complexity and diversity.

The changing face of the modern state

States, even if they possibly show 'hollowing-out' tendencies, are still the central and omnipresent interventionist societal entity. Although other constructions are tested, and are becoming more and more accepted, hierarchy is still the most common attribute for public governing bodies. They continuously intervene, they steer and control, their structure is hierarchical from local to international level, and for all practical purposes they are expressions of the modern state.

From ancient times there has been interest in the state as a subject of scholarly study and analysis, resulting in an abundance of theories on it. For my purpose a relevant theory is by Cerny, working explicitly within a structuration framework, using structure and agent concepts and the relations between them.[10] In his view the state is a contingent phenomenon, being the product of:

> a certain amount of historical accident, of circumstantial choices made by political agents, and of pre-existing structures being in flux due to a wide range of interconnected changes … changing patterns of economic inequality; changing forms of coercion and violence, changing ways of looking at the world culturally; and of course, classic forms of political conflict and change.[11]

Four sets of state tasks can be identified, each one in itself, but also in their interrelation, shaping the behaviour of state actors, and in doing so structurally reproducing themselves somehow. These tasks, according to Cerny, can be defined as: 1) the definition of society, its character or 'fabric' and its boundaries; 2) the 'political' process by which access to office is gained and the state can be influenced; 3) the design and care for state apparatus itself, such as control of its organisation, decision-making structures and division of authority and responsibilities and 4) decisions by state actors with an impact on the wider society.[12] Major areas of state activity such as these are the foundation for the state as a governing entity. They shape the behaviour of social-political governors, and by these governing actions these governors influence concurrently its structure.

Before discussing a few major interventions by the modern state, and the arenas structuring them, some changes that have received attention in the literature recently will be examined. The outcome of these transformations is a matter of speculation and discourse, because such developments as follow are in progress. I present these tendencies under the *epitheta* given to them in the literature. However, the custom, often found, of taking the features and exalting them to the state as a whole will not be followed. In my opinion there is no such thing as an 'enabling' or a 'regulatory' state. There are, within and around the state, 'enabling' or 'regulating' tendencies, but also there are many other changes, and sometimes these are contradictory. This is not new: elsewhere we find examples such as the 'sovereign' state, the 'institutional' state, the 'supermarket' state, the 'corporate' and the 'bargaining' state.[13] All these 'formulas' together show the dynamics of the modern state, and '[w]hilst the state … may be in retreat in some respects, its activity may be increasing in others. And nowhere … has its key decision-making role been seriously undermined'.[14] What follows are three examples of changes in such key roles.

> The state may change its ambitions, but seldom will it give up or wither away completely. It will redefine its hierarchical mode of governance in the light of shifting aspirations.

From command to regulation

The commanding state has, according to Majone, three major ways of intervening in the economy: income redistribution, macroeconomic stabilisation and market regulation.[15] Redistribution includes transfers of resources from one group to another as well as the provision of 'merit goods' that citizens are compelled to consume. Stabilisation attempts to achieve and sustain satisfactory levels of economic growth and employment. Market regulation aims at correcting certain types of market failure. All modern states use these methods of intervention, although to what extent differs from country to country, and from period to period. The redistributing interventions called for its own structural *epitheton*: the welfare state or varieties of those. This – in my view – commanding state has or had the following characteristics:

- tax-and-spend as the major instrument
- budgetary allocations as the main arena of political conflict
- parliament, ministerial departments, nationalised firms, and welfare services as characteristic institutions
- political parties, civil servants and corporate groups as key actors; the political style is discretionary
- policy culture corporatist and political accountability direct.

This commanding state being at its height in the 1970s, showed or was believed to show all kinds of defects, so it moved to another *epitheton*, the regulatory one.

This regulatory state is characterised by privatisation, liberalisation, welfare reform and deregulation. In the regulatory state the emphasis is less on direct, rigid and restrictive rules and interventions, than on administrative decentralisation and regionalisation. These new and indirect interventions require new structures of responsibilities and new forms of control and accountability. The regulation is aimed at third parties, who provide the merit goods, according to rules set by central authorities or bodies especially created for that purpose. According to Majone, the regulatory state can be characterised by its main function, of correcting market failures, using rule-making as its main instrument. The main area of political conflict is review and control of this rule-making; characteristic institutions are parliamentary committees, independent agencies and commissions and tribunals; key actors are single-issue movements, regulators, experts, judges; the policy style is rule-bound legalistic, the political culture can be described as pluralist and political accountability is indirect. Because of these specific features the regulatory state may have problems with its legitimacy, which might be best tackled by strengthening its accountability structures.

> The transformation from command to regulation shows a considerable change in aims and tools, however, the state remains the central governing entity.

From procuring to enabling

In another vein, withdrawing tendencies of the state in areas of service provision such as welfare, social security, health and education, demand attention. In the classical notion of the welfare state procuring such services was a major public task. This retreating process expresses the notion that the state should limit itself to a number of core activities: those which it considers cannot be left to others. Control instruments are put in place, instead of procuring those services or products itself. Although other terms are used, they will here be brought together under the term 'enabling'. Important in this move from procuring to enabling is the introduction of market thinking and market mechanisms either directly, such as by introducing competition into the delivery of those services, or indirectly, by the use of instruments such as contracts and evaluation to control these provisions. The idea of enabling is also linked with notions of removing constraints and creating incentives, thus offering providers and clients opportunities to achieve individually tailored solutions, which the state itself could never produce. This move towards enabling results in the question 'who is enabled by whom to do what?'[16] Although the state always had some kind of an enabling role, the recent shift in emphasis has been from the citizen being enabled by state provision, and thus being the enabled party, to enabling the providing agency, either on a profit or non-profit making basis. There are also elements in the concept of the enabling state to reduce or replace influence of organised (corporatist) interest groups, and to enhance the role of the voluntary and informal (civil society) sector.[17] Next to these ambitions, there is the shift towards privatisation, not only to reduce costs but also to improve the performance and effectiveness of tasks and services.[18] All these changes have their positive and negative points, which in the literature and in practice are subject to (sometimes heated) debate. It would be too narrow a view to see all this in terms of management, either 'new public', or otherwise.

> By using market mechanisms for the provision of (public) services, the enabling state raises serious questions about its functions and competencies, its boundaries and role, in other words about the nature of its governing and governance.

From benevolence to activation

A third direction, through which the traditional state does not give up, but changes its focus while retaining its basic pretensions, is in relation to the citizen. In German public governance the 'activating' state is, in theory as well as in practical politics, a rising star.[19] One can take different starting points to mark this re-orientation, but an original one is Max Weber's concept of 'legitimate or legal authority', expressing the hierarchical element of the relation between citizen and state, as well as principles of legality. This form of state appearance can be found in concepts such as the 'liberal democratic state', with its emphasis on individual rights and a retaining role of the state; or in the *Soziale Rechtstaat* and comparable notions, consisting of an almost unlimited involvement of the state in, and responsibility for, the life and well-being of its citizens. All these substantive state roles in relation to its citizens are based upon principles of 'legal hierarchical authority', i.e. the benevolent state.[20]

In the concept of the activating state a new position and role is suggested that trys to find a way out of the situation of the state structurally being unable to fulfil all the tasks requested of it (overload) or leave them to others (communitarism, subsidiarity or privatisation). In the concept, the initiative for societal activities emanates from the state, but it is not held responsible for full implementation of the goals to be achieved. Key elements are: mobilisation, guiding, support, R&D (*Entwicklungsagentur*) and 'public grease' (*Öffentliches Schmiermittel der Gesellschaft*). The realisation that the state cannot solve all societal problems is not considered to be an argument for a 'minimal state', but for a state that systematically scrutinises which tasks can be most effectively carried out by whom, either by doing so itself, by developing and stimulating self-governance, or in co-operation. It has a strong dynamic dimension externally because it operates in continuous interaction with activated citizens and citizen groups at all levels of governance, particularly in areas where goals are vague and instruments under-developed. This external interaction requires an internal reform strategy, in which innovative external initiatives constantly demand new priority setting, demand-supply orientation, quality control, and guarding of negative external effects.

> The essence of the activating state involves the promotion of civic potentials by means of sharing tasks and duties. Overall responsibilities of the state are not abandoned but given a new, dynamic and innovative substantive quality.

Arenas of hierarchical governance

The most classical and characteristic mode of governing interaction between the state and citizens – individually or organised – takes the form of interventions. As discussed above, the state is not the only societal institution where this governance mode is practised, it can also be found in the market, and less so, but still, in civil society. Because state interventions are structured in a systemic way, they have become a specific mode of hierarchical governance, needing special attention. The systemic nature of state or public governance is mainly due to the use of two major instruments, laws and policies. For almost any subject, on almost every level of public involvement in societal affairs, laws, policies or combinations of the two, are standard governing practice. The systemic nature of law was encountered earlier, when discussing its assumed *autopoietic* features (Chapter 6), and bodies of policies as found in public task fields often show the same attributes.

Each pattern of hierarchical governance has specific qualities at their intentional level, at their structural level and in the relation between these two levels as well, for which the label 'arena' seems appropriate.

The legal arena

The relation between the state and the rule of law is close, as modern positivist legal theory acknowledges, but certainly not an exclusive one.[21] Many areas of social life are governed with the help of self-governing norms and rules, and co-governing procedures are becoming more popular (see Chapters 6 and 7). All modern states engage in comprehensive legal action, and by doing so influence many aspects of the private lives of their citizens, individually and organised. The state intervenes using legal instruments in other entities in society, governing them internally and externally, but also protecting them, including protection against the state itself. The constitutional state requires this multifaceted interaction to be governed by legal principles, as equality before the law, legal security, unity of the law and due care. The more directly the state intervenes in the private sphere, the more formal guarantees are required.

Next to direct intervention by legal means into the lives of individuals and organisations, interventions in life conditions, including employment and welfare, health and education, constitute, as it were, a layer inbetween the interventionist state and individual citizens, groups and organisations. Intervening directly and indirectly in the private and public life of the citizenry at large, mean that the terms interventionist at the intentional level of legal interactions, and hierarchy at the structural level, is in the legal sense, quite appropriate.

It also has to be noted that many of these legal interventions have a broad co-ordinating, modifying, controlling or steering purpose, and thus almost by necessity have partly a legal and partly a policy basis. For the state, as ultimate authority, the relation between policy and legal interventions is very close and modern law-giving is as optimally targeted at the setting of norms (legal) as at bringing about changes (policies). There is a growing interconnection of interventions by law and administration on, and between, levels of sub-national, national and supranational regulation. This almost becomes a handicap. In the course of extending steering and control by legal and administrative means, the limitations and disadvantages of hierarchical governance present themselves.

However, the continuous amplification of governing by law and other legal instruments, is an answer to increasing societal complexity, diversity and dynamics. This is not easily avoided. The question becomes one of whether legal and administrative systems can cope, or even more crucially if they themselves may have become obstacles on this path. Every rule calls forth other rules, because of expected or unexpected side effects in complex intervention situations. A paradoxical effect is highlighted by remedying this tendency by deregulation. It is often observed that to deregulate, you have to re-regulate, only resulting in more confusion. Societal diversity as represented in law-making makes for progressive refinement in legal interventions. Also, societal dynamics exert their influence on hierarchical governance by legal means. Many interventions are already outdated at the moment they are enacted because of the time it takes to fulfil all juridical, political and administrative requirements. This inflexibility calls forth its own reaction: new measures to 'update' earlier versions, or as the Dutch say, legal 'repair'.

Observations such as these fit within the theoretical approach that considers the legal system to be a largely autonomous, self-referential and *autopoietic* system, which itself has precarious relations with the political or state system (see Chapter 6). Legal systems – compared with other societal subsystems – have strong autonomy promoting tendencies, we should take these tendencies seriously, but not to the extent that *autopoietic* theory does. Such a view is of importance, because next to observing legal systems as being relatively autonomous, they also show inclinations to broaden their scope and influence. This raises the question of the inter-penetration of law within other societal sectors. The juridification of modern societies, as many observers see happening, is, next to its assumed autonomy, also an important governance matter.

Because of difficulties previously mentioned, legal-administrative rule-making at the intentional level of state-society interactions not only diminishes its effectiveness but also its legitimacy. At the structural level hierarchical governance loses its meaning, resulting in a sense of power-lessness and a growing alienation from the legally interventionist state. The obeisance of the law, being the basic notion on which interaction between the state and its citizenry is built, erodes in varying degrees. Resistance against the state as a distant and omni-present, but not inter-acting legal machine, seems to be growing. Counter-moves in terms of guarantees, publicity, participation and other forms of citizen involve-ment are not lacking, but in practice they are restricted to special groups or interests and to issues of a 'not-in-my-backyard' (NIMBY) nature. In terms of interventions the balance is highly dis-equilibrated, and the hier-archy in that sense skewed. An effort to search for a better balance in this respect is the subject of the next section.

Responsive regulation   For decades there have been efforts to introduce a 'co-' element in more traditional rule making (called responsive law) in the USA. At the end of the 1970s this concept found a trend-setting formula-tion when 'responsive law' was positioned next to 'autonomous law' and 'repressive law'.[22] The central argument for responsive law is that the dynamics of legal development increase the authority of purpose in legal reasoning. Legal obligation becomes more problematic, relaxing the law's claim to obedience, gaining more flexibility and openness, generating forces that help, correct and design legal institutions.[23] A recent version of this basic idea of responsive law is that 'regulation should respond to industry conduct, to how effectively industry is making private regula-tion work'.[24] The responsive regulation concept builds on the concept of responsive law, but treats it rather as an innovative effort rather than an evolutionary stage in legal development. According to Ayres and Braithwaite it is more in line with the idea of 'interactive corporate com-pliance'. The building of 'co'- and self-governing elements ('enforced self-regulation') into hierarchical governance, is an expression of 'the shifting balance between the key institutions for securing social order'. As these authors see it, responsive regulation fits the 'republican' tradition better than the corporatist one, because of its emphasis on direct participation and on communitarian sources of order in the regulatory arena. Responsive regulation contains a number of elements that seem to answer some of the requirements for legal interventions particularly in the face of societal diversity, dynamics and complexity. As such, one speaks of 'regulatory pyramids' with ranges of interventions: escalation or de-escalation in response to industry's conduct. This can be called the dynamism of a responsive regulation strategy. In the same vein partial regulation is also an element of responsive regulation: if parts of an industry are regulated, the rest will follow as a result of (the dynamics of) market mechanisms. The concept also allows for the introduction of tripartism, by empowering citizens' associations to participate in responsive regulation. According to the authors this may serve as a means to facilitate, among other things, attainment of regulatory goals, the prevention of corruption, and in general, nurture democracy. The inclusion of citizen groups in responsive regulation offers an opportunity to take diversity and probably complexity aspects of regulating into consideration.

> Problems with hierarchical governance by legal means are mainly to be located at the structural level of governing interventions. Initiatives such as responsive regulation are no answer to these problems, unless they are raised to the legal system in general.

The policy arena

For a long time policies have been considered one of the major instruments governments have at their disposal to bring about politically preferred societal changes. In most policy theories the perspective taken was from the governmental or public side of policy processes. Recent developments in policy theorising place greater emphasis on the institutional framework in which policies are prepared and implemented. This might signal a shift in governing focus from the political to the social-political nature of policies and the arenas in which they are developed. In recent approaches to policy-making, social aspects and public-private aspects receive greater attention; governors are becoming more 'open' towards societal aspects than their predecessors. One of the major contributions to this awareness is articulated in the idea of 'overload'. There are two main arguments concerning overload. First, it is argued that the political system with its dominant policy model is unable to 'process' all claims upon it. Second, it is argued that in the policy process too many actors are involved, that boundaries between public and private are vague, and that no prioritisation of demands is made. This change in thinking doesn't only relate to the rationality of models used by taking more social variables into consideration, it also expresses the realisation that contexts in which policies are prepared and implemented are becoming less – rationally – controllable.

Overlooking recent work on policies as a major tool of state intervention, these shifts from more closed to more open models can be observed in many aspects: policies as substance (agendas), policies as process (input-output) or policies as interaction (communities, networks).

Notwithstanding the many different ways that policies have been and are defined, most have distinguishing stages or phases within them. There is a stage that is mainly concerned with translating a problem into a subject for policy; a stage in which alternatives are considered and choices made; and finally a stage in which the chosen policy is implemented and executed. All these stages have been theoretically refined, aiding a greater understanding of the factors influencing them. The more we get to know about these influences, the more open that policies as means of governing become. What is evident is that these stages themselves become governing arenas, with all the intentional and structural features of the interactions characterising them. A good example concerns the way policies are implemented. In traditional policy approaches, implementation was considered to be 'just' a technical aspect, concerning the technical-administrative specifications of political decisions taken earlier in the process. Recent theorising puts more emphasis on the realisation that implementation takes place in an arena of its own; an arena with other players, all pursuing their specific goals and interests. Some of these may be in line with those of the policy as it was 'originally' designed, others completely at odds with them, resulting in resistance, evasion, improper use of means and so on.

Each of the approaches mentioned, stress a particular aspect of policies, and of the arenas at least partially structuring them. This enhances the neatness of the partial explanations they offer, but decreases their utility in the development of more generalisable ideas on policies as major means of state intervention and hierarchical governance in modern societies. For this purpose I suggest a somewhat different path, stressing the interrelation of the different elements and aspects of policies. The major tools to be used are: the two levels distinguished in governing interactions, the intentional and the structural levels and their interrelations, in this case to be applied to policy interactions with an interventionist purpose (see Chapter 2) and; the three governing elements, of image, instrument and action, distinguished above (see Chapters 3–5). At the intentional level of these policy interactions we look primarily at variables such as information exchange, communication and discourse, knowledge creation and learning, in other words, the formation of policy images. Also, there is the choice and selection of policy instruments, varying from formal to informal, from broad to specific, from those with a short-term or a long-term effect, and those with an information, organisation or rule character. And finally there is the action component, where we look at aspects such as the political will to act on the governors' part, and mobilisation to support or resist, on the part of the governed. At the structural level of policy interactions we find those distinguished before as fact and value systems, instrumental resources and social-political capital. These will vary from policy issue to policy issue, and from policy sector to policy sector, but we can also look for general structural patterns. One analytical possibility is to link these patterns to the governance modes distinguished, and the mixes of them to be found in policy areas or arenas. In the governance perspective it makes a lot of difference which of these modes or mixes of them dominate in a particular arena where policies are formed and executed. In the next section I will allude to this, when I come to speak about the introduction of forms of interactive policy-making in relation to the co-mode of governance.

Summarising, the literature presents a broad spectrum of conceptually and empirically-oriented policy studies, offering enormously varied insights in its aspects. For a long time the more intentional or actor-oriented notions of policy processes have been the subject of much analysis. More recently the interest in its structural aspects has grown in relation to broader societal processes. Along the way, positivist, neo-positivist, modernist and post-modernist, analytical and constructivist tendencies in policy studies have appeared, flourished and shrunk. Unfortunately there is not much debate concerning them, making it difficult to say that progress in the overall understanding of policies as means of public intervention has been made. It is more a matter of taking your pick and using what is on offer. In developing my own ideas on social-political governance and the place of policies as government-society interactions, there exists much conceptual and analytical-empirical insights, however the theoretical status of these policy contributions is somewhat limited because of their often rather narrow focus.

Interactive policy-making   Recently (in The Netherlands) a form of policy-making has been developed and quite widely exercised, known as 'interactive' policy-making. It is being described as a way of making and implementing policies in which the government involves citizens, social organisations, business firms and/or other governmental agencies at as early a phase as possible in relative openness.[25] The reason for early and open decision-making is to give the parties involved sufficient room to make their contribution. The openness towards these other parties can be substantive, e.g. room for new ideas and plans and also room for opinions deviating from the intentions of those initiating a policy proposal. The openness can also apply to the process, e.g. its transparency, meaning more interaction at one time, and less at another. In practice, interactive policy-making serves different purposes. First is the broadening of a support base. A second objective could be the enrichment of the substance of a policy, for instance improving the quality of its content, clearing up issues and points of view, better underpinning, generating new ideas and mobilisation of knowledge.

Although the introduction of interactive policy-making certainly can be regarded as an effort to open up more traditional hierarchical forms of policy-making, the method itself can result in problems, or at least dilemmas. Questions such as: in what way are political actors involved? How is the number of those actively involved being determined? How independent are those involved, how binding are the outcomes of inter-actions taking place and for whom? Issues like these are important in determining how interactive policy-making is conceptualised. This can be seen as a contribution to developing the governance approach, because it is a serious test of the boundaries of the hierarchical governance mode. If one sees this mode, next to the 'co' and 'self' governance mode, as indis-pensable in certain steering or controlling governing situations – which I do – then a critical analysis of its boundaries such as in interactive policy-making cannot be missed. In such an analysis intentional-level consider-ations have to find their place (which actors, what kinds of roles) as well as more structural aspects (which resources, what kind of social capital, mandates, rules) and normative ones (responsibilities). Only then can an initiative such as interactive policy-making be judged on its contribution to developing new modes of governance, within or next to existing ones.

> Problems with hierarchical governance caused by public policies are predominantly to be located at the intentional level of governing interventions. Initiatives like interactive policy-making are a step in the right direction of solving (one of) them.

Conclusion

In this chapter I have presented an overview of some developments within and around the modern state, demonstrating that in recent years the state as an institution of governance has been in flux, but has none the less retained many of its core features. We might hypothesise that these changes are – at least partially – due to the influence of the diversity, com-plexity and dynamics of modern society on the state. One might argue that the shift from command to regulation is a governance response by the state to the complexities of modern economic processes. In the same sense the shift from procuring to enabling is due to an inability of the state to deal with the diversity of the client-service relation. The activating state concept might resolve the dynamics of the tension between demand and supply of government tasks in constantly changing conditions.

One can also point to other factors that have an impact on the modern state in its many manifestations, such as post-modern culture, social and economic globalisation, the assumed IT revolution, and most recently terrorism. Within the governance perspective a number of interpretations can be given for what these changing situations or conditions mean for the role and position of the state as a major interventionist societal institution with a strong emphasis on the hierarchical governance mode. This is what I have attempted in the previous sections. An over-riding conclusion I draw from this exposition is that the state in modern society is still very much alive, although its classical position, of being elevated above its subjects, either as individual citizens or groups, is being eroded, either unwillingly or on a voluntary basis. This changing role and position is expressed in many ways and directions. One can take almost any concept traditionally related to the state, only to discover that either the substance is not as it used to be, or new concepts have been coined to underscore the differences between the old and the new. Authority is an example of the former trend, where traditionally its use for state operations was almost never questioned; these days authority is a quality to be earned. Steering and rule-making are examples of the latter trend where modifiers like 'at arm length' or 'responsive' governance, emphasising the shift between traditional and more recent interpretations. It seems quite clear that most of the classical or primary public responsibilities are still solidly under the umbrella of the state. However, there is also a range of governing tasks where we see shifts towards co-governance, such as in responsive and interactive policy-making, or to self-governance, either by privatising them or leaving them to profit or non-profit parties. Some of the more established shifts in governance modes have already been discussed in the two previous chapters, but others such as is manifested in the 'enabling' or the 'activating' state, are not as widespread and accepted, although in some cases experience with them already has a relatively long tradition.

As an institution of governance the state is still very much alive. New modes of governance, in which the state participates in varying degrees or different forms, are on the agenda, not only in theory but also in practice. However one has to be careful. As experience shows the state is perfectly capable of giving with one hand and taking with another. More analysis is necessary to recognise changing emphases of governance.

Notes

1 Mayntz, 1968.

2 Dahl, Lindblom, 1953, p. 23.

3 ibid, pp. 227–230.

4 Quoted by Witteveen, 1985, pp. 31–34. The publication from which this quote is taken is called: 'Ship of state'.

5 Quoted by Witteveen, 1985, pp. 32–33.

6 Beer quoted by Gunsteren van, 1985, p. 279.

7 Wirth, 1986.

8 Campbell et al., 1991, p. 323.

9 Fligstein, 1996.

10 Cerny, 1990.

11 *idem*, p. 11.

12 *idem*, p. 30.

13 Schuppert, 2000, pp. 55 ff.

14 Müller, Wright, 1994, p. 1.

15 For this section, I make use of Majone, 1997 and 1999.

16 Taylor, 1996.

17 Evers, as quoted by Taylor, 1996.

18 Gormsley, 1994/95.

19 Blanke, 2001; Schuppert, 2000; Bandemer and Hilbert, 1998.

20 Citation from Weber, in Blanke, 2001, in German; transl J. Kooiman.

21 In this section I make extensive use of Cotterrell, 1992.

22 Nonet, Selznick, 1978.

23 *idem*, p. 78.

24 Ayres and Braithwaite, 1992.

25 Pröpper and Steenbeek, 1998, pp. 292 ff.

PART IV

ORDERS OF GOVERNANCE

9

PROBLEMS AND OPPORTUNITIES
(FIRST-ORDER GOVERNANCE)

In first-order governance, governing actors try to tackle problems or create opportunities on a day-to-day basis. In this chapter, I aim to deal with these two governing activities, keeping their basic diversity, complexity and dynamics in mind.[1] In modern societies the responsibility of finding solutions to societal problems and creating opportunities belongs to the collective realm. The 'classical' distinction of turning to the government for problem solving, and to the private sector for creating opportunities, is an outdated idea. Problem solving and opportunity creation in complex, dynamic and diverse societies is a public as well as a private challenge. At one time one party takes the lead, in another situation it is another, and there seem to be a growing number of social-political challenges that call for shared responsibilities and 'co-arrangements' (see Chapter 7). I do not intend to develop a comprehensive perspective on problem solving and opportunity creation in this chapter, but to conceptualise these subjects to fit within the governance perspective. I also use this occasion to make the diversity, complexity and dynamics of social-political issues tangible.

To begin, we need to ask ourselves, what in fact a problem is, and apply this to social-political problems. This chapter is written from the perspective of problems, however I also introduce the opportunity concept, not in as great a detail, but to highlight the direction thinking about opportunities could go. The chapter ends with an elaboration of two kinds of governing challenges, moral issues and risk issues. They serve as examples how some of the ideas advanced can be applied to two quite different societal issue areas.

Problems

The first thing to do when tackling the phenomenon of problems is to define them. What in fact is a problem? This question is easier asked than answered. Even an uncomplicated description of a problem – as a subjectively and negatively experienced difference between an actual and a desired situation – can result in much obscurity. Someone working with a problem definition composed from this formula has to deal with a three-pronged construction. The definition presupposes consensus on the actual and the desired situations as well as the coupling between them. It is self-evident that such a three-fold construction is quite liable to obstruction: the construction of the actual situation can be denied, the value construction can be dismissed and the relation between fact and value can be opposed. In general, however, the definition is a satisfactory one. Such a definition emphasises its moral or evaluative dimension. In addition to this dimension, the definition has a cognitive aspect. Events and situations are not only opinionated in the evaluative sense, but also observed as facts related to causes. The cognitive element also includes the belief in the changeability of the existing situation.

I see social-political problems, their description and definition as social constructions: a social-political situation becomes a problem as soon as it is social-politically defined as such. This means that (definitions of) such problems are not objective givens outside of the actors who experience the problems, or actors who want to solve the problems, or even researchers who want to look for problems and possibly others who are involved or have a stake in problems. Problems are defined in mutual and common processes. For this reason, the formulation by those experiencing a problem is an important part of its definition process, and thus can be considered to be the 'reality' or the 'essence' of the problem. In the governance perspective, there is a possibility of a problem if the actors involved in interactions regard certain tensions within and between the different elements of interactions as unwanted and changeable. Sometimes such an experience can be strictly individual or limited to small groups, sometimes it can take on such collective dimensions that there is the possibility of a social-political problem. In such cases the experiences of those who 'have' the problems are the main criterion. This assumption implies by definition that not a single irregularity or regularity, not difficulty or the lack of it, tension or weakness, chance or disturbance can be excluded from what a problem can be.

It should not be concluded on the basis of the above, however, that problems are merely subjective. In social-political situations one can always speak of the inter-subjectivity of problem definitions on the basis of the commonality of subjective problem experiences. The fact that problems are 'social constructions' does not imply that no more or less objective elements can be recognised in them. There are almost always certain objective measures. For example, rights and duties are institutionalised in laws; breaches of such rules can in a certain sense be considered an 'objective problem'. However, the perception of such measures will always contain a certain element of subjectivity. In these degrees of subjectivity and objectivity, different positions can be taken. My conceptualisation certainly does not consider 'objective' to be, by definition, of a higher order than 'subjective'. Subjective and objective aspects of social-political problems do not exclude each other; they are complementary. They deal with different perspectives. Objectivity consists of a system of agreements that are products of their time and place. They have an inter-subjective character. It can be considered a task of governing to create the necessary conditions to arrive from the 'chaos' of subjective experiences to an 'ordered' problem definition that is satisfactory to those involved, characterised by a higher degree of objectivity than of the individual experiences. In this process the diversity, dynamics and complexity of the problem situation should be justified or at least justifiable. In order to do this, individual subjective experiences are put in a relevant perspective of identifiable tensions and conflicts in social conditions or developments. Should these attempts fail, in other words, should these experiences remain purely subjective, one cannot speak of a social problem. Every problem that is objectified in social situations can, by definition, be considered a social problem.

> Through a process of relating the subjectivity of those experiencing a problem to an inter-subjectively shared reality, a more objective problem definition can be arrived at.

Social-political problems

When we discuss problems, we do not refer to private problems, but to social problems with a political component. That much seems evident. But not all social problems are political and the boundaries aren't equally clear in each case. Most problems people experience occur outside of political consciousness. This is not to say that they are of an individual character. The democratisation movement of the 1960s demonstrated that many individually experienced difficulties also have a common, social and collective component. The second wave of feminism was supported by the slogan: 'What is personal is political'.

Many problems hover at the fringes of public debate. Interest groups keep them alive there. Only a few attract public attention or become a focus of it. There is no telling how a problem gains public status or how long it will remain in the limelight. Some remain there for years, others only for a couple of days or even hours. Some come up, never to appear again; others return at regular intervals. To a great extent, the carrying capacity of public arenas determine the competition for attention, and the winners and losers in this competition. The feedback processes between arenas and the characteristics of the groups and associations of interested parties influence the definition as well. Administrators, politicians and social leaders have to translate the diverse, complex and dynamic questions within these tension fields into problems that are solvable, or at least controllable by those involved in them.

Some problems look self-evident, people define them almost the same, excluding any alternative perspective as unimaginable. In these situations, warns Gusfield, one has to be careful.[2] It is quite possible that this 'homogeneous consciousness' of the problem among all involved is a form of social control that eliminates conflict or divergence by declaring other definitions or solutions unthinkable. These subtle, unnoticed implications of cultural ideas are perhaps the most potent form of power. The existence of open conflict and debate at least assures that such forms of cultural power exertion are suppressed and that the political character of issues is brought out into the open. But not even political debate can solve such dilemmas in all respects.

There are different theories available about how 'social constructions' come into being and are developed. Globally, two perspectives can be distinguished: one takes a linear path; the other opts for a non-linear process of problem definition.[3] The advantage of the linear mode of explanation is the surveyability of these processes. This, however, is also the source of their limitations. First, most of them are strongly government-oriented, and often take one particular characteristic as the dominant one. Second, they are often too 'smooth', in that problems and solutions are conceptualised in isolation from each other. In non-linear processes, the definition of a problem as a social-political one is seen as a dynamic process. In such a view, there is scope for all kinds of different forces at work in the definition of social-political problems. In these processes, the thinking about solutions is considered to be part of the definition process. It is necessary to think about 'post-solution problems' and their solutions. This can be a way to combat stopgaps. The specific advantage of the non-linear mode is that the problem definition enhances the solution space and that problems and solutions are considered to be in constant interaction: one cannot be conceptualised without the other. The importance of a definition process in which both perspectives find a place should be recognised. In the early stages, attempts are made to form images of the problem experiences, the involved interactions etc., in isolation from solutions. Solutions then become part of this process before the process is over and the problem system as such has been defined.

> The translation of a private problem into a social-political one, of a social-political into a governing one, of a governing one into a solvable one, is a governing interaction process with quite specific characteristics for each of those phases.

Opportunities

Several times I have mentioned opportunities as a specific category of social-political situations, which can be set apart from problems. A few reasons can be advanced for paying special attention to them. In the first place, the distinction between problems and opportunities enables us to correct a false sort of dichotomy, in which too easy societal problems and problem-solving are allotted to the state, and the creation of opportunities allotted to the private sector. This conception denies the interdependent character of modern societies and their governance. Second, there is reason to distinguish problems and opportunities because of the (categories of) actors involved in them. Generally speaking, in societal problems there is a – sometimes drastic – separation between those confronted with or experiencing a social-political problem, and those involved in trying to do something about them. In opportunity creation we don't usually find this sort of separation: because of societal differentiation those creating and implementing opportunities may not necessarily be the same people; however both will be in the realm of experts and professionals. This means that in social-political problem-solving and in opportunity creation the governing interactions will be of a different nature. For instance the representation aspect of those experiencing a problem in the professional arena will not apply similarly to issues with an opportunity character. Third, attention needs to be paid to a possibly confusing aspect of the difference between problems and opportunities. Quite often we will see in practice that what is a problem for one category of people is an opportunity for another, especially for those professionally involved in solving social-political problems. From a conceptual point of view this does not affect the distinction between the two. Finally, problems and opportunities can be distinguished because the way societal diversity, dynamics and complexity are expressed in them differ. How to deal with these societal features in this context is the subject of the next section, and I will come back to this difference after the discussion in the final part of the chapter.

> Opportunities require another type of interactions than problems, although in practice they may become part of the same governing activity or issue.

Dealing with diversity, dynamics and complexity

In this section an approach to problems in the governance perspective is suggested. The priority here is to make a systematic effort to 'translate' the three societal features, diversity, dynamics and complexity of problem situations into steps that place these features at the centre of governing attention. This, in my opinion, is what governance is about and it could be argued that the model sketched is operationalising governance for the sake of solving problematic governing situations. Each section deals with a phase of this model and the ways it can be applied to social-political questions and issues. The steps are as follows:

1 Stocktaking and ordering of those experiencing a problem: dealing with diversity.
2 Identification of relevant interactions and their mutual relations: first reduction of complexity.
3 Bringing the sources of problems to the surface by locating pockets of tensions in interactions: analysing dynamics.
4 Deciding on the solution space: diversity, complexity and dynamics, but this time from the solution side.
5 Drawing a boundary around the problem-solution system, which will be the focus of governing: second reduction of complexity.

Ordering diversity

Drawing on the assumption that problems are social constructions, it follows that in the governing of social-political problems it is of the utmost importance that those who experience problems are, in the first place, identified. Usually the ones who first publicly draw attention to a problem are not the ones who experience them, only articulate them. Through them or through other means such as social research or public-opinion polls it becomes clear – or clearer – who is involved in the problems, and what their problem experiences are. At later stages, others may surface who have not yet expressed themselves, and measures can be taken to ensure that these 'silent' people also get involved in the defining process. The identification process in dynamic, diverse and complex problem situations is far from simple. An inventory of those experiencing problems also implies that they are involved in formulating potential solutions. The ordering of diversity in problem situations includes those experiencing them and those involved in solutions. The problem experiences will predominantly have to be ordered according to the kinds of interactions with which they are interconnected. In addition to this, the ordering has to be presented such that, in the diversity of experiences, it becomes visible in and between which intentional and structural aspects of the involved interactions the problems are experienced: do they concern predominantly the intentional or actor level of those interactions, or do also structural aspects of problem issues play a part. Only in this way can the close relation between diversity and complexity, and the dynamic character of the relations within those interactions, be made transparent.

First reduction of complexity

This part of the process deals with the first stocktaking of the relevant interactions between those involved and the ordering of the interactions in partial problems. Next we shall examine which patterns, relevant to governing, can be distinguished in and between partial problems. In this phase, the experience of problems will be abstracted from those experiencing them; they will be placed in the context of social-political interactions. The description of the problem experiences in terms of social-political partial problems and the definition of the patterns between and within those partial problems derives from the perspective of the problem-solving capacity of those involved. Governing usually cannot proceed without first taking account of any problem-solving structures already in place. In the identification of partial problems, any form of governing is at least partly linked with that already existing. The lines along which those directly or indirectly involved try to solve their own problems will have to serve as a starting point for the definition of partial problems and their interrelations. This does not mean that these lines are constant and unchangeable.

At this stage of complexity reduction, problem experiences are described in terms of the different types of interactions in which the partial problems manifest themselves. Although, at this stage, the subjectivity of the problem experiences is, to a large extent, released, no unequivocal image of the problem will arise. This is purposeful. It is important for those involved in the process to get a surveyable and at the same time representative image of the social-political relations and the forces connected with them. In determining partial problems, the skill is in distinguishing which are most important/relevant to the problem, and to work from that image. What the most important relations are can only be established by certain complexity reduction methods, according to the principle of 'nearly (de)-composability', that demonstrates that not all partial problems are connected with all others with equal intensity (see further Chapter 12). It is for problem-solvers, together with those directly or indirectly involved in the problem, to decide which partial problems and the relations between them should be considered serious and which ones less serious. They have to decide, mutually and collectively, which partial problems to bracket with the problem, and which ones not to.

Analysing dynamics

Now that the relevant interactions have been described, the problems within these interactions can be localised. The objective is to find within the interactions those pockets of tensions that lead to problematic situations. The challenge is to arrive at agreements between those involved, at images that are acceptable and, because of their acceptance, legitimised. If applicable, this may be done by way of models, but any usable working hypothesis about the nature, coherence, dynamics and directions of problems and their solutions, can serve this purpose. In certain instances such an image may take shape as the reconstruction of a policy theory, at least if the condition is satisfied not only to reflect certain pre-established administrative or scientific insights.[4]

In the context of the social-constructive character of problem definitions it is of the utmost importance that any appearance of 'objectivity' of scientific or bureau-political rationality be avoided, and if they are found to play a role, tested against the constructions of other participants. This does not mean that we should refrain from asking questions about what causes problems. Each social-political problem is the consequence of, and embedded in, societal structures and cultural patterns. These often assume the character of non-linear processes with self-amplifying forces within them, making it even more important to locate where the tension 'causing' these processes are coming from. Together, these factors determine how a problem becomes a social and a social-political one, and these contexts will more or less contribute to, or be the cause of, a negatively experienced relation between an actual and a desired situation. Many authors who are influential in this context remark that too little attention is paid to the fact that societal problems are always interconnected with other societal problems, and that these are embedded in complex and dynamic systems of problem formulation and dissemination. Without a serious effort being made to locate the pockets of tensions assumed to bring about problem experiences, the search for solutions will be a haphazard enterprise.

The solution perspective

At this stage of the process, systematic attention to solutions is needed. In earlier stages, potential solutions may have sporadically appeared, but not yet in an orderly way. Solutions to problems form an integral part of problem experiences. Within the boundaries drawn during the problem analysis, more and more solution elements will present themselves, until finally the problem system becomes a solution system. The way a problem is defined not only influences the attention it receives, but also the way it might be resolved. A range of potential solutions offers greater scope for definitions of problems than situations where only a limited number of feasible and acceptable solutions seem to be present or evolving. To create some order in scrutinising what feasible and acceptable solutions might be available, the first three steps have to be repeated. Step one requires that an inventory is made of the diversity of solutions and that these are ordered. In step two the range of solutions is examined, and in step three an analysis is made of which solutions will neutralise which tensions, and which tensions might be expected to heighten, due to the implementation of certain solutions. Each of the participants will want to place their problem experience or their proposed solution at the centre of the interaction, resulting in clashes of interest. These clashes are part of the problem and solution space. In the formulation of this space (political) decisions are taken as to what should and should not be considered to be solutions in relation to legitimated problem images. These decisions should be made according to democratic principles. The result of these three steps scrutinising the diversity, complexity and dynamics of solutions will be an image of the solution space as is lived through with all its snags, and practised by those involved.

Second reduction of complexity

Problem definition processes can be seen either from the perspective of experienced problems, or from the perspective of (potential) solutions, or from both more or less at the same time. Finding a problem-solution space is a way to lend form to an experienced reality. This search also includes the question of which norms and values are at stake. This is expressed in the subjective approaches of reality, problems, situations, relations, systems and their boundaries. Implicitly or explicitly, these influence (in combination) the opportunities of, or possibilities for one or more solutions. On the basis of the solutions that are available in the final instance, the problem-solution image will be singled out as the focus for governing action. This implies a second reduction of complexity. The first took place during the partitioning of the interactions involved into partial problems. The same partitioning occurs now for the problem as a whole, so as to designate its boundaries. It is important that the drawing of this boundary constitutes the final stage of the definition process, when a broad insight on problems and solutions is available. Decisions as to which problems and solutions not to be taken into consideration can be defended and legitimated vis-à-vis those involved. At this stage, the decision has to be taken on which entities are experiencing problems, which partial problems are going to be part of the problem-solution space, and which pockets of tensions are going to be the focus of governing. This decision has to be justified to all parties involved. In these decisions, practical as well as political considerations will play a role.

The final definition of the problem-solution system will always imply a reduction of the broad analysis in which those experiencing problems, partial problems, pockets of tensions, and solutions are described. Such reduction is representative of the total analysis. Often this ideal situation will not be feasible. Even then, it is of consummate importance that limitations that occur during image formation regarding problems and solutions, are made explicit, either during the process or as part of the final stage.

In the definition of social-political problems more is at stake than simply what the problem 'is'. Much implicit or partially explicit conflict material is usually, hidden in such 'simple' definitions. The temptation to simplify definitions too rapidly must be suppressed. It should now be evident that the way diverse, complex and dynamics problem-solution systems can be looked at in a governing perspective are not quite the same as the prevailing analytical models in policy-analytical circles. Not that those models are false, useless or outdated, but arguably they are applicable only to certain types of problem-solution situations, i.e. relatively simple ones. Of course these do occur in social-political governing, but they are not representative of issues central to a social-political governance context. In the next section I will give two examples of such issues.

> Retaining the diversity, complexity and dynamics of problem situations for as long and as completely as possible, is a certain guarantee that their images will remain close to the reality they are supposed to represent.

Governance issues

Many efforts have been made to design typologies of problems. Much literature exists concerning the solving of group problems, including distinctions made between highly, moderately or ill-structured problems, with respectively algorithmic, heuristic and creative responses.[5] A well-known and often applied example in politics involves differentiating between distributive, regulatory and re-distributive problems,[6] later complemented by dividing regulatory issues into fragmented and emotionally symbolic ones.[7] For the structure of problems two Dutch scholars drew up a typology of types on the basis of crossing degrees of value content with available knowledge. These also related to solutions to be found for them, including aspects such as government intervention, public participation and democracy.[8]

My starting point in the direction of identifying special types of governing problems and/or opportunities can be found in the governance perspective itself. In fact all the distinctions made so far could be used to sort out problems or opportunities, or construct typologies on them. Many if not most societal governing issues are multi-dimensional. That is why they may become governing issues to begin with and one has to be careful not to reduce these dimensions beforehand, which usually is the case with typologies. So I will refrain from this course of action and will instead use two examples of sorts of governing issues as illustration. Of importance are their complex, diverse and dynamical features, as are their actor and structure dimensions. Other aspects will merely be hinted at.

Moral or other normative governance issues

The first kind issues to be discussed are those with a moral or normative loading. Societal issues with strong moral overtones, such as genetic manipulation or euthanasia, have interests connected to them, but the main tensions arising out of them in a governance perspective are principle driven rather than compelled by interests. In policy literature ethical or other types of normative issues figure as 'position' issues. These are problems considered difficult to resolve. They are goal oriented – in contrast to 'valence' issues that have a means orientation – for which a common or consensual base is not easy to be found.[9]

In moral issues diversity is always present. Diversity of opinions, evaluations and traditions are at the base of moral or normative governing issues. But there are varieties in diversity at this point, making for different governing situations: some relatively easy to be solved, while others cannot be solved at all and will remain governance issues unless, perhaps, evaluative schemes at the structural level change, or no challenges at the intentional level of governing interactions take place. To operationalise the diversity of normative or moral issues Lukes has suggested three types that apply: diversity of morals, next to incompatible and incommensurable moral questions.[10] Moral diversity may become an issue when there is a confrontation between different outlooks, when there is a group of people for whom each of the outlooks is a real option, which means that they can live with such an outlook in their actual, historical circumstances.[11] Such moral issues involve differences of life-world and life-styles, and they will often arise in multi-cultural societies and multi-ethical situations. Difficulties will arise, but to govern them practical solutions must be found. Next to moral diversity issues are issues of incompatibility. These arise when choices or trade-offs can be made between values, such as between equality and liberty. In such issues normative principles are at stake, but there are ways of finding acceptable answers, for example by the formulation of legal rules. Finally there are incommensurable moral issues. These arise when no trade-offs can be found and no standard or scale can be invented on which to measure or compare them. These are the most difficult, and Lukes cites a number of authors who have tried to define why certain questions, choices or dilemmas are incommensurable. Some approach this from a structural level by speaking conceptually of good and evil, of sacred and beautiful, of value spheres of the world; others point at actor's ways of life in actual choice dilemmas where no standard can be applied, such as between interpersonal relations (friendship, marriage) or 'calling'. It seems that the greater the normative diversity at the structural level of governing interactions, the more difficult it will be to find at their intentional level solutions for problems experienced by some, because of opportunities arising for others.

Traditionally, moral issues and their diversity, are especially to be found in the civil society domain. Churches were considered to be, and still see themselves as being, major governors of morals and ethics. However this role has diminished due to increasing secularisation in most modern societies, and by the fact that between and within religions opinions differ on many moral and ethical matters. Church and state are – sometimes uneasy – allies in upholding aspects of morality at the structural level of governance. In moral issues, especially in incommensurable ones, the state is moving more and more centre stage either as guardian, or in modern terms as 'regulator' of morality, perhaps assuming the role that the church is unwelcome to.[12] Legally two schools of thought have developed here, with different – almost incommensurable – ideas on this subject. One school promotes the role of the state as upholder of morality as a condition for societal unity and cohesion, using the law as a major instrument in this endeavour. The other school defends the rights of individuals to set their own moral standards, and to refrain from setting standards in ethical issues raised. It is clear that diversity is an important feature of moral issues, either as problems or increasingly as opportunities, therefore raising a number of interesting governance questions.

In a dynamic perspective it is clear that recent moral and ethical issues are often related to social, economic, technological, medical and related developments in modern societies. Conceptually then, moral and ethical issues can also be looked at from a dynamic angle. Tensions within governing interactions at the actor and structural level arise when in these developments moral or other normative values are at stake. At the actor level this may be expressed by a particular person or small group attempting to break through a current normative practice allied to such developments; others will resist this. The motives for such action and counter-action and the images on which these are based, are always part of broader normative patterns, such as a value system or moral codes. This shows the intimate relation between the intentional dimension of governing interactions and their structural component. In normative issues, moral or otherwise, there are always tensions in this relation because moral dimensions of societal questions are usually well entrenched structurally, or even institutionalised, particularly when the state is involved in them. The dynamical aspects of moral issues not only concern tensions between preconceptions and their structural counterpart, usually having a conservative make-up, but also concern facts, embedded in broader factual knowledge systems, often of a more progressive nature and displaying opportunity traits. This we see expressed in new (governing) coalitions between the state, market and experts in civil society. Because many of these 'modern' moral and ethical issues are acted out in the social-political public sphere, the media also play an important role in influencing public opinion about them (see Chapter 3).

Therefore, in the dynamics of moral issues, interdependence between state, market and civil society actors is an important factor, as the form of inter-penetration at the structural level between them (see Chapter 13). 'Modern' moral issues are predominantly driven by market and civil society actors. The state normally does not have strong ambitions in moral issues, to the contrary, it prefers to stay out of them indefinitely for political reasons, especially in incommensurable moral questions. The state has one major resource at its disposal, the monopoly of formal rule making, so in the dynamics of moral issues it will try to narrow the issues to instrumental choice. In which case it is not the substantive pro's and con's of the issues at stake, but the pro's and con's of certain rules or regulations that can be applied. In Luke's terms: the state translates issues from incommensurable into incompatible or even to moral diversity issues so as to be able to handle them procedurally. Governing discussion will focus on the details of legislation, while the ethical aspects remain as much as possible in the background. Due to the fact that civil society has insufficient capacity at the structural level to institutionalise moral issues within its own realm (nor does the market for that matter) if by doing so makes them subject to self-governance. As a result the governing of these issues is mainly becoming a matter of state intervention, sometimes subject to a 'co'-mode. In this way problems and/or opportunities with a (strong) moral or ethical nature are reduced to instrumental ones instead of part of a broader societal image formation. As such, the dynamics of moral issues have a more controlling than an enabling outcome.

Primarily, in moral and ethical governance problems, societal diversity is expressed. Because they have inherent dynamical tensions that are difficult to handle by governance, social-political action will concentrate on instrumental issues to come to grips with them.

Risk as a governance issue

Contrary to moral issues, which are basically of a subjective nature, in risk objective and subjective, appearances are both present, and in risk theories, emphases on one or the other vary. Quite significant in recent theorising on risk is a shift from looking at it from a technical-management perspective to a much broader social-political one. Although it is quite clear that risks related to technological and/or biological possibilities now present are new, the question seems justified if risk in a broader sense is indeed something new and special for our times. Much depends on the way it is defined. In classical approaches 'objective' manifestations figured prominently, while more recently objective or technical aspects of risk are supplemented with subjective qualities. This makes risk a much richer concept but at the same time more diffuse.[13] Three perspectives on risk will be presented each emphasising different aspects of it.

The question of how a particular kind of risk or danger becomes a (governing) issue has been put on the scholarly agenda by Douglas and Wildavski in their book *Risk and Culture*. The answer they give is that the choice of risk and the choice of how to live with it have to be taken together. 'Each form of life has its own typical risk portfolio ... acting in the present to ward off future dangers, each social arrangement elevates some risks to a high peak and depresses others below sight. This cultural bias is integral to social organization ... people who adhere to different forms of social organization are disposed to take (and avoid) different kinds of risk'.[14] Against this background three risk cultures are sketched based within three types of social organisation. Hierarchy and hierarchists emphasise continuity and do not see any real threat, danger or risk in the long run (state). Individualists will take responsibility for long term risks as long as they can collect the rewards (market). And there is the culture of the 'border' or the 'periphery', which is alarmed (civil society). Although *Risk and Culture* was controversial, in later publications its approach has been developed and it is considered to be an influential school of thought in risk theorising.[15] In my conceptual terms, this theory is saying that any subject that gets sufficient 'risk' attention can become an issue in social-political governing.

The question of whether risk as a central societal phenomenon is new and a product of our time has been answered quite conclusively by Beck.[16] He argues that modern society has changed radically because of the increasing risks of technological processes. These days social processes do not distribute goods or wealth as used to occur in the (primary) industrial or class society, they instead distribute risks: the bad sides of modern society. This results in new patterns of social differentiation and other political conflicts. Beck states that a risk society is a catastrophic one, because the exception threatens to become the rule, and averting or managing it necessitates the reorganisation of power and authority. In earlier periods risk had a predominantly personal character, but the dangers that present themselves now are of a global nature. In the past risks had to do with under-supply (such as of health) but now are due to overproduction and supply. By politicising risk as Beck does, risk problems and solution issues assume a central place on the social-political agenda, leaving no doubt about the structural nature of the involved governing interactions.

A final example from the literature on risk cannot be overlooked. Evers and Nowotny's (less alarming) work on societal risk did not get the attention Beck's work did. According to them the paradox of modern society involves both life risks due to self-development and self-management, and a growing dependency on 'mega' developments and institutions.[17] In this perspective all social activities (micro) and developments (macro) go hand in hand with dangers and uncertainties. If and how societies take on political or social responsibilities for risky social processes depends on historical conditions reflecting power relations, especially of guarantees or mediation by the state. New governance challenges in coping with risks, uncertainties and dangers, are the consequence of individualisation as a modernisation process and the division of responsibilities between individuals and the state. In the same vein Berting sees Europe also as developing into a 'risk society', where risks at the individual and the European level may lead towards a *société vulnérable*.[18] The importance of both these views for the governance approach is the relation they establish between actor and structural factors in the governance of modern risks. By taking both levels of risk seriously, both theoretical approaches may be helpful in advancing ideas on how to govern risk issues in modern societies.

Although diversity and dynamics are aspects of risk as problem or opportunity issues, complexity is arguably the major component requiring attention in governance. In modern risk issues so many interrelations occur, that causes and effects are almost impossible for governing interactions to 'follow'. This is often the case in modern governance issues, but if one speaks of societal risks one doesn't want to 'take a risk' handling the consequences of their complexity the wrong way.

A diversity of actors increases complexity, and dynamics influence risk situations because of tensions and conflicts between perceptions of, and interests in, risk. Psychological/psychometric studies of risk show an enormous diversity of risk perceptions (images) embedded within risk cultures, and dynamical aspects of risk are clearly expressed in what is called its social amplification. This approach to risk includes diversity and dynamical aspects by combining hazardous events with psychological, social, institutional and cultural factors in ways that can heighten or attenuate perceptions of risk and shape risk behaviour.[19] In doing so, the social amplification approach to risk gives an insight into the diversity of risk situations, but helps in particular in operationalising the dynamics of risk situations.

Technical, economic and psychological perspectives on risk tend to reduce its complexity to one or a few dimensions in able to make 'harder' analyses possible; systems and sociological exercises take more dimensions into consideration, but the price to be paid is a greater choice of interpretations.[20] Examining the risk and management of risk literature, one finds case studies describing and analysing actors involved, techniques used, conflicting interests and values at stake, giving the impression that there is an inescapable and often inevitable complexity to risk issues, summed up as being societal problems or opportunities, usually both. A good – if not unbiased – example of operationalising the complexity of risk issues is in the legal arena, where different systems of assessing risk are integrated to evaluate the health, safety and welfare of people at work in court.[21] In the first place there are concepts of risk based on calculating probabilities, that some kind of risk may happen in specified categories of work situations. Then there are legal risk concepts that demand causal relations be established and proved beyond any reasonable doubt. And there are 'lay' concepts of risk (employers and employees alike) weighing immediate injuries against long-term health risks. Each of these approaches reduces the complexity of health risks by applying their own logic to it. According to the author of this study there is general agreement that it is much easier to know and understand the complexity of risks from past experience, expressed in the fact that the law operates much more comfortably retrospectively, tending to favour reactive rather than pre-emptive behaviour in risk situations.

Summarising the above insights on risk as a societal issue, be it as a problem or as an opportunity, I am inclined to say that risk issues occur at the intentional as well as the structural level of governing interactions. Beck emphasises the structural aspects of risk in modern societies mainly because of technological developments. Evers, Nowotny and Berting believe attention should equally be paid to both levels, and to the relation between the two. Social, economic, technological and cultural processes stimulate risk situations of a structural nature, while actors take or create more risks individually, and by doing so contribute to new patterns of societal risks. Because in my governance thinking I put great emphasis on the diversity, dynamics and complexity of governance issues, a step should be made to evaluate risk and risk situations along these lines. Overlooking these three features of risk, their diversity aspect can be seen to be articulated in the mix of subjective and objective risk notions. The dynamics of risk in modern societies is, arguably, particularly related to the interrelation between structural and action dimensions of risk processes, which may build up pockets of tensions, which may run out of hand, or become ungovernable as Beck suggests. The complexity of risk issues is due to the many interrelations so characteristic of risk situations in the modern world, varying from multi-facetted risk at workplaces to risk in its global technological, economic and other structural dimensions.

The studies discussed give a glimpse into such complexities of risk at different levels of societal aggregation.

My personal assessment of which of these three features is the most dominant or pressing in a governance perspective is that complexity comes first, followed by dynamics and then diversity. As to which governance mode or mix of such modes might be the most appropriate to cope with risk issues in modern societies, apart from moral issues, where I saw a place for hierarchical, and self governance mades for risk issues, I am inclined to say that in light of the above insights, there is little place for self-governing in risk issues and because I see complexity first, dynamics second and diversity last, a mix of hierarchical and co-governance seems to me the appropriate mix to govern risk situations in modern societies (see further Chapters 12 and 13).

From this brief description, three important contributions detailing the role of risk issues as diverse, dynamic but especially complex societal phenomena have been given. Cultural theory emphasises the subjective character of risks, while its social and organisational embeddedness hints at the diversity aspects of risk: where one sits decides how one appreciates risk. Beck, and Evers and Nowotny, argue that risk, both objectively and subjectively, is related to modernisation, and that risk dynamics involve social and political processes. The complexity of risk is expressed in the fact that scholarly disciplines and even inter-disciplinary approaches reduce risk to a size that suits and is applicable to that particular discipline.

> The uncertainty because of the coincidence of many simultaneous cause and effects relations of modern risks issues and the (potential) dangers involved in the iterations involved in them, makes their complexity and dynamics the dominant governance feature.

Conclusion

In this chapter I have taken a first step in conceptualising first order governing and governance, that is, the day-to-day activities of social-political governors in solving societal problems or creating opportunities. This is not to say they don't display other primary activities, I see these two as most important. In the chapter I have tried to make clear how to view problems and opportunities. The central qualification for them is as social constructions, meaning that in fact the images of them are highly subjective, both as categories of knowledge and in the way they are assessed. When subjective notions about problems or opportunities are shared by large numbers of people, governed as well as governors, they may acquire certain objective qualifications, but these have always to be considered with great care.

One of the major themes of this book is the idea that because modern societies are complex, dynamic and diverse, these qualities are reflected in the issues that get on the public agenda as governance issues. So the next step in the chapter was to see how these traits could be operationalised in problem solving or opportunity creation. In a model type exercise I suggested steps or procedures to design, as it were, problem-solution schemes that could handle the diversity, complexity and dynamics of societal problems and opportunities. I limited this exercise primarily to the image formation part of this first order governing. For a more thorough review the choice of instruments and the action component would have to be included. Next I discussed two prototypes of problem/opportunity issues in modern societies as exemplars, showing how different elements of the governance perspective can be used to make problems and opportunities part of the broader conceptual exercise, and also as a contribution to synthesising these elements into a whole. These deliberations are small steps on the road to developing such an inclusive picture, but steps they are nevertheless.

Notes

1 An earlier version of this chapter was published in Dutch as Kooiman, 1996.

2 Gusfield, 1981.

3 Dery, 1984; Hoppe, 1989; Hisschemöller, 1993; Rochefort and Cobb, 1994; Schmidt, 2000.

4 This is a body of literature focusing on the assumptions or hypotheses on which policies are based. Particularly in the Netherlands this concept has been widely discussed. See Hoogerwerf, 1987, 1989, Ringeling, 1987.

5 Cohen and Silver, 1989.

6 Lowi, 1972.

7 Smith, 1975, see also Outshoorn, 1986.

8 Hoppe, 1989; Hisschemöller, 1993.

9 Outshoorn, 1986.

10 Lukes, 1991.

11 Williams, as quoted by Lukes, 1991, p. 10.

12 Krabbendam, ten Napel, 2000.

13 Kaplan and Garick, 1993; Renn, 1992; Rayner, 1992; Bechmann, 1993.

14 Douglas, Wildavski, 1982, pp. 8–9.

15 Rayner, 1992.

16 Beck, 1986; transl., 1992.

17 Evers, Nowotny, 1987.

18 Berting, in press.

19 Kasperson, 1992.

20 Renn, 1992.

21 Hawkins, 1989.

10

INSTITUTIONS (SECOND-ORDER GOVERNANCE)

Social-political problem-solving and opportunity creation (first-order governing) are embedded in institutional settings. The care for and maintenance of these institutions I call second-order governance. In first-order governing the emphasis is on governing as a process, whereas in second-order governing attention is focused on the structural aspects of governing interactions, controlling or enabling problem-solving or opportunity-creating practices in modern societies. Attention to second-order governing is not only a question of analytical distinction, I am inclined to think that responsibility for institutions is a governing order in itself, with its own character and taste. It would be naive to assume that problems are solved or opportunities created within 'ideal' institutional conditions, or that such institutions are explicitly designed for optimal first order governing. This is usually not the case, because the creation and development of societal institutions are the result of historical 'path-dependent' processes. On the other hand we see institutional settings designed, created, maintained, reformed and even ended all the time. There are even specialised professions and bodies looking after such matters. In the public sector, often very little will happen with recommendations made, in the market place these are usually taken more seriously. One could even propose that fluctuations in economic life shape market institutions more than changes in political life do their public counterparts.

In order to systematise our considerations on second-order governing we need an analytical framework. Can we use the one applied to first-order governing? Can the approach developed for 'coping with' the diversity, complexity and dynamics of social-political first-order problems or opportunities be used for institutional problems and opportunities? In principle, comparable principles seem to be applicable; but differences will arise as well. Three of these are worth mentioning. First, the emphasis on 'social' and 'political' varies in first- and second-order governance. In social-political first-order governance the emphasis usually will be on the 'social', whereas in second-order governance the (definitions of) issues rising, because of their institutional nature, will have more of a 'political' stamp. Second, in first-order problem-solving or opportunity-creation the main direction of the governing 'system' perspective emanates from a part, runs through considerations for the whole, and refers to the part in question again. In second-order governing when a governance issue is formulated, the main perspective is the whole. During the process considerations focus on a part or a number of parts, relative to the needs-capacities of those parts, but eventually the perspective will again be holistic. This difference in perspective is an important element in the totality of what social-political governing is about and the differentiation between the three orders I make. In the first order the emphasis is on parts, while in the stages of the problem-solving process within parts as much attention as possible is paid to consequences for the whole of the system to be governed. In second-order governing the opposite occurs: governing needs and capacities are phrased with an emphasis on the system as a whole. In the process the consequences for a particular set of interactions are scrutinised. But finally the measures (which might apply to a part or a set of parts only) will be taken with the whole as a frame of reference.

A third difference between the two orders is the object of governing. In first-order governing these objects are social-political interactions in which problems are noted. In second-order governing it is systems of interactions that are the object of governing. Needs and capacities are expressed in terms of categories, classes or systems of social-political interactions. It is qualities or dis-qualities of types of interactions that are the main focus. We will continue our analysis of second-order governing using in particular the three forms of interactions we have distinguished: interferences, interplays and interactions.

To stress that in second-order governing other things are at stake than in first-order, I have 'coined' two new concepts: *needs* and *capacities*. While we can see first-order governance as a balancing act between problems and opportunities and solutions and strategies, in second-order governing I conceptualise a balancing act between governing needs on the one hand, and governing capacities on the other. In accordance with the general idea that governing interaction has an intentional and a structural level we might say that in first-order governing the emphasis is on its intentional level, whereas in second-order governing the structural level of governing interactions will be predominant. Another way of saying that in second-order governing the institutional framework within which first-order governing problems are solved or opportunities created, is 'problematised'.

Besides the use of needs and capacities as concepts to accentuate the difference between first and second-order governance, I will also make use of the concept of representation in this chapter. By representation I mean that institutions have a dual role in societal governance, in that they both reflect somewhat abstracted and generalised traits of first-order governing, and also reflect broader aspects of societal features such as societal diversity, complexity and dynamics.

What are institutions?

Institutions always have been a subject of interest for social science scholars. In the last decade the subject has received renewed attention, focussing on their role in influencing the behaviour of actors or organisations under the heading of 'new institutionalism'. This endeavour has revealed many important factors for the governance perspective, however it has not created a common perspective on institutions.[1] Four institutional theories will be reviewed, the first two see institutions arising from the intentional level, the third and fourth argue the opposite, that institutions arise from intentions.

First, in the 'upward' mode, studies identify institutional influences by 'calculating' the behaviour of actors. Governing actors trying to maximise the attainment of certain goals will be influenced by institutions and the way they help or hinder them. For example enforcing agreements or allowing penalties for defection. If one wants institutions to be 'efficient' formal arrangements such as contracts, administrative hierarchies, decision-making procedures and budget mechanisms are mentioned as being applicable. One might also think of interactions between basically 'self-governing' actors who institutionalise the parameters they work within by rules, because by doing so the interaction parties expect a maximum possible result. Theories in this school have a relatively narrow definition of institutions, basically as formalised rules of the game.[2]

Second, in the 'upward' approach, institutions are looked at as contexts for organisations. Rules have a normative character, they shape interactions between organisations and by 'isomorphic' tendencies institutions-as-cultures are created and maintained. Theories in this perspective tend to define institutions relatively broadly, '[t]hey include not only formal rules, procedures and norms, but also ask attention for symbol systems, cognitive scripts and moral templates that provide "the frames of meaning" guiding human action'.[3]

In the structured 'downward' perspective, studies also emphasise that rules form the contexts, the 'room for manoeuvre' for societal actors, either individually or collectively. Four features are relatively distinctive for theories in this perspective: broad relations between institutions and individual behaviour; asymmetries of power relations; path dependency; and unintended consequences and openness for including other explanatory variables.[4] This kind of theorising is particularly valuable in showing – historically developed – governance patterns, tensions between 'inclusion' or 'exclusion' or dealing with the relation between 'wholes and parts', keeping the ever-growing complexities, dynamics and diversity of modern societies in mind.

A second 'structure-down' institutional theory to be mentioned is the 'rediscovering of institutions' as March and Olsen have termed their reaction to the behavioural and rational-choice approaches in explaining political outcomes. According to this 'rediscovery' human action attempts to 'satisfice' and not to maximise expectations, it is context specific and embedded in cultural, socio-economic and political structures. Choices are not as clearly defined as decision theories suppose, and decisions must be sought in complex environments including institutional constraints and opportunities. Utility maximisation is just a small part of what institutions are about. Institutions come into existence out of processes of legitimisation of rules of conduct and power related behaviour, and as such they represent the establishment of social, cultural and political norms. Rules define and shape not only the behaviour of actors, they also define the appropriateness of what actors do. Therefore institutions have a clear normative element.[5]

Not all types of governing interactions and their institutional settings are the same, to the contrary, they vary enormously from institutionalising governance at 'street corners' of local communities in public-private partnerships to institutionalising regimes governing international political-economic global arenas. It would be hard to imagine that one institutional theory would suffice for understanding of or coping with such a broad scala of institutionalising governing interactions. Some institutional theories are better equipped to handle institutional aspects of small-scale informal face-to-face governing interactions, others for the analysis or creation of formalised multi actor arenas. The institutional theories presented attempt varying answers to questions raised in a governance context, and I agree with Lowndes that '[i]nstitutional analysis stands to benefit enormously from the surfacing of diverse theoretical and intellectual positions ...'[6]

> The variety of institutional theories is rather an asset than a hindrance to the understanding of governing institutions in a diverse, complex and dynamic world to be governed.

State, market and civil society as institutions

If we accept that the societies we live in have diverse, dynamic and complex traits, we might also assume that our institutions will reflect these qualities, and it would be strange to take it for granted that the institutions in which governing interactions are embedded 'suddenly' would become uniform, static and simple. Because institutions can be seen as 'thickened' forms of human behaviour, this condensation is probably expressed in less diversity of forms, less dynamic in patterns of change, and maybe less complex in architecture than the interactions they define, order, constrain or enable; but diverse, dynamic and complex they will be. In this section the issue of the relation between these societal features and societal institutions will be examined. To make the discussion more tangible the three major societal institutions state, market and civil society are used as examples, and as mentioned above, representation serves to conceptualise the intermediate position of these institutions in societal governance.

Representation as a concept is widely used in political discussions. In political theory formal representation is considered one of the key criteria to judge the democratic state with. The way I will use it has a wider meaning, although political aspects are part of this broader concept. This broad meaning has been nicely summarised by Pitkin in the term 'standing for'.[7] She distinguishes two types of representation, a descriptive and a symbolic one. In the descriptive variant the representative does not 'act' for, but 'is' something rather than 'does' something. Standing for is by virtue a correspondence or a connection; it is the making present of something absent by resemblance or reflection, as in a mirror or in art.[8] In the symbolic version of representation no resemblance or reflection is required and the connection is of a different kind. Symbolic representation can be seen as 'an exact reference to something indefinite' and 'vehicles for the conception of what they symbolize'.[9] Symbolic representation also draws attention to emotions, to attitudes, to satisfactions. Because of this symbolic representation can be looked at as a two-way correspondence.[10]

Drawing upon these insights, the representation concept I have in mind has the following characteristics: it is a 'standing for' and it is a two-way indefinite correspondence. On the one hand first-order governance is represented in 'what is going out there' as societal problems and opportunities, and thus this governing order represents within its institutional settings specific governance issues at large. On the other hand institutions reflect broader societal governance issues, being representative of societal diversity, complexity and dynamics at large.

This two-fold representative role can be demonstrated more concretely when we look at the state, market and civil society as major societal institutions. Partly it is state institutions such as parliaments who act out this representative role, but partly this role is much broader. Other institutions also play this dual representation role. Thus, next to the state, the market and civil society participate in reflecting generalised day-to-day problem-solving and opportunity-creation into broader societal governance institutional issues. And the market also reflects societal diversity, complexity and dynamics, as does civil society in the institutionalising of broad societal trends. This concept of representation is what I set out to elaborate.

A central argument in the governance perspective is that governing as an activity and governance as its structural component, is not something governments do (or don't do). They are sets of activities and structural arrangements in which public and private actors participate. Next to governments, market and civil society parties have governance roles, at the intentional and the structural level of governing interactions, from local to global. Attention should be paid to the institutional arrangements of all these roles, and the way they represent what is at stake in societies these days. The duality of the representation concept can be of help in the analysis of the governance contribution of the state, as well as the market and civil society.

> Governing institutions play a central two-way role in the representation of 'those being governed' and 'those governing'.

State as institution

Although in Chapter 8 the state already figured quite extensively as representing the hierarchical governance mode *par excellence*, some of its institutional aspects have not yet been treated as fully as seems necessary. It is generally acknowledged that within the state, next to hierarchical principles, various other forms of co-ordination are practised that play out the dual representative role as explained above. Growing and more complex governing tasks are tackled with mixes of interactions, in my conceptualisation to be seen as mixes of interventions, interplays and interferences. Thus the image of the state as a homogeneous societal institution, governed by uniform rules, has to be replaced by others, representing a scala of components with varying attributes, differentiated degrees of autonomy, mixes of involuntary and voluntary co-ordination and formalised and informal authority patterns. The German theory of *Politikverflechtung* ('political interlacement') is an important example of the possibility to develop a coherent set of propositions around public organisations 'interwoven' in many mutual interrelationships, and thus being able to represent the diversity and complexity of modern societies.[11] The relation between the state and societal dynamics has always been arduous, because of the built-in sluggishness of state institutions. What is known as 'public management' has in essence much to do with making the state more sensitive to societal dynamics, and to represent this dynamics in its operation. To make these thoughts more tangible I will apply them to the European Union (EU).

Much of the political and scholarly discussion on the EU as an institution, and its institutionalisation process from the Treaty of Rome on to its most recent changes, are exactly about its role in representing the diversity, dynamics and complexity of Europe as a society. The *diversity* of Europe, in particular cultural diversity, is considered one of its most important features. However, it is appreciated in quite different ways. Some see it as an impediment, others as an element of strength. Europe as a culturally divided, fragmented and socially heterogeneous entity, is said to be less united than it was in earlier periods, when a European cultural and political system existed, strengthened by alliances and marriages. According to Touraine Europe is moving from a collection of production societies with strong national-state orientation, to a consumption and communication society, with weakened or disappearing links between culture, society and personality.[12] European integration serves as a new mediating institution in these processes, which he finds positive and desirable. Others regard difference and heterogeneity to be barriers to European integration. They see national cultures as distinct ways of life that define to a large extent people's collective identities. Different institutional models have been developed within Europe, with cultural and emotional energy invested in those societal solutions. These should be kept alive.[13] 'The quest for European unity presupposes citizens conscious not only of their multiple roles in contemporary society but equally of their multicultural identities ... the recognition of diversity and pluralism, the mediation of cultural and political identities and allegiances'.[14] How these twin aspects, diversity and identity should find their institutional expression and representation is a matter of debate, but it is certainly a major governance issue.[15]

The *dynamics* of the EU have been a scholarly issue almost from the beginning. Its growth pattern has led to many different theoretical explanations and connected extrapolations for its future development.[16] There are neo-functional or neo-federal perspectives that see European integration as a smooth linear process involving not qualitative jumps, but incremental steps. Then there is the view of a cyclical process, of 'fusion and diffusion'. There is also a 'realist' option, stressing the influence of geopolitical processes, and foreseeing a radical transformation process of European integration. Whatever these interpretations, they all point at the importance of the dynamics of an EU with all its entities and cultures creating tensions in the balancing processes between governance needs and capacities making the creation and maintenance of institutions, modes and orders of governance necessary.

The *complexity* of the EU is also a major source of discussion, in popular as well as specialised writing. Its formal bodies, the relation between them and those of the member states are increasingly becoming subject to debate and research. So the recent 'transparency' issue is directly related to the issue of the complexity of EU institutions. A theoretical approach putting the complexity of the EU squarely on the table sees it is a *Mehrebenensystem*, a multi-level system.[17] In this perspective the complexity of the EU system is expressed in the cross-wise relation (*Verschränkung*) of the allocation of competencies, rights of consent and control, and veto powers of the European actors at different levels. The reduction of the complexity of all these state and supra-national interests has to be reflected in organisational and institutional forms, in which a subtle balance is struck between representational demands of the member states and efficiency and rationality criteria in the decision-making processes of the Union. This balance between inter-governmental and supra-national is a redefining and restructuring process that started with the Treaty of Rome and remains a major and permanent governance issue, as is the case for all living institutional frameworks.[18]

> For the EU, representation of complexity is the most serious institutional governance issue, and *ceteris paribus* stands as an example for this second order 'state' governance issue in general.

Market as institution

Markets as societal institutions consist of mixes of all types of interactions, interferences, interplays and interventions, and they have their own diverse, complex and dynamic features. As early as 1890 Marshall (although according to Swedberg, as an exception) showed that markets can and should be analysed by criteria such as space, formal organisation, informal regulation, and the presence or absence of social bonds between buyers and sellers. And in the Austrian School, von Mises said: 'The market is not a place, a thing or a collective entity, but is a process, actuated by the interplay of the actions of the various individuals co-operating under the division of labour'.[19] The organisation of markets is in recent 'institutional economic theory' and receiving serious attention. So Coase suggests that in principle the organisation of a market by the enforcement of the rules can be left to the members. However, when this is not the case, external control such as by state intervention has to regulate buying and selling, if 'there is to be a market at all'.[20] Swedberg develops a concept of the market as 'a special type of interaction that begins as competition between number of actors (buyers and/or sellers) and that ends up with an exchange for a few of the actors'.[21]

What has become known under the heading of institutional economics can also give us a hand – albeit a small one – in sketching a picture of the market showing some of its real features. This school of thought has chosen transaction costs as its central institutional device, and its central presumption is that economic organisations try to economise on transaction costs. It uses a variety of economic, legal and organisation concepts to analyse this phenomenon. Two key behavioural assumptions count: the cognitive limitations of market actors and their opportunism in self-interest; and at the structural level limitations such as political, social and legal rules are considered as institutional arrangements governing the way in which economic units co-operate and/or compete. There is also what Williamson calls governance, which in institutional economics denotes the institutional framework, broadly consisting of markets, hierarchies and hybrids, through which transactions are channelled.[22] This amounts to a departure from general economic laws explaining market interactions, but demonstrates some governance aspects.

If we agree on the basis of these examples that the market exists through different kinds of interactions, the question must be of how these can be differentiated. Perhaps *interferences*, the most spontaneous variety of interactions, with the entrepreneur as the central actor are most pertinent. In the classical description by Schumpeter, the entrepreneur is a revolutionary, 'changing conditions of supply, combining new resources, setting up a new production function. Entrepreneurial innovation is a creative act, breaking through a wide array of ordinary constraints'. More recent theories of entrepreneurship also stress that the great variety of entrepeneurial interactions are interactions within specific social contexts and reference groups, making it impossible to define a single entrepreneurial role.[23] These ideas about the entrepeneurial role in the market point to the importance of interferential interactions in the market. It is clear that those spontaneous and creative aspects of the market are also an indication of its *diversity*.

Interactions such as *interplays* occur frequently in markets. Recent scholarly work has recognised interplays, and in particular networks, as important forms of governing interaction in the market place. Castells is even of the opinion that the whole (capitalist) mode of production in our time will fundamentally change because of them, becoming 'network societies'.[24] And another study states that '[i]ndustrial development need not involve vertical integration or standardised mass production but may rely instead on horizontal networks of production. Trust, mutual forbearance, and reputation may supplement and/or replace the price mechanism or administrative fiat'.[25] Networks as governance configurations in the market are forms of inter-firm collaboration, strategic or otherwise, and can be explained by economies of scale, scope, specialisation and experience, as by the asymmetry in resources controlled by different firms.[26]

In a structural perspective on market interactions, the idea of embeddedness is an important one. Granovetter argues that all interactions between firms take place within a web of pre-existing social relations and he warns of a Hobbesian or atomised-actor explanation of economic interaction in which only self-interest is the driving force.[27] To say it somewhat differently, network or interplay forms of interactions between firms can be seen as 'inter-penetrations of markets and hierarchies in the formation of co-operative relations'.[28] What we see in the market domain are societal interplays in the form of networks that analytically should not be neglected. Finally I shall touch upon *interventionist* interactions in the market. I already quoted Coase in this respect, and many other studies can be mentioned. Even in the American economy 'degrees of formal integration in the form of bureaucratic controlled structures' are recognised, as well as hierarchies in the (non-state) governance of industries, according to an authoritative study of the governance of the American economy.[29] All this hints at those forms of interactions I conceptualise as of an interventionist nature. These short notes on the composition of the market in terms of interplays and interventions add up to a view of the market being quite a bit more *complex* than is often assumed.

The *dynamics* of the market has for a long time been the subject of scholarly attention. Many theories have tried to identify key determinants for transformation in the governance regimes of markets.[30] Campbell et al. recognise as many as five, all emphasising a particular driving force for dynamic transformation of the market: efficiency, technology, power and control, culture and even policies of the state. The authors themselves have developed a model of dynamics in the governance of markets containing elements of the five approaches mentioned. Their model stresses the interactions between actors as a key factor in the transformation of governance systems of the market, within a context of exogenous and endogenous factors. Combinations of these make for pressures of change, which according to them, seldom go smoothly.[31]

> The market can be considered to represent many societal features in all kinds of societal interactions, but it is in serious need of an approach translating questions around them into a blend of governance issues.

Civil society as institution

Civil society is a much debated, but relatively vague, concept. There is a line of thought bringing all governance outside 'pure' states under the heading of civil society, including the market, and elements of politics. Remarkably, authors promoting this 'broad' line of thinking can be found in literature of a European neo-Marxist tradition (Keane) and in American citizenship theorising (Somers).[32] My own idea on civil society is a more limited one, excluding the market from it as well as differentiating it from the state. A good start for this point of view is empirical. Most observers see as typical elements of civil society organisations like churches, professional bodies, spontaneous groups and movements such as neighbourhood groups. An important new category are Non-Governmental Organisations (NGOs), by some even seen as the nucleus of international or even global civil society. Characteristic of most organisations and groups mentioned is their voluntary nature. However, to simply equate institutionally the voluntary sector with civil society is in many respects unsatisfactory. There are for civil society important 'boundary' cases that cannot be considered as voluntary ones: academic institutions are usually at least partially financed by the state, and what of the media? Where do these institutionally belong, in civil society, state or market? And what about the pure private sphere of the family, and informal social groups, do they belong to civil society, or only as far as they are involved in 'civic' activities? So a descriptive start has its merits but also its limitations, bringing me to a partly analytical descriptive, partly conceptual attempt based upon governance considerations.

In the governance perspective we will look in particular at non-state societal actors or entities being in one way or another involved in governing by means of image formation, choice of instruments or social-political action, and to the structural contexts in which they operate: public sphere, resources, social-political capital (see Chapters 3–5). They may be voluntary groups, professional bodies, academics, media, or firms: what characterises them as civil society is involvement in social-political governance, on the intentional as well as on the structural level of governing interactions. However, at the structural level of governing interactions in particular, we might also look at those parts of social life in the family or group sphere, where interest in governing might start and grow, in the long run evolving into social-political participation of one kind or another. If, in other words, we think of civil society also as the breeding ground for civic socialisation processes, we can fully comprehend what, in my view, typically belongs to social-political capital.

A more conceptual route can also be followed, that sees civil society as the societal domain predominantly characterised by interferential and interplay types of societal interactions. These are the interactions with a somewhat spontaneous, semi-formalised, mainly horizontal, non-interventionist nature. Therefore, in principle it is not the formal status of individuals or organisations, but the way they interact with each other, that is decisive in deciding if they belong to civil society or not. This way of looking at civil society comes close to, but is not quite the same as how Cohen and Arato conceptualise it. These authors see the development of civil society, as with the market and the state, as a consequence of the rationalisation of society and societal differentiation. In these processes these institutions become relatively autonomous societal spheres, specialising in certain tasks. State and market were successful in institutionalising this autonomy and task differentiation, civil society less so.

According to Habermas the essence of civil society is communicative rationality or undisturbed public discussion. However these basic activities have been insufficiently institutionalised within civil society, partly because of colonisation by the state (power) and the market (money).[33] I will come back to these broader issues later, of colonisation as interpenetration, suffices to say here that we can conceptualise civil society as the societal domain consisting mainly of interferential, occasionally of interplay interactions, and rare use of interventions. This comes close to what these, and other, authors see as the essence of civil society, stressing its voluntary communication at the actor and the structural level, but now in a slightly more integrated view.[34] It should be noted that this forms also a conceptual answer to those who put civil society and the market under one heading: in civil society the intervention form of interactions, which one finds regularly in the market, is almost completely missing in the civil society domain.

Although, as argued above, civil society and the voluntary or non-profit sector can not be equated as being indivisable, enough similarities can be assumed between them to allow the steadily growing literature on the voluntary or non-profit sector to say something about the diversity, complexity and dynamics of civil society. This literature stresses the special character of the voluntary sector, for example its institutionalisation and governance issues, the diversity of its power relations and elite structures, its rules and codes, division of labour, horizontal and vertical inter-organisational networks. Some of this theorising aims to establish commonalities, however it seems to me that more theoretical progress would be made by exploring its qualitative differences. Voluntary and solidarity elements of civil society point to a principal freedom of organisation and interaction, by definition emphasising its diversity.[35] Cultural or symbolic approaches place even greater emphasis on diversity as a basic aspect of civil society. In this theorising civil society is considered the realm of structured, socially established consciousness, as a network of understandings to be studied by distinctive symbolic codes.[36] This approximates a vision on civil society close to what in earlier literature was conceptualised as civic culture.[37] Civil society certainly also has a complexity of its own. However, compared to the other two domains, state and market, this cannot be seen as a crucial institutional dimension. Complexity, in terms of overlapping relations between interacting societal entities, is exhibited in civil society particularly at its margins, especially in its relations with the state (see further Chapter 13). In a dynamical sense there is more to say. For example there is a school of thought relating the dynamics of civil society to the dynamics of democratisation, or rather to the liberalisation of the developing world and recently in Eastern Europe.[38] In this analysis there is a constant balancing of dynamics between the state and civil society: 'neither of the two can monopolise public life without provoking a reaction from the opposite realm to retain political space'.[39] To this external dynamic aspect, an internal one can be added due to tensions within civil society itself, between co-operation and conflict, between public and private, between organisational and cultural tendencies, or between individual and collective dimensions of voluntariness and solidarity.[40] Ideas about features like this change, and as always one finds dynamics of interactions between those wanting to keep such concepts, and others who seek to change them.

> Civil society represents in particular societal diversity at the intentional level of governing interactions. However because of its open boundaries, and its institutional weakness, it is easy prey for predators at the structural level of those interactions.

Governance, representation, needs and capacities

In the introduction to this chapter I suggested the possibility of capturing second-order governance in the twin concepts of needs and capacities, comparable to the problems and solutions for first order governance. Now I want to return to this suggestion and try to substantiate it. What was said about problems is true of needs: they are subjective constructions, and in the process of being formulated they can acquire a certain degree of objectivity or a sufficiently shared status to become governance issues. Needs are not self-explanatory, value-free or neutral matters at all, but as Foucault expressed it – albeit in another context – 'needs is also a political instrument, meticulously prepared, calculated and used'.[41]

Turning to capacity, an interesting example is an exploration of state capabilities analysed under the title *Do Institutions Matter?*[42] In this book capabilities are seen as patterns of influence of governments in their environment, and operationalised in elements such as setting and maintaining priorities, targeting resources, co-ordinating conflicting objectives, ensuring political stability, and (above all) managing political cleavages. The study concludes that:

> although institutions affect governmental capabilities, their effects are contingent; specific institutional arrangements often create both opportunities and risks for individual governmental capabilities; there are direct trade-offs between some institutional capabilities and governments gain some room to work around basic institutional arrangements by generating countervailing mechanisms.[43]

In this book, capabilities are closely related to tasks, two sides also to be found in my coining of the dual concept needs-capacities. Governing capacity is therefore the generalised institutional ability to structure frameworks, conditions or contexts for solving generalised societal problems or occasioning societal opportunities (needs). The care for this dual notion of formulation of needs and structuring capacities at the institutional level of governing interactions is the essence of second-order governance.

The representation concept serves to clarify the relation between governance needs and capacities. I defined institutional representation as a two-way relation: from society to institutions (downward) and from first-order governance to institutions (upward). It is two-way position of institutions that give them their pivotal governance role. Both second-order governing needs and capacities can be deduced from this two-way posture, and it will be clear from the way they are defined, that needs and capacities are not 'givens', but themselves diverse, dynamic and complex societal configurations. If categories of governing interactions dealing with problems or opportunities are insufficiently available or not geared to their tasks (needs), and or institutions of governing unable to develop insufficient solution or strategy structures (capacities), governing overload or other unbalances in governance will be the consequence. This is, in practice, what second-order governance or institutional care is about: the handling of the balance between governing needs and capacities in the way societal institutions represent or misrepresent them.

Finally these ideas can be specified according to the three major societal institutions. Because of the nature of its main governing interactions – interventions and interplays – the state is the societal institution best able to cope with societal complexity in a representative manner. The market and civil society, because of the dominant interferential nature of their interactions, are less able to handle complex societal issues. The creation of institutional frameworks for solving complex societal problems or creating complex societal opportunities would easily amount to arbitrariness and unfairness. However there is no doubt that the state and the market also contribute to societal complexity in a considerable degree. The state, by the multitude of its organisational settings, and the maze of its rules and regulations covering all spheres of life and all societal levels, is itself a complexity-creating institution. In particular the often overlapping and even contradictory nature of its interventions contributes to societal complexity. Once in a while efforts are set in motion to reduce this bureaucratic maze, but often the result adds complexity instead of reducing it (see Chapter 10).

The market is, next to a complexity-reducing institution (such as by the price mechanism), also a complexity creating one in its unwillingness or inability to take care of the consequences of its own imperfections.[44] It points to the state to cope with the complex governance issues it brings about, because of these imperfections. I am inclined then to say that the state has a central role in the representation of societal complexity, in its needs as well as capacities dimensions. The role of the market in the representation of societal complexity is more one sided: it does contribute to reducing societal complexity, but is less able/willing to handle the complexity needs it also creates.

The position of civil society in representing societal complexity is a less outspoken one. This runs contrary to societal diversity, where I see a prominent place for civil society. Patterns of cultural identities and other differentiating qualities as expressed in societal diversity will develop most freely within the domain of civil society, that is to say in its 'downward' representation, from governance to day-to-day governing. But is it the institution best equipped to handle governance issues arising from representing societal diversity in an 'upward' direction, that is to say from first to second order governance? Because it is the institution characterised mostly by interferential and somewhat by interplay forms of societal interactions, the coping with diversity issues occur mainly on a voluntary basis. However, there are diversity issues, which cannot be handled solely on a voluntary basis. This is where the state intervenes. Representing societal diversity seems to be a shared one, by civil society as well as by the state. The role of the market here is neutral. It produces and delivers services creating diversity effects, in doing so it also reduces diversity by ordering consumers into market segments. I am inclined to say that civil society plays a dominant institutional role in the representation of societal diversity, however the state offers assistance. Finally in the representation of societal dynamics in its upward as well as in its downward direction, the market is the dominant institution. Of the three institutions it is most able to react quickly to societal changes, and it also has the capacity to create such changes by stimulating amplifying trends and tastes.

> The state, the market and civil society each represent specific societal needs and capacities. As long as the state is expected to intervene where the other institutions fail, it will remain playing the 'all-round' role in representing the society in governance.

Conclusion

Second-order governance involves care for the operation and maintenance of governing institutions. From the outset I have tried to make it clear that second-order governing differs qualitatively from first-order governing. Compared to everyday problem-solving and opportunity creation, addressing institutional questions usually has a political rather than a social character, and second-order governing reasons more from wholes to parts, than from parts to wholes, and deals with categories of governing interactions instead of interactions as such. Qualities or lack of qualities of governing institutions are not objective givens but depend on the way they are defined, and what is expected from them. Ideas about these vary a great deal. For example, if one approaches institutions from a normative rational point of view emphasising the categorical nature of actors interacting as calculating entities on the basis of self-interest, quite different institutional questions are raised than when one considers institutions as historically developed entities reflecting outcomes of longer-term societal processes.

Remaining within the governance perspective I have chosen, second-order governance questions circle around issues like the institutionalisation of different types of governing interactions and the way governing institutions represent societal diversity, complexity and dynamics, as capacities or needs. Because discussions on institutions easily become rather abstract, I seized this occasion to introduce the three major societal institutions, state, market and civil society as frames of reference for developing some conceptual ideas on second-order governance. Fields covered are immensely broad and complicated. My aim in this chapter was limited to attempting to show that conceptualisation of societal institutions in their role and position is, in principle, possible. The recent interest in institutions is catching up on a neglected subject of scholarly interest. However, the forms this interest has taken vary a great deal, with quite different theoretical and analytical assumptions, methodologies and outcomes.

The question 'do institutions matter?' is only the beginning of an inquiry into what institutional theorising for governance purposes might offer. The exploration in this chapter, especially on institutional aspects of state, market and civil society, has made it quite clear that in my opinion institutions matter very much. Governing qualities of these institutions have great conceptual promises, yet much work has to be done to bring them in line. The deliberations in the chapter only scratch the surface of the role of societal institutions in governance. Important matters such as on design and reform of these institutions have to be left to future contemplation. In the final chapter the role of institutions for governance will return as an element in a synthesising effort. The discussion on the representative, intermediate role of institutions as second-order governance media between societal features on the one hand and societal problem-solving and opportunity creation on the other will be continued in the final part of the book, when I come to speak about governance and governability.

Notes

1 Hall and Taylor, 1996; Lowndes, 1996; Scott, 1995; Powell and DiMaggio, 1991; March and Olsen, 1989; Goodin, 1996.

2 An important example of this approach is Scharpf's theorising on 'games real actors play' (1997).

3 Hall, Taylor, 1996.

4 *idem.*

5 See March and Olsen, 1984.

6 Lowndes, 1996, p. 195.

7 Pitkin, 1967.

8 *idem*, p. 5, p. 61.

9 *idem*, p. 97.

10 *idem*, p. 106.

11 Scharpf et al., 1976; Benz et al., 1992.

12 Touraine, 1994.

13 Zetterholm, 1994.

14 Nelson et al., 1992, p. 5.

15 Grote, Bgikpi, 2002; Berting, in press.

16 Wessels, 1997.

17 Scharpf, 1994; König et al., 1996.

18 Sibeon, 2000.

19 Quoted by Swedberg, 1994, p. 260.

20 *idem*, p. 264.

21 *idem*, p. 271–272.

22 Williamson, 1975.

23 Martinelli, 1994, p. 479 and p. 487.

24 Castells, 1996.

25 Powell and Smith-Doerr, 1994, pp. 370.

26 Grandori, Soda, 1995.

27 Granovetter, 1985.

28 Grabher, 1993, p. 7.

29 Campbell et al., 1991.

30 *idem.*

31 *idem*, esp. Chapter 11.

32 Keane, 1988, Somers, 1995.

33 Cohen, Arato, 1992; Dubbink, 1999.

34 Alexander, 1998a.

35 Powell, DiMaggio, 1991.

36 Alexander, 1998b.

37 Almond, Verba, 1963.

38 Bendel, Kropp, 1998.

39 Biekart, 1999, pp. 36–37.

40 Ahrne, 1998.

41 Quoted by Fraser, 1989, p. 291.

42 Weaver and Rockmann, 1993.

43 *idem*, pp. 446–452.

44 Dubbink, 1999.

11

META (THIRD-ORDER GOVERNANCE)

Several building-blocks for the governance concept have so far been examined, these blocks fit together in the form of a norm oriented framework, which I call 'meta'. Normative preconceptions have variously crept into the analysis, explicitly but certainly implicitly as well. This can hardly be avoided in treating a theme like governance that is value-ridden from top to bottom. In fact 'social-political' or 'interactive' governance is much more than an analytical concept. It is a highly normatively charged one and its entire development can be regarded as a normative exercise. In other words, governance explicitly phrased as 'social-political', or 'interactive' is advisable and sensible at the beginning of the twenty-first century, as far as I am concerned. As such, this chapter is devoted to an overall view of what has been discussed before, from a normative point of view.

So far I have identified two orders of governing and governance, first-order governing involved in day-to-day problem-solving and opportunity creation, and second-order governing dealing with institutional governance conditions. A third order of governance can be added, conceptually the place dedicated to normative governance issues. I want to make clear from the start that meta governing is not simply governance at a higher level. This aspect of governing is already subsumed in the first two orders and concerns layers or stratification according to organisational or constitutional principles. Meta as third-order governance is of a different type. It folds back on the theory and practice of governing and governance *as such*. Meta governing is like an imaginary governor, teleported to a point 'outside' and holding the whole governance experience against a normative light.

A meta perspective

It is accepted usage that meta-x is something over and beyond x. Meta thinking is thought-about thinking, a meta system is a system of systems, meta governance is the governing of governing. According to Sklair, a meta theory is a set of assumptions about the constituent parts of the (observed) world, and about the possibility of knowledge about them.[1] An effective meta theory is one that manages a high degree of coherence between epistemology and the objects of knowledge. At a meta level there are basic questions to be addressed if one wants to be consistent in the way one conceptualises. The admittedly limited ideas I am able to formulate on the meta- (theoretical) aspects of governance are only a few steps towards an effective meta theory.

I attempted in the previous chapters analysing from different angles what I consider to be a perspective on governance. In the course of this were reviewed all kinds of partial images, of governance as activities, as modes of interactions, as solving problems or creating opportunities, as institutions. All these partial views contribute to shifting insights on governance, and in this chapter the focus will once again shift. The focal point is the imaginary meta governor wanting to formulate a set of norms or criteria to judge governance with. Assuming such a meta-focus and invoking norms or criteria, meta is associated mainly with evaluating 'how to'. This seems plausable: 'how to' implies higher-order judgements based on higher order norms or criteria based upon ideals, ideals for sustaining and improving. Human systems are ultimately self-designing. We continuously change and design implicitly or explicitly the social and governing world we live and participate in. Governing these change and (re) design processes from a normative point of view is the essence of meta governance. In my perspective such meta governing activities focus in particular on the continuous dynamic (re) construction of societal elements (diversity) in their interrelations (complexity). Somehow social-political systems are self-contained – they resolve their own internal contradictions – within the context of the ever changing relations with their environments. Ultimately social-political entities are (normatively) self-governing, both actively and creatively. They maintain their own will and identity, react to internal or external influences, and continuously create new states of affairs. In meta governance norms and criteria are advanced according to which existing practices are evaluated, new directions suggested, existing goals examined and new ones formulated and pursued.

Meta governance also 'binds' in another way. In reality, governing elements and levels, and governance modes and orders, are seldom clearly separated, and governing action in one direction has repercussions in one or more others. What from one governing element, mode or order may seem to be quite sensible, can be quite insensible from another. Following Hofstadter, these interrelations are known as strange loops or links.[2] In fact, many such loops are built-in in society. From a governance point of view, the one central 'loop' of interest to us is the 'democratic' one: who (or what) is above the governor, who or what 'governs the governor'? In a democratically governed society the governed are governed by their governors, who are likewise governed by those they govern. A central meta governance question must be: how are the strange loops between governors and governed organised, and what is the quality of these arrangements? This is a strange loop process, being both input and outcome at the same time. Because meta itself is a two-way interacting governing order, it is not necessarily paradoxical or contradictory to define meta governance both in terms of process and the outcome of that process.

In meta theory it is deemed important that meta considerations are cast in other terms than the subject itself. This leads me to couch my ideas on meta in two qualitatively different ways from those before: first, I have not made use of these concepts as yet, and second, I apply them as normative measuring rods. However, the conceptual path is maintained by applying to my meta deliberations the distinction between intentional and structural levels of governing interactions. Beginning with the intentional level, the three governing elements image, instrument and action will be placed under the meta scrutiny of *rationality*. This will be followed by an evaluation of the governance modes as structural level of those interactions, by applying '*responsiveness*' as a norm. Finally the orders of governance will be reviewed, including meta governance itself, by using *performance* as a criterion.

The three meta standards, rationality, responsiveness and performance, and the sub-criteria derived from them within the chapter, are my personal choice as a 'meta governor'. Colleague meta governors would undoubtedly prefer other normative notions. That is exactly the purpose of a meta exercise like this: let them come forward and we will cross (meta) arms.

> In meta governing interactions, governors and governed alike, 'take each other's measure' in formulating the norms and criteria by which they want to judge each other and the measuring itself.

Rationality: meta considerations on governing elements

Governors (public or private) with all their ambitions, emotions and intuitions have to be able to underpin their – interactive – governing proposals with reasoned arguments. Governing has in some way to be rational: based upon verifiable facts and data, logical choice of instruments and defendable action routes. Doubts will always remain, because governing facts or data are no more than observations that have passed through many filters of social-political communication. Instruments are often unreliable and, in combining them, they even may become counterproductive. Action seldom will go undisputed. Rationality in governing thus means the acceptance of certain degrees of uncertainties, the realisation of partial knowledge and provisional insights, and learning by doing.[3] Still it is an important normative consideration in modern governance, because rationality implies a condition of 'relevant considerations', as the Dutch philosopher Derksen phrased it.[4] In his view there is nothing particularly 'good' about rationality, but it helps: to act rationally, relevant considerations are needed; otherwise behaviour can be called irrational, which in social-political governing is not common or advisable.

Despite this, rationality has strong roots in many (meta) sciences and is simultaneously highly controversial within and between sciences. A Symposium on the subject in which many renowned philosophy scholars participated, concluded: 'We certainly have not been able to build a general theory of rationality for to-day's world, not even to lay any firm foundation for such a theory'.[5] As such, claims for an all-embracing rationality concept seem to be overstated, a more modest interpretation is as follows: '[a] rational person as methodical and precise, as tidy and orderly, above all in thought. He does not raise his voice, his tone is steady and equal; that goes for feelings as well as his voice. He separates all separable issues, and deals with them one at a time. By doing so, he avoids muddling up issues and conflating distinct criteria for interaction'.[6] This is the kind of actor I have in mind when I think of a governor acting 'rational in a governing situation' (see below).

Can something sensible be said about how 'rational' social-political interaction might look or, in other words, is there a version of rationality appropriate for meta norm-setting within the governance perspective? There are several ways to approach this question. The first would be to start with a view on rationality as applied in public choice or game theories and 'stretch' this to make it applicable for broader governance purposes. However, even mild critical reviewers of this theoretical scene concur that we are still far from any generally applicable insights on the rationality of governing actors, notwithstanding Scharpf's capturing title: *Games Real Actors Play.*[7] Second, we might start from accepted types such as value and goal-means rationality and work from these. The attraction of such an approach is of releasing an overall rationality concept and allowing a variety of rationality notions. However, this might open the door to as many rationality concepts as one sees fit: someone even distinguished eight different rationality notions in Weber's writing,[8] thus hollowing out its normative and synthetic power.

My choice for rationality as a meta criterion follows a third route, involving my own ideas on governing and adding some rationality concepts to them. In fact I take the three elements of governing: image formation, choice of instruments and action, and for each of these I select a (sub-) rationality concept as yardstick: for 'proper' image formation communicative rationality (Habermas); for choosing an appropriate instrument Simon's bounded rationality concept, and for taking action Boudon's perception of rationality. Boudon's interpretation can also be seen as an integrating one in the sense that in the action component of governing the image and instrumental element are subsumed.

> Governing elements can normatively best be evaluated by principles of
> rationality: how rational they are, how rational they can be, what their
> contributions to governing should be.

Communicative rationality – evaluating images and image formation

Images in the governance perspective have a broad meaning, covering,
among other things, governing problems, opportunities, needs and
capacities. The most important event in image formation is arriving at collective images, either shared ones or the acknowledgment of differences.
This comes about by communication in interaction between those involved
in governing. Actors producing patterns of interactions use language to
co-ordinate their actions. In this co-ordination, says Habermas, actors are
oriented towards 'reaching an understanding' in concrete practical situations. 'Communicative rationality' characterises interactions between
social actors striving for a common definition of reality by means of communication.[9] Four demands fulfil this purpose: what actors say is com-
prehensible, it is true, it is right – i.e. there is a normative basis for its
utterance – and it is a sincere expression of the speaker's feelings. Good
reasons given and found by arguments in discussions connect communicative rationality with actual co-ordination of actions. The essence of
communicative rationality is of a striving for consensus based upon the
critical weighing of arguments. This may lead to acceptance of an argumentation by one party as given by another, or by mutual adaptation of
views by all parties involved in a particular interaction. Even if no agreement is reached there is always the opportunity for a new sequence of
argumentation resulting in better and more convincing arguments. The
norm regulating communicative rationality is legitimacy based upon the
acceptance of its justification by all involved. An important procedural
guarantee belonging to the practice of communicative rationality is checking and comparing each other's intentions with ensuing actions.

Communicative rationality, as phrased by Habermas, and the debate it
provoked is a prime source for evaluating image formation in governing
at the meta governance level in a coherent and stimulating manner.

Bounded rationality – evaluating the instrumental condition

Within the governing space created between images of governing challenges, and courses for action, governors have to select instruments. The

bounded-rationality concept, as developed by Simon, is an ideal method of selecting an instrument to evaluate processes in a meta governance perspective.[10] In contrast to perfect rational decision theory, which locates all constraints in the context not in the actor self, Simon assumes that actors are severely limited, particularly cognitively. This causes them to act within what Simon calls limits of bounded rationality. Rational actors 'satisfice' instead of optimising or even maximising. They aspire for acceptable costs versus benefits, simplify calculations, and routinise searches for (new) information. Bounded rational actors are rational within limits, and satisficing behaviour is rational in that it responds to finite means towards a particular end.[11] The bounded rational actor overcomes his limitations, by setting out procedures or following operating rules to reach a satisfactory outcome.

The bounded rational actor model as a normative model for (meta) governance is based upon two recognitions: (1) the world is too complex, dynamic and diverse to be fully understood and thus the scope of analyses for a satisfactory outcome should be reduced; (2) tools, techniques and arrangements are needed to extend the cognitive limitations of actors. Although Simon does not explicitly place the bounded rational actor within an interaction perspective, his ideas fit quite well with my view of the instrumental element of governing as the 'middle ground' between a relatively open image (formation) part of the governing process and a more closed decision and will-formation part.

Integrating the rationality concepts: rationality of action in a situation

The communicative and bounded form of rationality is a good place to begin building a meta governance norm for image formation and the choice of instruments. However, we also must integrate the third component of governing, the action element. The first two contribute to governing, but nothing 'happens' if no action is taken: action, in governing interactions, 'binds' them together. In terms of rationality the following line of thinking serves this purpose. The least stringent rationality criterium, the communicative one, applies to image building. This governing element is the most 'open' of the three and its rationality yardstick is not as high, for example, irrational beliefs are not beforehand excluded from consideration. As long as the participants in governing interactions try to reach understanding by rules and norms as set out by communicative rationality, interaction may lead towards shared governing images, in my terms. Interactions in which governing instrument(s) are chosen can be evaluated within the stricter boundaries of 'bounded' rationality as defined by Simon. After all, choosing a governing instrument usually goes through many stages of deliberation, in which the cognitive limitations of actors are – within boundaries – overcome by discussions between experts, and the weighing of alternatives. The application of supporting tools and techniques to extend the cognitive limitations of actors by means of thorough interactions are quite common. Ultimately, rationality is a good instrument to employ.

For the action component of governing, rationality demands should be even more strict. Taking action often means making binding decisions, which in the public arena are accompanied by strict procedural guarantees. Can a rationality norm be formulated able to evaluate this last, integrating and decisive step in governing in a meta perspective? A promising one might be Boudon's concept of 'situational rationality' meaning if I were in the same situation as the observed actor, pursuing the same goal with the same information available, 'would I do the same thing'?[12] In Boudon's view rationality of behaviour can be explained as a function of the structure of the situation of an actor, as an adaptation to this situation. Behaviour directed at achieving a particular goal in a rational manner has to be understandable for an outsider, when this observant has sufficient information at his disposal to judge the way the actor interprets his situation and the goals he or she wants to pursue. Boudon adheres to a rational choice model in which cost-benefit considerations play a central role (Weber's instrumental rationality). At the same time, he is aware that in many – important – situations this model has little explanatory power, e.g. when actions are inspired by beliefs (Weber's value rationality). He interprets value rationality in a way that such beliefs 'are grounded in the minds of social actors on reasons which they see as valid, and consequently as likely to be considered as valid by others'.[13] Beliefs can be partly scientific, when it is 'trans-subjective', when a generalised other will share this belief, such as 2 + 2 = 4. But we always have to take into consideration that a belief at one time completely valid – such as power and movement within Aristotelean physics – may turn out in fact to be invalid.

This situational rationality – I would do the same thing *ceteris paribus* – is broad and at the same time precise enough to be applicable to the action element of governing. It seems fitting to integrate the two other rationality criteria, the communicative and bounded rationality one. There is more to be said on the use of the rationality concept to evaluate governing activities, but a first step has been made to make meta governance applicable to this element of governing activities.

Varieties of rationality are applicable as meta governing principles to systematically evaluate the intentional image, instrument and action elements of governing interactions at their intentional level.

Responsiveness: meta considerations on modes of governance

In this section attention is paid to the structural component of governance interactions. This level has been conceptualised as modes of governance, of which three are distinguished, self-, co-, and hierarchical governance. Now a criteria must be developed with which these three modes can be evaluated each of them apart and as a cluster. As a central concept for this exercise 'responsiveness' seems appropriate. In contrast to rationality, which is typically actor-bound, responsiveness has a more structural connotation. In the literature examples of both can be found, but in my opinion, the more authoritative ones, Pitkin, Etzioni and Kaufmann et al., give it an interpretation leaning towards the structural or institutional side.

With varying emphases responsiveness is regarded as the quality to respond to wishes. Pitkin discusses responsiveness in the context of a theory of representation: 'For in representative government the governed must be capable of action and judgement, capable of initiating government activity, so that the government may be conceived as responding to them'.[14] And she also says: 'There need not to be a constant activity of responding but there must be a constant condition of responsiveness, of potential readiness to respond ... there must be institutional arrangements for responsiveness'.[15] From a broader point of view, but still focusing on the public realm, Kaufmann et al. aim their analysis at 'modes of coordination which operate jointly or separately to maintain order, efficiency and responsiveness within the public sector'.[16] The normative notion is emphasised by saying that public services are to be evaluated by a multidimensional set of standards such as legality, economy, effectiveness and responsiveness.[17] An even broader concept of responsiveness is formulated by Etzioni, who sees it as an essential element of an 'active society', puts it squarely in a meta context by using phrases such as 'to be active is to be responsive' and 'as some mechanism for converting the aggregate demands of its members into collective directives, and it is its responsiveness to these directives that can be assessed'.[18] Although interaction as such is not explicitly part of the examples mentioned, the two-way character of responsiveness is a key element of it. So, it would appear that at a meta level responsiveness is an appropriate criterium guiding the evaluation of the structural level of governing interaction, in my terms modes of governance.

Governance modes can normatively best be evaluated by principles of responsiveness: how responsive they are, how responsive they can be, and what their contributions to governing should be.

Responsiveness and self-governance

In Chapter 6 the concept of self-governance was discussed and three positions dealing with it were defined. In the *autopoietic* school of thought social systems have an inherent self-referentiality and operational closure quality. To distinguish themselves from others they create self-identities. They communicate with the outside world by communication on a voluntary basis and they interpret outside signals self-referentially. In this line of thinking, responsiveness is by definition limited. In the 'actor constellation' perspective on self-governance social, political and historical processes explain why societal (sub) sectors show tendencies towards autonomy and self governance. Variation in autonomy depends on all kinds of internal and external factors, and responsiveness to outside influence is by this school seen as variable. The governance view considers societal self-governing as embedded within the sphere of societal interferences, the most spontaneous and variable form of governing interactions. They can be found in all societal sectors, in particular within civil society, to a lesser extent within the market place and least commonly in the state domain. Responsiveness related to self-governance can be expected to vary according to the presence of interferential interactions. To paraphrase Etzioni 'being spontaneously interactive is being responsive', to new insights (images), responsive to new techniques (instrumental) and responsive to new issues/movements (action).

But responsive to what? In the definitions given above, the main argument is that on the side of the governors there should be responsiveness to the wishes of the governed, and with the governed there should be responsiveness to measures taken by the governors. This responsiveness basically applies to all those belonging to the self-governing entity, and thus might be called 'internal responsiveness'. This 'internal' normative conception of responsiveness for self-governing systems appears, in principle, to be uncontroversial, but in practice all kinds of qualifications can be made. In all three perspectives on self-governance, this internal notion of responsiveness is shared in principle, but different answers will be given to different practical questions raised.

What about 'externally' directed responsiveness, with the adherent normative notions? Self-governing social entities don't live an isolated life, they are part and parcel of other, broader societal contexts, also raising normative responsiveness demands.[19] One cannot take for granted that governance of self-governing entities, adhering to internal responsiveness criteria, automatically also means being responsive to the outside world, or in other words being 'external responsive'. If the self-governance of a societal entity has effects which will be appreciated by other entities in its environment as detrimental to their governance, and this entity is not willing or able to adapt (no external response) it might be expected that governance from the outside will (try to) limit or change this self-governance. One might say that the better self-governing societal entities can fit with expectations or conditions in their environment, the more this self-governing nature will be respected and maybe even re-enforced. Conceptually such environments consist of other self-governing entities, 'equal among equals in self-governance'. It is to be expected that the two-way notion of responsiveness also applies to them, and the question then becomes what we can say about such 'mutual' responsiveness expectations.

A solution to finding some answers is to realise that the world these self-governing entities 'live in' is complex, dynamic and diverse. In an *autopoietic* theoretical perspective with its emphasis on self-identity one might expect that self-governing societal units will be particularly sensitive to diversity and complexity in their environment. A societal subsystem with a strong self-identity will try to handle mutual normative responsiveness expectations by ordering the qualities of other societal subsystems according to their own responsiveness criteria. That is the kind of 'responsiveness language' they understand and are able to deal with. In the actor-in-constellations perspective societal entities are particularly sensitive to societal dynamics and complexity. A standard response to dynamics is flexibility, which normatively can be translated, in the presence of feedback circuits with frequent responses, to, in particular, non-linear events. The answer to complexity is reduction, and according to complexity theory this is normatively best expressed in appropriate (de-) composition rules (see Chapter 13). Finally, the interaction perspective points to the spontaneous and creative qualities of interferential external interactions of self-governing societal entities. One might expect self-governing entities to be adept at responding to dynamics and diversity in their environment. However, the (growing) complexity of modern societies defined as multiple and often overlapping interrelations, might diminish this responsive quality of self-governing societal entities. From a meta normative point of view this is a plea for not 'exporting' complexity of social-political issues to all societal domains, but to be selective in doing so.

Responsiveness and 'co'-governance

'Co'-modes of governance are the structural arrangements for the societal interactions of interplays. Such interplays are defined as collaborative and co-operative interactions whose aim is the pursuit of a common goal, usually assuming a (semi-) formalised character. The question now is of whether we can formulate responsiveness norms for co-governance, and if the different types of these arrangements require different norms of responsiveness. These – again – can be distinguished in internal and external norms, respectively the way the partners in those arrangements are responsive to each other and the manner these arrangements are responsive to their environment.

It should be remembered that co-governance itself might be a response, a reaction, to growing societal interdependencies and interpenetrations (see also Chapter 13). The acknowledgement by societal entities of dependencies on others can be due to different reasons, such as the realisation that coping with societal complexity, dynamics or diversity might be better done with others than done so alone. This can apply to pooling knowledge (image), finances (instrument) or action potential (social capital). Distinctions and considerations like these are the beginning of phrasing normative expectations for the design, maintenance or even ending of such arrangements. For example a co-arrangement for enhancing common knowledge might be a 'lighter' response than pooling financial resources or sharing action potential. 'Lighter' arrangements require less outspoken and formalised responsiveness norms; 'heavier' ones demand greater investments in these norms in the way they are implemented and sustained. What 'lighter' or 'heavier' might mean in this context can, for example, be demonstrated by examining concepts such as trust, reciprocity and binding, each having a normative notion of its own. So one can see trust is a minimal norm, reciprocity builds on trust and binding makes for co-arrangements for a longer time span. With the aid of concepts like these communicative governing, PPPs, co-management, networks and regimes as forms of 'co' can normatively be evaluated. Such refinements will depend on the purpose at hand, but quite easily normative scales or other measuring rods can be applied to them.

For external responsiveness such scales can also be conceptualised. For example, the degree of transfer of tasks and responsibilities by participating entities to the co-arrangement can vary from very little to a great deal, externally giving the impression of a trade-off. The more a co-arrangement gains independence from the parties engaged in it, the more it becomes an entity of its own, and the more it can externally be seen as self-organising societal entity. One sees this sometimes in public-private networks, as Mayntz and her colleagues point out, and their external responsiveness will be, accordingly low. However, when parties invest only a little of their autonomy in a co-arrangement such as in a communicative governing project, they can be seen as 'the lengthened arm' of the participating parties. Their external normative responsiveness expectations will vary according to those of the participating members. Generally it might be said that external responsiveness of co-governance arrangements depends to a great extent on the quality of their 'boundaries'. This quality, probably more than anything else, can be seen as decisive for the external responsiveness to be expected of co-arrangements.

Responsiveness and hierarchical governance

With responsiveness of hierarchical governance we come close to the more common discussions on this concept. Pitkin (see above) puts the subject directly in relation to public governing. Most of the literature deals with responsiveness in this context and the contours of the discussions on it, and in particular the lack of responsiveness of modern governments, are quite well-known. One way of looking at responsiveness as a norm for hierarchical governance is to see it in relation to interventions at the intentional level of hierarchical governance interactions (see Chapter 13). Hierarchical governing interventions are highly formalised, have a command and control character and often have sanctions attached to them. Although they can be found in the market and in civil society, they predominanty feature in public authorities and the state. Public interventions, as opposed to those in the other two domains, are usually a response to a social-political problem, are to be legalised by public bodies, are generally binding, and the sanctions attached to them have in the final instance physical force attached to them. Defects of hierarchical governing can also be attributed to interventions in the private sector. It is generally understood that much hierarchical governing has a symbolic character, and where it has substance, it is poorly controlled and seldom fully enforced. In the market sector this lack of response may be problematic, but in the long run competitive forces will deal normatively with such defects. In the civil society domain with its emphasis on voluntariness, lack of responsiveness because of low quality interventions is the least pressing, although long term it may have disintegrating effects. For the public sector responsiveness issues are the most complicated and the most serious, because the state 'does not end'. It may change, and in Chapter 8 several examples of this were given, from 'command' to 'regulation' and from 'procuring' to 'enabling'. Adaptations such as these usually are responses to broader societal developments or demands, and they may make hierarchical governance more responsive in its interventions.

In passing, I have already mentioned difficulties that the state faces in first and second-order governance due to the diversity, dynamics and complexity of the modern world. These 'macro' predicaments will effect its response at meso and micro levels of interventions. Notwithstanding strains in responsiveness, traditional hierarchical governance by the state, expressed in multi-facetted interventions in all spheres of societal activities, will remain an important mode of governance. This mode of governance, however, has to be continuously placed under normative scrutiny, and also, from a normative governance point of view, has to be supplemented with other governance modes as well.

> With responsiveness, the two-way institutional capacities of the three governance modes can be evaluated in a meta governance perspective.

Performance: the three governance orders in a normative perspective

Meta governance also applies to the three governance orders: problem-solving/opportunity creation as first-order governance, care for institutions as second-order governance, and meta governance for meta governing itself. The governing activities comprising these three governance orders differ substantively, consequently normative notions about them also differ. However, there is also a binding element between them: together they form the core of what governance is about, and they can't function without each other. Concrete problems cannot be solved if institutions lack the capacity to generalise them into governance needs. And second order governance cannot play its linking pin role, if normative principles detailing the balance between governing needs and capacities are not made explicit, and shared by the majority of governors and governed alike. First, a criterion must be found, able to cover norms relating to these three different types of governing activities.

Performance appears to be a concept that might serve this purpose: it has an evaluative connotation, it can be applied to quite different settings, public as well as private, at different levels of governing (actor, inter-actor, organisational and institutional) and it can be considered a multi-dimensional or composite normative concept. The authoritative study by Kaufmann et al. makes this quite clear.[20] However, we have to realise that 'the tools we use and the calculations we make are only imperfect measures of performance that depend for their meaning upon shared communities of understanding and agreement'.[21] This warning by Ostrom bears upon all norms applied, because there are no objective standards or criteria to operationalise meta considerations with.

My conceptual choice is to operationalise performance in dimensions or sub-norms, showing varying degrees of concreteness. To evaluate first-order governance – day-to-day problem-solving and opportunity creation – I introduce *effectiveness* as a concrete standard to measure performance. For second-order governing – institutional care – the *legitimacy* might serve as a standard. It is less tangible than effectiveness, but is given a central place in judging the performance of a two way representative role of institutions by the relevant 'community of understanding and agreement'. For the normative evaluation of meta governance itself, *ethical principles* seem to be the proper evaluative criteria. After all, without shared ethical norms, governance, in the final resort, will have no normative foundation, and thus ethical norm-setting as the central meta measure to evaluate the performance of meta governance itself seems appropriate.

> Governance orders can normatively best be evaluated by performance principles: how they perform, how they might perform and what their contributions to governing should be.

Effectiveness as norm for first-order governing

Effectiveness can be considered a relatively reliable normative meta criterium for evaluating problem solving and opportunity creation as first-order governing activities. Literature on evaluation in the public sector provides a rich source of developing conceptual ideas on how to apply effectiveness criteria to these activities. General concepts and theoretical notions used in this literature can – with certain modifications – be made usable for the purpose of meta evaluating first-order governance. There is much more available on problem-solving than on opportunity creation, but recently this aspect has also been subject to scholarly attention under the banner of 'policy strategy'.[22] Research traditions on evaluation and effectiveness – and there are many – all have their specific contributions to make. My own experience, as a long time member of a scientific advisory board sustaining policy analysis in Dutch national government, has taught me that meta debates in this area are sailing between the *scylla* of simplifying norms to make them applicable for model-building and other methods to measure effective governing activities, and the *charybdis* of phrasing realistic norms applicable to real life value orientations in governance. As might be expected, scholarly opinion on how best to sail between these tendencies differ, for example some emphasise 'rationalistic' versus 'hermeneutic' values.[23] Rationalistic approaches rely heavily on deduction of causal relations and ex post-evaluation research has developed a broad array of relatively simple to highly sophisticated methods, models, techniques and tools for tracking down such causal relations. In the hermeneutic approach relations are not deductively arrived at, but induced by observation and interpretation. In studying effectiveness we find concepts such as understanding, intentionality, functionality, empathy and detailed description.[24] The approach, as examined in Chapter 9, combining substantive requirements (coping with complexity, dynamics and diversity) and process aspects (interaction, participation, feedback) offers space for both model and observation or interpretation types of evaluation methodologies, depending on the meta purpose of the normative exercise at hand.[25]

Legitimacy as norm for second-order governance

Discussing normative notions for second-order governing, that is the care, maintenance and design of institutions, mention was made of 'new institutationalism', which defines institutions almost exclusively in terms of normative concepts (see Chapter 10). Legitimacy conceptually fits this line of thinking. Institutions play a two-fold representative, linking or intermediary role between societal diversity, dynamics and complexity, and day-to-day governing activities. The question is of whether legitimacy is an appropriate conceptual candidate for meta norm setting and evaluating institutions for that role.

The legitimacy concept has its foundation in a long tradition of social-political theorising and it has a focal place in recent discussions on institutional matters. Overlooking the classical and more recent literature, it seems that legitimacy is the victim of erosion, by broadening the concept and the theoretical notions implied in it to such an extent that almost everything, from participation, political accountability and democratic control to efficiency and effectiveness are included.[26] Legitimacy, like responsiveness, has a two-way character. It assumes the opportunity for those governed to express their preferences genuinely, and based upon this condition obedience to those governing as justified, 'because collective fate control is increased when powers of government can be employed to deal with those problems that the members of the collectivity cannot solve individually, through market interactions, or through voluntary cooperation', according to Scharpf.[27] He adds that the normative binding force of legitimacy is enhanced when it is combined with elements of truth-oriented debates and discourses, which however require political leadership.[28] A normative meta task *par excellence*.

For legitimation of public authorities these normative requirements seem to be relatively clear and can serve as guidelines for discussions on the design and maintenance of institutions, for instance as recently can be seen in the institution building of the EU. However, for the legitimacy of governance arrangements in which the market and/or civil society are involved, justifications for them as legitimate governance institutions are less clear and certainly require more substantial conceptual consideration. A possible direction for such an effort can be found in the regime concept, considered as a collection of relatively stable normative expectations of co-operating public and private actors (see Chapter 7). Easton in his classical work on political systems sees regimes 'as sets of formal or operating constraints that are generally accepted … by rulers and ruled alike and that give at least broad indications of what are or are not permissible goals, practices, and structures of the system'.[29] This is exactly the way I want to interpret regime, applied in particular to governing 'systems' (in Easton's way of using it) of a mixed, public-private character. And regimes also can be objects of legitimacy, based upon ideological, structural or personal sources.[30] Put differently, when certain interaction patterns between public and private actors have evolved into relatively stable relations they can become legitimated on the basis of 'their permissible goals, practices and structures'. The realisation that legitimacy as a normative governance concept is a dynamic one, always subject to tensions within and between their intentional and structural level of the governing interactions implied in them, is an important one. This applies to more traditional patterns of legitimation processes between public governors and governed as well as to more experimental forms of social-political interactions, which involve public as well as private governors and governed.

Moral responsibility as norm for meta governance

Finally I come to norm-setting for meta governing itself. This can be formulated by making the most fundamental principles on which governance is built explicit. How do we want meta governing itself to be governed, and by what, is the question to be answered in this setting. Conceptually, we speak about governing norms, governing processes and those responsible for governing interactions as a whole. In fact it seems to me that 'responsibility for' is the most fundamental norm and evaluative criterion available in meta governance. This is what – in my opinion – meta-meta governing is about: the governing principles of governing itself. Taking this position, I underline that 'responsibility for' has a moral or ethical dimension for governors and governed alike and that moral and ethical questions are of central importance for governance. Phrasing and answering them is not something to be left to discussions between moral specialists or to the exclusive agenda of ethical institutions. To the contrary, ethical and moral questions are the essence of the governance domain. They are not only part of meta social-political interactions, but in a final sense are also the foundations of them. But what are these moral norms for which all involved in social-political interactions have to take common and shared responsibility for?

Moral systems are practice-oriented imperative answers to the question '[h]ow should we live … they are multifaceted: they address problems of the possible realization of ethical projects: they set priorities among aims and provide principles for coordinating a range of primary ideals and values'.[31] This definition of a moral system is the general description of what I mean when I speak about a set of norms and values that might be able to 'govern governance'. According to Oksenberg-Rorty there are advantages in the *diversity* of these moral systems, they are often organised in *dynamic* systems of checks and balances, and the *complexity* of most communities with distinct and layered sub-communities set the stage for negotiation and sometimes conflict among a range of moral systems, each attempting to define a dominant configuration of ethical projects. Meta-governance questions and answers of such an ethical nature cannot be separated from the general moral culture of which they are part. It has been remarked upon that there is a growing interest in the discussion of governance issues with a moral character.[32] There is a call for the 'restoration' of a public morality, which emphasises that societal developments ask for a redefinition of what a concept like public morality might mean. Then there is the growing importance of what is called 'practical ethics', which is to say that answers have to be found for moral issues and societal dilemmas. As a matter of fact, in many moral or ethical issues the boundaries of the public realm are at stake, and the responsibility of the state, next to the responsibility of civil society and the market, for moral codes is in discussion. Who is responsible for what is a central question in many moral or ethical issues already on the governance agenda, and in some of them one can see an interest in meta governance aspects of them.

There is a tradition in ethical discourses on 'taking responsibility for' and its relevance for (meta) governing seems to be beyond doubt: 'The links between representation, legitimacy, authority and power provide the basis for a deepened analysis of responsibility'.[33] The same can be said of ethical/philosophical literature where 'to be responsible for' is ascribed to individuals, to individuals as members of groups or organisations and also to collectivities. All these ascriptions have raised moral questions, which have been the subject of philosophical and ethical debate.[34] Ethical theories offer different notions of what an individual's responsibility (for governance) might be.[35] Next to individual moral responsibility one speaks of collective or shared moral responsibility which applies to collectivities, but also to individuals as members of them. Responsibility, individually or collectively, for the interactions one participates in, is one of the issues being debated. Ultimately, moral responsibilities are by their nature shared by all those who themselves count as moral agents, notwithstanding the fact that (collectively) we may assign special responsibilities to particular people.[36] Another aspect of individual as well as collective moral responsibility, of importance for meta governance, is the distinction between prospective and retrospective responsibility.[37] Prospective responsibility concerns things it is up to us to attend to, which may be attached to particular roles, often related to collectivities we are members of, and in which we are considered to be morally responsible, invidually as well as collectively. Retrospective responsibility concerns things we have done or have failed to do and the effects of our actions or omissions. The retrospective variant especially has been subject to much discussion such as about unforeseen and unintended effects or for harm we did not prevent. For meta-meta governing the distinction between these types of responsibility is relevant, because it makes clear that in governing interactions (and all the aspects to them as discussed above) there is a moral responsibility at the individual as well as the collective level for the things we do, but also for the harm affecting others for what we fail to do.

These considerations should not be seen as a plea for the development of a set of normative responses for action or inaction in governing situations, which is what much of the ethical or moral theory seems to be about. My purpose is to make a plausible argument for looking at aspects of moral responsibility at the individual and the collective level as part of normal and continuous governing interactions, as part of our roles in these interactions. Moral conflicts or even dilemmas may arise when these governing roles are taken seriously, as when 'taking responsibility for', and not left to ethical specialists. It is widely assumed in moral theory that 'the existence of moral dilemmas is evidence of the inconsistency in the principles or obligations giving rise to the dilemma'.[38] And it is exactly from the conflicts and inconsistencies between principles and obligations of interactive governance at and between the different governing levels, and the moral dilemmas they may give rise to, that meta governance gets its importance.

If, as I claim, moral issues such as concerning responsibility in governing and responsibility for governing, not only play an important role in governing, but (in relation with the three other central evaluative concepts rationality; responsiveness and performance) are the normative foundation on which in the last resort governing-as-practice is built, we should be able to see what the outcome of such evaluations are, i.e. test them. But can we test moral theories as we do (other) scientific theories? Opinions differ here.[39] At the least, we may ask for coherence, such as between general moral principles and particular claims in specific situations. We also need experience, which is not the same as observation. Third, such testing will usually not have a generally agreed result. There always will be different opinions, whether the 'tests' in question are really relevant and crucial or not: 'In the end we are each of us responsible for the moral theories we accept or reject, and we must make judgements about acceptance or rejection ourselves'.[40] Here we have closed the circle: we are only ourselves – individually and collectively – responsible for which moral theories we think will apply to governance questions. In this section, the chapter, and in fact in the book as whole, I have tried to make this clear for myself, and thus take responsibility for the conceptual choices made and for those left out.

With performance as a composite criterion, and with effectiveness, legitimacy and moral responsibility as sub-measures, normative standards can be set for the three governance orders in a meta-governance perspective.

Conclusion

In this chapter I have tried to conceptualise a meta perspective on governance. I established a basis for this effort by applying a set of normative meta principles to the major aspects I distinguish in my governance perspective: elements, modes and orders. To keep this survey manageable, I reduced the scope of the subject by searching for a particular norm for each of the major aspects, serving as an exemplar for the normative dimensions of governance as a whole. These norms have a dual function. On the one hand they guide the behaviour of actors involved in governing interactions directly in their activities. In this way they form the meta normative framework that directs and sets boundaries for actual governing at the first and second governance order. This is the world of governing-as-practice in which meta norms are followed or neglected, tested out or changed, in the constant tension between the intentional and structural level in governing interactions. On the other hand, these norms themselves should be the subject of governance debate. This use of meta might be called a helicopter view scrutinising these norms for their appropriateness, their relevance, how up-to-date they are and how to-the-point. This critical review at the meta governance level addresses individual norms but also looks at them in their mutual relations. This pertains to both governors and governed alike, and belongs to their 'taking responsibility for' governing role. One can even say that because of the 'strange-loop' character of meta, the roles are reversed: in meta governing it is, in particular, the governed who take the primary role as meta governors and the governors are the ones being governed.

What I have tried to show in this chapter is that phrasing norms for each of the dimensions of governance serving these two purposes is, in principle, possible. Of course one can debate about which norms for which dimensions, about other norms, or about other definitions of them. I tend to believe that this is exactly the sphere or level of governance where such differences of opinion should find their most free expression. This can, or should be a value free discussion on norms and criteria, ethical or otherwise. People, collectivities and whole societies have invested a lot of energy and even power in norms and other parts of normative systems that guide their governance.

This chapter has outlined the contours of what I consider to be meta governance. For governance I translate the meta concept into 'governing how to govern'. Meta governing is an essential part of social-political or interactive governance, because it is the forum where the normative principles for governing are formulated and tested. Meta also contains ideas about the way the process of how to come to such criteria or norms is made explicit and how this process itself should be governed. This meta governance programme is – admittedly – an ambitious one, and in the chapter I could only sketch a few lines of 'how to do this'.

Notes

1 Sklair, 1988.
2 Hofstadter, 1985.
3 Berting, 1996.
4 Derksen, 1992.
5 Geraets, 1979, p. xi.
6 Adapted from Gellner, 1992, pp. 136–137.
7 Scharpf, 1997.
8 Wallace, 1994.
9 White, 1995, pp. 36–43.
10 Simon, 1983.
11 Simon, 1957.
12 Boudon in Berting, 1996, p. 21.
13 Boudon, 1996, p. 124.
14 Pitkin, 1967, p. 232.
15 idem, p. 233.
16 Kaufmann et al., 1986, p. 212.
17 idem, p. 792.
18 Etzioni, 1968, p. 7, p. 430.
19 Mayntz and Scharpf, 1995, p. 19 ff.
20 Kaufmann et al., 1986, Chapters 11, 13, 30, 35.
21 Ostrom, 1986, p. 242.

22 Special issue of the Dutch Journal Beleid en Maatschappij, 1999/93.
23 Vught van, 1987.
24 idem p. 171.
25 Nÿkamp et al., 1996.
26 Höreth, 1998.
27 Scharpf, 1999, p. 268.
28 idem, pp. 284 ff.
29 Easton, 1953, p. 192.
30 idem, p. 287.
31 Oksenberg-Rorty, 1992, p. 42.
32 Koelega and Noordegraaf, 1994.
33 Friedrich, 1963, p. 309.
34 Duff, 1998, pp. 290 ff.
35 Scheffler, 1995.
36 Goodin, 1998.
37 Zimmerman, 1992.
38 Mason, 1996, p. 5.
39 Held, 1982.
40 idem, pp. 361–362.

GOVERNANCE AND GOVERNABILITY

12

SOCIETY, GOVERNANCE AND GOVERNABILITY

In the final part of this book I want to discuss governability. I left this to the end because I see governability as an overarching concept, as the quality of a social-political entity as a whole. Governability is not a static quality; to the contrary, it is always changing, depending on external factors, such as natural disasters, which can hardly be influenced by governing, external ones which can be influenced, such as by co-operating with others, and internal ones such as changing governing images, instruments or social-political action potential. The role of governance in relation to governability should neither be exaggerated, nor underestimated. What may be high governability at a particular time, may be medium or low governability at another. This we can see in the scheme, used in Chapter 1 as an analytical overview of the governance approach, but now as a synthetic framework pointing at governability as a quality to which all the distinguished aspects play a role, each by itself, but especially in their inter-relations. Together they give a picture of what governability is about.

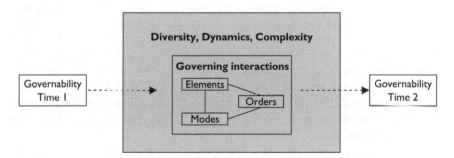

Figure 12.1 Scheme of synthesis

Social-political entities have special governability characteristics, partly based on heritage, partly on actual internal and external circumstances. This is the state of governability of an entity at Time 1. All governing interactions at the intentional and structural level will have their effects on the governance of that entity, which can be expressed in governability at Time 2. Therefore, the descriptive-analytical model of governance can be transformed into a theoretical-analytical one, allowing us to spell out ideas on supposed governance qualities influencing governability. In this and the following chapter, I will begin to attempt just such a theory formulation, as well as explore a few concepts alluded to in the previous chapters in more detail. The statements in these two chapters are summary ones, but can, more so than in the earlier chapters, be considered as propositions with a more theoretical calibre.

Diversity and governance

Interest in the diversity, heterogeneity, and difference in the social-political realm has grown in recent years. However, what it might mean is far from clear: 'Diversity has become one of the most often used words of our time – and a word almost never defined. Diversity is invoked in discussions of everything from employment policy to curriculum reform and from entertainment to politics ... All this was known long before the word 'diversity' became an insistent part of our vocabulary, an invocation, an imperative or a bludgeon in ideological conflicts', as Sowell summarised this state of affairs.[1]

One of the most important diversity constituting factors in the continuously moving patterns of societal developments are the self-images that individuals, organisations, groups and even nations create. They do so to maintain and to protect themselves against the ever-present dangers of disintegration. Social and political actors will invest a great deal to realise their self-images, while self-images take shape in the opinions, goals and interests they strive for. Cultural diversity at the macro level is a more debated issue. On the one hand we find theories arguing that values tend to converge, because media such as television and advertising level out cultural differences, even globally.[2] On the other hand we see a (re) discovery of regional and local cultures, often combined with regional or national demands for political autonomy. All these ideas point out that diversity, at the actor and probably also at the structural level of (governing) interactions, is a factor to reckon with.

Governing diversity means influencing diverse social or natural entities by protecting, maintaining, creating, promoting, or limiting the similarities or dissimilarities of their qualities. The more diverse the qualities to be governed, the more diverse the necessary governing measures, and the more diverse the relation between the two. This is the essence of Ashby's famous 'Law of Requisite Variety'. Wilden has since added a principle of 'requisite diversity in representation' to this, stating that it is not the diversity of a whole system that has to be represented, rather a governing system must be able to represent the basic types of variety found in the system to be governed.[3] The qualities of the governing and the governed system must correspond two-ways, is the basic message of these two 'laws', and of the ideas on representation as developed earlier. If in governance such insights on the dual representation of diversity are ignored, forces and counter-forces that are difficult if not impossible to govern will result. In collaborative public–private interactions in community situations, diversity in the representation of the respective organisations is an important factor; the way it is handled is a strong explanatory factor in their success or failure.[4] This is an important argument for taking the diversity of values, goals and interests of those involved in interactions into account.

However, diversity has its boundaries. Social entities cannot function without a certain measure of uniformity in inter-human, inter-organisational, inter-regional and inter-state interactions. Unlimited diversity may rapidly become counter-productive, because with growing diversity the similarities needed for communication will decrease rapidly – possibly even exponentially. The ancient Greek philosophers and poets were conscious of this. Fear of diversity was an important subject in their thought, exploring the tension between human diversity and what binds them together, fear that diversity and differences might bring chaos, resulting in demands that the world be put in an orderly pattern.[5] Early Greek thinkers express this in tragedies exploring the dilemma of the one and the many, while Aristotle looked at the political consequences of diversity in relation to the political world as a whole. This according to Saxenhouse is the way in which Aristotle 'gave birth to political science'.

Informal and formal rules form the frameworks in which the fundamentally unlimited diversity of goals, interests and aspirations of actors on different levels of aggregation are expressed and can be developed. These two sides of diversity occasion a constant tension between freedom of action and expression of actors and entities, and the rules and customs these actions and expressions have to comply with/conform to. This is a theme that runs through recent thinking on how to cope with difference and diversity. Diversity, next to individualism, is considered a cornerstone of liberal societies.[6] Liberal purposes undergird liberal diversity and provide the basis for *e pluribus unum*, meeting the challenge of forging and maintaining unity in the face of centrifugal forces of diversity. Another approach emphasises the relation between difference, diversity and democracy.[7] In this view, the theoretical understanding of democracy and democratic legitimacy are on the move, and the politics of identity, difference and diversity generates a good deal of that motion. The search then is for a democratic theory that enables the expression of diversity in politics and stresses its importance for attaining justice and legitimacy. In the development of such a democratic theory of difference and diversity, the 'public sphere' and a direct role for civil society, are essential.

Actively employing a diversity of values, goals and interests in governing interactions in modern governance means developing an operational grip on it. This requires processes of ordering and re-ordering diversity (creating) qualities. This looks simpler than it is. Definitions are hardly given (see above) and efforts to operationalise diversity qualities are scarce. Feminist thinking and literature on ethnic experiences provide examples of differences or diversity being described in terms such as of daily *experiences* (housework and childcare, low-paid employment and exclusion from key centres of political and cultural power); *social relations* (mechanisms for exclusionary and discriminatory practices); *identity* (modes of being); and finally how *subjects* are formed, how are 'symbolic order' and 'social order' articulated in the formation of a subject?[8] When we discuss diversity and how to order or classify differences we are also discussing physical and symbolic distinctions creating boundaries that separate societal entities. Distinctions can remain latent, but also may become focal, especially in times of social change, when boundaries blur and mechanisms come into play to reinstate them. Boundaries are societal facts, they distinguish but can also be crossed.[9]

This raises important questions for governance: how to identify (changing) similarities and differences and (re) order them, how to acknowledge boundaries, but also cross them? Recent insights from 'classification' theory may help answer these questions. Classification should not be seen as the simple outcome of an ordering process, but this ordering process 'itself is embedded in prior and subsequent action'. It is a middle part of a circle of questions and answers, in which 'self-classification is an important element of a democratic community'.[10] Official categories and ordering procedures as used in modern states 'do not float above societies, but are sewn into the fabric of the economy, society and the state'.[11] To understand official social classifications both the historical context and political choices have to be taken into consideration. Classifications have consequences: some cause damage, others are beneficial. This particularly applies to official categories, and many social-political conflicts have been fought regarding their establishment or elimination.[12] Ordering or classifying diversity in governance is basically a process of ordering qualities. In a number of steps, qualities can be ordered and re-ordered whereby similarities and differences of and between entities find their place. Such an ordering process has an iterative character, in which searching, recognising, and categorising of similarities are alternated with the same kinds of procedures on differences. In social-political governing such ordering processes will undoubtedly have multiple outcomes that continuously overlap and exclude each other. For classical (top-down) governing, this is an almost Sisyphean task. For interactive governing, iteration is one of the 'basics', it may be difficult, but it is not an impossible task. It is exactly in the interactive character of governance that the possibilities of iterative ordering can be explored, at its intentional level, as well as in their contexts. The 'model' for problem-solving or opportunity creation is an example of how this might be done (see Chapter 9).

Governance means making systematic use of the richness of societal diversity, (re) order it, and define its boundaries in iterative governing interactions.

Complexity, governing and governance

More often than not, 'complexity' doesn't mean anything other than that something is difficult to understand, or complicated to handle. However, complexity is more than that: it is a basic aspect of the phenomena we are dealing with, and as such it has baffled practitioners and scholars alike. The most typical attitude towards 'real' complexity is in fact not to confront it head-on: 'Whatever success has been achieved in modern public administration – or, for that matter, in modern society – owes much to the human capacity to organise, simplify, and reduce perceived reality to manageable size and forms. Put bluntly, our typical approach to complexity has been indifference, intentional ignorance, or illusion'.[13] For definitional purposes I concur with LaPorte et al. who conclude that most approaches to complexity share the basic notion that it is about manifold interactions of many parts within a system; a characteristic certainly applicable to the social-political systems we are interested in. These authors also emphasise that there is no single way of coping with complexity.[14]

How 'fundamental' social complexity is, has been a subject of scholarly interest and debate. Does the complexity of social phenomena prevent the formulation of scientific laws, as we see in the natural sciences? Hayek is a representative of the notion that 'there is a fundamental difference between natural versus social science as such – that human phenomena are somehow inherently complex, and therefore that social scientific laws are unavailable in principle'.[15] McIntyre, on the other hand, finds such an approach 'naive' and prefers a more 'mature' version, which states that 'social phenomena are not complex as such, but only as described and defined at a given level of enquiry ... Complexity of human phenomena is not inherent, but derivative, in that it is dependent on the nature of our interests'.[16]

Central to my perspective is the idea that in societal development the road of differentiation and specialisation has been predominantly followed. The sciences and bureaucracies are good examples of this. As a consequence, there has been great progress in the knowledge of parts, but much less in the knowledge of the relation between them, and the relations between parts and wholes. This raises numerous governance questions. In handling complexity by governance, the many interdependencies between and within social systems are subject and object of our interest, and in doing so we are facing a number of rather difficult conceptual and practical issues.

We assume that there are limits to the human capacity to know and to act. This means that, in coping with complexity, we have to follow the path of combined strategies. Several come to mind. Three intellectual sources can be mentioned guiding ideas on the relation between governance and complexity: Luhmann, Weaver and Simon. We have already discussed Luhmann, who grappled most systematically with complexity as a 'red thread' through most of his (voluminous) writings. In the course of his work the way he 'reduces complexity' goes through several stages.[17] Initially he sees complexity as a question of whether social systems have enough opportunities to react to a constantly changing world. Later on this system-environment paradigm shifts, and the issue becomes not only adaptation to an environment, but also adaptation to internal complexity. This insight brings him still a step further, and complexity becomes a matter of (self) observation and by self-referentiality construct (their own) reality.[18] This led Luhmann finally to his radical insight of the *autopoietic* nature of social systems (see Chapter 6).

A second important line of thinking about complexity and governance is the distinction between organised and disorganised complexity (Weaver). According to him there are two sorts of complex systems: one where few units interrelate in many ways (deterministic) and two systems in which there are many units but undetermined (random) interrelations. In fact Weaver places complexity on a scale with organised simplicity (deterministic) on the one hand and extreme disorganised complexity (random) on the other. He argues that many, if not most important problems, lie in between these two extremes. This is what he calls organised complexity, consisting of a considerable number of parts related in interdependent ways. Social systems in particular possess the characteristics of organised complexity, and are thus difficult to handle with statistical or probability methodologies.[19] Many theorists on complexity have applied Weaver's distinction. One considers international relations as having the worst of both worlds: at the systems level it is an anarchy, and at the actor's level the actors behave in an indeterminable way. This creates enormous governance problems, because successful predictions can neither be made by statistical means (random) nor through knowledge of the position of the unit in relation to the whole (deterministic).[20]

Finally, there is Simon's discovery of the hierarchical quality of complex systems. In his classic paper 'The architecture of complexity' Simon considers a complex system consisting of a large number of parts, interacting in a non-simple way.[21] In such systems the whole is more than the sum of the parts, not in an ultimate, metaphysical sense but in the important pragmatic sense that, given the properties of the parts, and the laws of their interaction, it is not a trivial matter to infer the properties of the whole. Among such systems, hierarchy is one of the central structural schemes. Simon defines hierarchy differently than most other users, which complicates the matter somewhat. Hierarchy in his view means that a system is composed of interrelated subsystems, each being in turn hierarchic in structure until the lowest level of elementary subsystem is reached (the 'Russian' doll: a doll within a doll within a doll). It is for scientists to decide what the partitioning looks like and what subsystems are taken as elementary units. At this point Simon introduces a distinction, which makes his contribution to complexity theory so important. Types of partitioning or decomposability can be distinguished on the basis of whether a system is completely or 'nearly decomposable'. In nearly decomposable systems interactions within subsystems may be highly complex, but the interdependencies among them are few and relatively weak. Social systems, in which each element is linked with almost equal strength with almost all other parts of the system, are rare. In other words in social systems nearly-decomposability is generally very prominent. To deal with complexity in such nearly-decomposable systems a combination of two procedures: composition and decomposition, can help us.[22] In the first, systems are (de) composed into parts that are as homogeneous as possible; in the second, a system is (de) composed so that they have as few interrelations as possible, into nearly autonomous parts. Both have their special governing consequences. (De) composition according to homogeneity promotes goal attainment, while (de) composition into autonomous parts, permits mutual adjustment. The principle of 'nearly decomposability' and the theoretical notions developed from it are a good starting point for dealing with complex social-political systems, e.g. in terms of solving problems or creating opportunities, or designing and maintaining institutional capacities.

Complexity is in the eye of the beholder. That is one reason why I limited and reduced my own use of complexity of my subject by making distinctions between types of societal interactions, modes and orders of governance. Other examples of complexity reduction in this study can be given as well.

> Societal complexity can only be partially understood and handled; combined strategies of composition and decomposition are needed to reduce it for governing purposes in a responsible manner.

Dynamics and governance

According to Mayntz knowledge of the dynamics of highly developed societies is quite limited. This is partly due to their enormous differentiation, and at the same time the immense connection between these differentiated parts, but partly also for lack of appropriate dynamic process theories.[23] The reality of dynamics involves societies moving from one state to another, in irregular and unpredictable patterns: pushed, drawn or in other ways influenced by technological, economic, social or political forces. Dynamics can be seen as a composition of forces that sometimes turn into gradual developments, but more often result in non-linear patterns of change. Traditional explanatory cause-and-effect schemes do not seem quite applicable to them. Recent developments in the natural sciences have stimulated the interest of social science in the usefulness of concepts such as (neg) entropy, non-equilibrium dynamics, and chaos and dissipative structures for the explanation of the dynamics of social phenomena.

To gain insight in dynamics, three intellectual sources can be mentioned: Sorokin (societal change), Prigogine (non-reversibility), Etzioni (chaos theory and entropy). Each of these highlight aspects of dynamics relevant to governing.

Sorokin, in his classic study on dynamics, sees two basic principles of social-cultural change: immanent dynamism and limits to it. The first points to the unexceptional, ever-present, permanent, universal and necessary causes of socio-cultural systems change. The second principle relates to the fact that the enormous number of socio-cultural systems and processes show a limited range of possibilities in their variation in the creation of new fundamental forms.[24] Developing these two principles systematically, and applying them to the problems of 'recurrence, rhythm, linearism, and eternal novelty', Sorokin arrives at the conclusion that the most general pattern of socio-cultural change is one of incessantly varying processes.[25]

According to more recent insights in dynamic processes, the 'why' of dynamics can be answered by means of a supposition derived from the theory of non-reversible processes. This theory entails that open systems such as social systems are usually unstable or disequilibrated; they 'fluctuate' constantly. By means of positive feedback processes these fluctuations can become 'irreversible'. New and higher order configurations may come into being – the so-termed dissipative structures. Irreversible processes are not necessarily chaotic or running a disorderly course, but on the contrary, can be seen as sources of dynamic order. Hence the title of the book: *Order out of Chaos*.[26] Also, different forms of non-linear social processes can be distinguished, such as 'cyclical', 'chaotic' and 'catastrophic', each with their own special forms of dynamics.[27] Next to non-linear processes social systems are characterised by equilibria, cycles, cumulations and other patterns of linear processes. Social systems can be said to be composed of many different forms of equilibria and disequilibria: near to equilibria, not-so-near or far removed from it.

What has come to be known recently as chaos theories makes new approaches possible that seem relevant to a discussion of dynamics (and its governing). The first is a new view of cause and effect prediction. Two discoveries can account for this view: one is that initial conditions of a process may be irrecoverable, and the other that such processes are critically dependent on these initial conditions: the 'butterfly effect'. Prediction is not the way to approach such phenomena. Second, there is feedback or in other words, the primacy of non-linear (historical) processes. In particular this new approach appreciates not only the role of negative feedback – returning to a stable original situation – but especially positive feedback – the production of new states and new behaviours not necessarily less stable. Third, there is the factor of time, not simply linear time, but also other views of temporality, such as non-linear, eternal and cyclical views. Concepts of time that make the non-reversible and irreducible character of changes taking place clear have important consequences for social and political analysis and governance. Fourth, there is the discovery of new and often quite beautiful forms and shapes, such as 'fractals and strange attractors'. They are expressions of an elegant order, where no such orders were recognised or considered to be disorderly before, 'on the edge of chaos'.[28]

Finally, entropy is a tendency present in any system to disintegrate and even disappear in the long run. All systems, physical, natural or social can do to fight this entropic tendency is to counterbalance this loss of energy. This counterbalancing is called negentropy. In most social-political systems such entropic states of (final) equilibrium will never be reached. Energy can be conceived of in the physical sense, but also as social energy, as Etzioni does. All social systems tend towards 'atomization and anarchy – unless continual investments are made in maintaining their levels of integration and organization'.[29] Any social order is considered a counter-entropic arrangement that not only requires explanation, but its maintenance also requires continual effort. Dissensus is, according to Etzioni, the entropic state of societal nature; consensus is not found but must be produced.

What this overview of theoretical approaches to dynamics indicates is that to cope with societal dynamics, new avenues can be opened, to conceptualise and understand them better. Non-linear as well as linear processes play a constructive role in these theories. Concepts such as bi-furcation, dissipative structures, catastrophic turning points, and stability at higher levels, shed new light on phenomena that have been known in social and historical analyses for a long time. However, in the light of these new discoveries they seem to take on a more solid basis. The importance of non-linear, next to linear, dynamics processes in social-political governance matters can hardly be exaggerated, although Mayntz warns that what these new insights might bring to bear is not a 'given' but has to be tested in serious social-political analysis.[30]

These insights in societal dynamics have direct or indirect relevance for governance, because each of them or combinations of them, condition at least partially the characteristics of the dynamic space within which governance takes place. They are important as heuristic tools and techniques to make us think differently and devise new perspectives on dynamics as described. Although these developments are a long way from original cybernetic principles, relatively simple concepts such as positive and negative feedback loops and their qualities point at important governance mechanisms, which are still relatively under-utilised in social and political sciences. Dynamic qualities of social-political systems, either linear (such as cybernetic) or non-linear, (such as chaotic) can be influenced. Loops with a 'positive' operation show in effect that tensions 'reinforce' each other: they have a tendency to 'run out of control'. 'Negative' loops show diminishing effects; they have the tendency to 'even out'/cancel. In cybernetic theory, two ways of 'controlling' such loops are distinguished: feed-forward and feedback. Feed-forward tries to control a fluctuation or disturbance in a loop by taking a controlling measure in advance; feedback controls by taking a measure after a disturbance or a fluctuation has taken place. For my purpose it is important to make a reasoned use of principles and theoretical notions in terms of the questions we ask about the cybernetic qualities of social-political systems. What kinds of loops can we recognise in social-political developments? What kinds of tensions can we expect to create dynamic situations, which show certain types of cybernetic qualities such as positive or negative feedback or feed-forward loops? How are these loops organised? What kind of actors in what kinds of processes under what kinds of structural conditions can be expected to develop positive or negative feedback loops? Answers to questions such as these are a first step towards theorising on the possibilities and limitations of governing dynamics in particular situations.

If we see the governance of dynamics as dealing with the tensions hanging together with these non-linear or linear dynamic principles it will be clear that this is only the very beginning of thinking systematically about their governance consequences. Two examples can be mentioned that use dynamical tensions for governance purposes. The first assumes that there is always, simultaneously, a tension between on the one hand a will to preserve the existing state and, on the other hand, the causation of change to that state.[31] In such a perspective dynamics can be conceived as social-political change potential. Governing dynamics then equate as taking such tensions as a starting point for governance interactions, either at the intentional, the structural level or the interrelation between the two (see next chapter). Tensions are often an indication of where to apply dynamic governing modes. In a second example dynamic tensions are used as a basis for stimulating positive and negative feedback and feed-forward loops. In this context Dunsire speaks of collibration, using 'counter-forces' as means of stimulating or weakening forces that are already present in societies.[32] This is a form of governing that takes advantage of the dynamics inherent in societal divisions of power in a purposeful manner. Other modes of governing will try to strengthen, diminish, bend or dampen particular forces in order to influence the dynamic potential that all societies and their interactions possess. But first this means that those dynamic potentials are recognised as such. Tensions can be defined as loops. Contrary to classic cybernetics, these loops should be seen as having open and closed elements, renewable and non-renewable, linear and non-linear, reversible and irreversible aspects. Recognising this is the beginning of developing conceptual, theoretical and practical notions on the use of dynamics in modes of governance. An important area of research and analysis with the use of dynamical concepts is conflict and conflict resolution.

> Societal dynamics are important for governance in two respects; (1) the linear and non-linear dynamical patterns of societal change form the basis for governing (object); and (2) dynamical forces can also be used for governing purposes (subject).

Societal diversity, complexity and dynamics and governability

Throughout this book, I have positioned societal diversity, dynamics and complexity as important elements in the development of my governance perspective. These features influence governability of modern societies considerably and at all levels of generality. I continue this line of thinking now by looking at them as raising governance issues, as a sort of independent variables. In what ways might we expect aspects of governance, such as elements, modes and orders, to cope with them, and by doing so enhance governability. However, there is still another angle to this, and that is to reverse the question: not asking how governance might contribute to handling these features, but how ways and means of governance contribute to 'causing' them. We might, for instance, speculate whether a particular governance element, mode or order creates diversity, by 'over' (too much?) ordering, dynamics by 'over' (too much?) steering and complexity by 'over' (too much?) co-ordinating. Questions such as these begin the process of theorising about the governability of social-political systems as the relation between qualities of the 'systems-to-be governed' and their 'governing systems'. What follows is not a systematic treatment of governability, but the phrasing of a number of propositions on it.

Diversity, complexity, dynamics and interactions

Governability can be made visible in the relations between the intentional and the structural level of governing interactions. Differentiating and contrasting these two levels of interactions results in potential governability

Table 12.1 Interactions and governability situations

	Structural level of governing interactions	
	Open	Closed
Intentional level of governing interactions		
Open	diversity: high dynamics: low	dynamics: high complexity: low
Closed	complexity: high dynamics: low	complexity: high diversity: low

situations. On the structural level of these interactions a distinction can be made between structures with a more open and those with a more closed nature, and the same at the intentional level. The difference between these qualities is expressed in the degree to which they are responsive to signals or pressures from their counterpart: structures for signals from the intentional level and vice versa (see also Chapters 3 and 13).

The four quadrants show four governability situations with different diversity, dynamics and complexity profiles. For instance in the first quadrant we find a situation characterised by openness at both levels of governing interactions, meaning quite an enabling governance situation. In such a case one might expect there to be a great diversity of interactional patterns possible, and because of the enabling nature of the interaction there won't be strong dynamics based upon tensions built up within such interactions. In the same manner the other three governability profiles can be hypothesised from the character of the interactions as defined.

Governability shows varying 'profiles' of diversity, dynamics and complexity, depending on the combination of open and closed nature of governing interactions at their intentional and structural level.

Diversity, complexity, dynamics and elements of governing

In the work governors do, the diversity, complexity and dynamics of the systems-to-be-governed will show up quite directly. The question I want to raise now is of whether we can say something more specific about the way in which these features are represented in the three elements of

Table 12.2   Societal features and elements of governing*

	Diversity	Complexity	Dynamics
Images/values	High		Low
Instruments/resources	Low	High	
Action/capital		Low	High

* Read this table vertically

governing, images, instruments and action. In Table 12.2 an approach to this supposed representation is given.

The idea conveyed is that societal diversity is first represented in governing images. Images and factual and evaluative systems have in contemporary governance relatively open meanings. Coping with societal diversity in governing is in particular a question of ordering processes in which the almost unlimited variety of images available in modern societies are sifted and ordered primarily by convincing and sharing. Interactive communication such as in the public sphere, rather than by imposition by public or other authorities, is the way in governing that diversity can be handled. In contrast with this, diversity is the least represented in the instrumental condition. As explained in Chapter 4 one of the great difficulties in governing is to find instruments that represent societal diversity. This makes me think that out of the three governing elements, the image element is the primary one in the representation of diversity in governing. As explained, societal complexity is a phenomenon that can't be helped. Although opinions differ as to its nature – either as limitations to knowledge, or as a reality 'out there', efforts to master complexity so far have not been very successful. Given this 'fact of life', reducing complexity by composition and decomposition procedures seems the correct route to take. This means that societal complexity, for all practical purposes should be considered as an instrumental one. As for the two other governing elements, the representation of societal complexity in image formation seems to be of greater governance importance than in its action element. Third, there is societal dynamics and the way this is represented in governing elements. As conceptualised, dynamics can be seen as the result of all kinds of societal forces, and the tensions emanating from them. From a governing point of view, many, if not most of the more dominant dynamic forces in modern societies can be influenced only marginally, despite the rhetoric around them. It is in particular their non-linear character that calls for modesty in the predictability of their effects. Cybernetic principles, such as feed-back loops, point in the direction of how to cope with societal dynamics. The action element of governing seems to be the primary one to focus on in this context. From such action the other two governing elements can be deduced, instruments more so than images.

> The representation of societal features in elements of governing can be differentiated. Diversity is primarily found in governing images, complexity in governing instruments and dynamics represented in governing action.

Diversity, complexity, dynamics and modes of governance

Next to the way in which societal diversity, complexity and dynamics show up in governing elements one can raise the question if something more specific can be said about ways in which these societal features are taken care of in governance. Table 12.3. displays some ideas on the supposed relation between these features and modes of governance.

Table 12.3 Societal features and modes of governance*

	Diversity	Complexity	Dynamics
Modes of governance:			
SELF : cope with/add to	Medium	Low	High
CO : cope with/add to	High	Low	Medium
HIER : cope with/add to	Medium	High	Low

*Read table horizontally

This table shows that, hypothetically the three different governance modes are, in varying ways, able to cope with societal diversity, complexity and dynamics. However, they also might add to already existing societal diversity, complexity and dynamics. For example, I hypothesise that self governance as the least formalised kind of governance is best able to cope with societal dynamics. It is the governing mode fitting within societal interferences, as the most renewing forms of societal interactions; so we may indeed expect this kind of governance to add most to societal dynamics. The same applies, if less markedly, to societal diversity. It being the most open form of societal interactions, diversity may be expected to be taken on by self-governance, and because of the variety of experiences with this, new diversity may be created. Because of its fluid nature self-governance is not well able to cope with societal complexity. It may add to it because of its tendency for 'closure' which might mean that self-governing societal entities do not have an eye open for the intended or unintended consequences of their behaviour for others. On balance I hypothesise that there is not a strong relation between self-governance and societal complexity. Now, looking at the way the two governance modes may be expected to cope with these societal features, a different picture arises. The arguments can be found in the relevant chapters. Summarising for co, and hierarchical governance, I suppose that:

- Co-governing can handle societal diversity best, somewhat less complexity and it is least able to cope with dynamics. Co-governing also adds to diversity, less to complexity and the least to societal dynamics.
- Societal complexity can be handled best by hierarchical governing, up to a point this mode is also able to handle diversity, and less able to cope with societal dynamics. However I hypothesise that hierarchical governing also contributes most to societal complexity, somewhat less to its diversity, and the least to societal dynamics.

> Of modes of governance self-governing has the strongest relation with societal dynamics, by coping with them, and adding to them, co-governing with societal diversity, and hierarchical governing with societal complexity.

Diversity, complexity and dynamics, and orders of governance

A further way of conceptualising governability is by trying to advance ideas on the way societal diversity, dynamics and complexity influence the three governing/governance orders I distinguished. In Table 12.4 some relations between societal features and orders of governance are hypothesised. Earlier in this chapter I argued that these three characteristics are often looked at negatively, primarily as creating difficulties for societal governance, but I also argued that there is just as much reason or maybe even more reason to see them in a positive perspective, to see them as chances. This point of view can be operationalised more precisely by 'crossing' them with the three different governance orders.

It is quite clear that the diversity, dynamics and complexity of modern societies create difficulties for governing, in particular when looked upon in the classical way of 'doing it alone', rather than searching for other governing/governance options.[33] Great diversity of problem definitions makes it difficult to reach a consensus for solving them. Strong dynamics, expressed in unexpected non-linear developments, puts institutional design and maintenance under pressure. And complexity, if not confronted head-on, makes classical governing arduous, especially when no meta rules are available to cope with it in a responsible manner. However, these features may also be considered from a more positive angle, from the way they can contribute to governance, to open-up governing options, to create chances and opportunities. Diversity scores a high potential in

Table 12.4   Societal features and orders of governance*

	Orders of governance		
	First (problem/opportunity)	Second (institutions)	Third (meta)
'Creating difficulties'			
Diversity	High	Medium	Low
Dynamics	Medium	High	Low
Complexity	Low	Medium	High
'Creating chances'			
Diversity	High	Low	Medium
Dynamics	Medium	Low	High
Complexity	Low	High	Medium

*Read table horizontally

first order governance (day-to-day opportunity creation). This I suppose is because in the future orientation of opportunity creation, diversity is a societal capacity to be explored and applied, and not so much historically based (vested interests), as is so often the case in traditional governing. This can be operationalised, such as my deliberations on interferences and self-governing make clear. Some view dynamics as an important factor in opportunity creation; others are of the opinion that coping with complex processes is an important quality of modern societies. My preference is with this second opinion, which is expressed in the score as indicated in the table. The same kinds of inferences can be made for the two other levels. The results of my own speculative thinking are recorded in the table.

> Societal characteristics show varying patterns of 'negative' or 'positive' representations in different orders of governance. Societal diversity seems to be the most 'crucial' in problem-solving as well as in opportunity-creating.

Conclusion

How do we make systematic and fruitful sense of a world of phenomena that are fundamentally complex, dynamic and diverse? In the terms of this book: how can dynamic, complex and diverse social-political systems be governed in a democratic and effective way?

These qualities do not only apply to those being governed, but also to those who govern and are of necessity in a relation with them. That is to say: governing, governance and governability themselves have highly dynamic, complex and diverse qualities of their own. The lack of insight in this might be one of the major reasons why so much present day governance is ineffective.

Each of these three societal features has specific consequences for governance and governability. Diversity is a source of creation and innovation, but carries the danger of disintegration, complexity is a condition for re-combining existing societal inter-dependencies but has to be reduced in responsible manners, and societal dynamics are the change potential of modern societies, however they can have disruptive consequences. All these aspects can be differentiated into areas of governance attention and activities. The governability of social-political systems as an input and an output of governance is largely dependent on the way their diversity, complexity and dynamics are handled as governing tasks. The responsibility for these tasks is not to be allotted to public actors or authorities, they are responsibilities for social-political systems as wholes with public, private and mixed task areas.

Separately, but in particular in relation to each other, societal diversity, complexity and dynamics are among the key building blocks of my theorising on social-political governance and governability. Only if we take these three basic characteristics of modern societies seriously can we begin to conceptualise how they can be used in the governing of those societies in a 'cross-modern' way; in other words, taking diversity, complexity and dynamics not only as aspects to be governed but also as main elements in a modern/contemporary mode of governing. In this chapter I started to advance a synthetic contribution of these societal characteristics to the governance perspective as a whole, i.e. to the governability of societal entities or systems. This exercise will be continued in the next chapter, where the focus will be on interactions, and the contribution of interaction and concepts related to them and to the governability of social-political systems as wholes.

Notes

1 Sowell, 1991, p. 37.
2 Ester, et al., 1994.
3 Wilden, 1987, p. 192.
4 Huxham, 2000b.
5 Saxenhouse, 1992.
6 Galston, 1991, pp. 4–10.
7 Benhabib, 1996.
8 Brah, 1992.
9 Fuchs and Epstein, 1992, pp. 232–238; Wolfe, 1992.
10 Douglas, Hull, 1992, p. 2, 11.
11 Starr, p. 154.

12 idem, pp. 161–162.
13 Dubnick, 1996, p. 1486.
14 LaPorte et al., 1975.
15 Hayek, as quoted by McIntyre, 1994, p. 132; Hayek, 1994.
16 McIntyre, Tiggy, p. 132.
17 Blom, 1997.
18 idem.
19 Weaver, 1948; see also LaPorte, 1975, pp. 5–6.
20 Snyder and Jervis, 1993.
21 Simon, 1962.

22 De Leeuw, 1994, Kickert, 1979.

23 Mayntz, 1997, pp. 15–37.

24 Sorokin, 1941, pp. 667, 710; Zentner, 1957.

25 Sorokin, 1941, pp. 731–732.

26 Prigogine and Stengers, 1984.

27 Bühl, 1990.

28 Turner, 1997.

29 Etzioni, 1968, pp. 309–390.

30 Mayntz, 1990.

31 Burns et al., 1985.

32 Dunsire, 1993.

33 Kooiman, 1993, pp. 249 ff.

13

INTERACTIONS, GOVERNANCE AND GOVERNABILITY

In this chapter I will resume the discussion on interactions started in Chapter 2. In that chapter I sketched the main outlines of the concept, in order to familiarise the reader with some of the main ideas implied in its conceptualisation, and to underline the importance of the concept for the book as a whole. I return to this exercise by working out some new aspects that in the earlier presentation did not receive full attention. This applies in particular to the 'twin' concept of interdependence and inter-penetration, helpful in sustaining the central position of interactions. Next to these two concepts more systematic attention will be paid to the three varieties of interactions, interferences, interplays and interventions. Placing these at the end of the book gives me the opportunity to make use of examples from previous chapters. The chapter also summarises a few ideas on the three societal institutions: state, market and civil society, and their relation to governance and governability. I conclude the chapter with a few remarks pertaining to the book as a whole.

Interactions, interdependence and inter-penetration

In the literature, interaction – as distinct from other types of relations – is connected with concepts such as renewal, evolution, and growth. Authors such as Luhmann and Münch distinguish interaction from other exchange relations.[1] I assume that in social-political (governing) inter-actions something new is created, that those participating in interactions contribute in some sense to the identity and the development of others, and by doing so also contribute to their own well-being, interest and growth. Mutuality is a central aspect of interactions. In my conceptualisa-tion of interactions I want to stress that entities contribute to each other's development: this applies to all parties involved in an interaction. Interaction influences the entities involved. The interaction of two entities implies that each has its own centre of autonomy, which serves as the point from which the co-activity with the other emanates. Entities inter-acting means that boundaries of one entity are accepted in the other's area or sphere of activity, and vice versa. Interdependence in interaction, there-fore, is more than just exchange; it is deeper and it must also be distin-guished from input and output relations. It refers to the constitution and reconstitution of actors or entities.

Not all relations between entities should be seen as interactions. Münch distinguishes three other types of relations in this connection: adaptation, rigidity and isolation. Adaptation takes place when a more controlled system acquiesces to a less controlled one. Rigidity is a situation in which a less controlled entity adapts to a more controlled one; mutual isolation takes place when no relations or exchanges come into being between systems. Using these concepts but interpreting them differently, one might say that these structural forms can be presented on a continuum, varying from domination at one end and isolation at the other. The two extremes can undoubtedly be seen as not belonging to the realm of interactions. Adaptation is a boundary case on one side, and reciprocity at the other end. Not only in the real world, but also from a theoretical perspective I wouldn't want to exclude those two structural arrangements from the discussion on interactions. The same kind of conceptual exercise can be carried out at the intentional level of interactions. Submission at one end of the scale and alienation at the other can be excluded from considerations of intentional interactions. However, again there are borderline cases. Not all forms of exchange can be seen as having a sensitivity interaction aspect to them (such as many economic transactions in the market). But to exclude all exchange relations from the realm of interactions would hinder conceptual development. On the other side of the continuum the same can be said of what can be called mimicry (civil servants behaving as if they are businessmen is an example of such a borderline situation). Summarising we might say that on the structural level interpenetration is in the centre of social-political (governing) interactions; the same applies to interdependence on the intentional level.

In Chapters 1 and 2 I argued that the realm of governing interactions, with their intentional and structural levels can be seen as expressions of, or reactions to, two societal processes. For the intentional level of these interactions this is the process of (growing) interdependence of governing activities and for the structural level I formulated the (growing) tendency towards interpenetration such as between societal sectors. The relation between the intentional and structural level of governing interactions was conceptualised in terms of enabling and controlling. The two levels were also seen as being mutually compliant, in the sense that at the intentional level the structural level is being considered more or less influenceable in the short term, while in the long term structural aspects of these interactions can change depending on efforts on the intentional level.

Now the question can be asked whether we can develop some general propositions about hypothetical relations between all these interactional elements. Figure 13.1 serves as a stepping stone.

What we might infer from this figure is that the two processes distinguished, the enabling and the controlling one, can also be seen as processes with 'cybernetic' qualities: the enabling process with positive feedback loops re-enforces existing tendencies, while the controlling

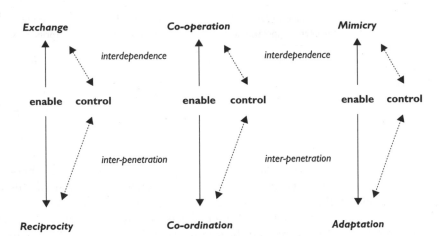

Figure 13.1 shows: Intentional level of governing interactions at top, with Exchange, Co-operation, Mimicry; interdependence, enable, control, inter-penetration labels; Reciprocity, Co-ordination, Adaptation at bottom; Structural level of governing interactions.

Figure 13.1   Dynamic relation between intentional and structural level of interactions

process, characterised by negative feedback loops dampens such tendencies. Supposing a starting situation of recognised interdependence, the governing reaction might be a propensity to co-operate, which in time might mean more inter-penetration. Supposing a starting situation of recognised interdependence at the actor level of a certain governing situations, by enabling forces exchange may evolve into reciprocity at the structural level, and thus interdependence may become inter-penetration. The same can be inferred with co-operation resulting in co-ordination and mimicry into adaptation. In a controlled pattern these movements between the intentional and the structural level will not take place. The interactions so to say 'remain' within the levels where they started. The same movements might also be hypothesised, reasoning from the structural level. By enabling arrangements reciprocity may give rise to new forms of exchange, but by controlling, this will not take place. The same applies to the other forms of governing interactions as indicated.[2]

Interdependence, inter-penetration and governability

Often, I have given the two related concepts interdependence and inter-penetration a place in the development of the governance perspective. At the intentional as well as the structural level of societal and governance

Table 13.1   Interdependence, inter-penetration and aspects of governance

	First order (problems/opportunities)	Second order (institutions)	meta (principles)
Interdependence (intentional level)	↓		↓
Inter-penetration (structural level)	↑	↑	

interactions differentiation and integration processes influence these interactions, and these twin concepts are the conceptualisation of this phenomenon. In this section I establish several hypothetical relations between these two tendencies and their effects on governability.

In the Table 13.1 the arrows indicate the main direction of influence to be expected in these situations. So in the case of second-order governing, that is to say in the governance of maintenance, care or design of institutions, I expect that the main influence will be from inter-penetration to interdependence. This means that inter-penetration at the structural level comes first, and that interdependence at the actor or intentional level follows. In practice this would imply, for instance, that in the movement from market concepts into public administration and its development into public management is to be seen as of a more structural character. This structural change then influences the role behaviour of civil servants into public managers. I suppose that the arrow in this case is not the other way around, where changes at the actor level, structural adaptations have been taking place. This can be learned from the fact that in many countries at more or less the same time this development took place, to be seen as a consequence of the strong influence of 'liberal' market philosophy globally in the last decades. For meta governance I hypothesise that the arrow points in the other direction. Here it is much more the initiative of certain actors, or groups of them, who bring certain 'meta'-principles of governance into the discussion related to certain experienced, changing interdependencies. The issues as described in Chapter 9 can serve as examples: moral, risk and commons governance issues start from the realisation of certain actors or actor groups that something needs to be done, in governance terms, about (changing) patterns of interactions. Moral issues demonstrate this clearly, when a particular group either for or against a certain practice of an ethical character starts voicing protest. New or changing forms of inter-penetration between public authority and civil society begin from there, not the other way around. For first-order governance I see potential movements both ways. Inter-penetration such as between state and market may give rise to new problems requiring resolution or to new methods to solve them; likewise for the creation of opportunities. But there may also be trends in the opposite direction, where a particular problem or opportunity situation will lead towards inter-penetration: the behaviour and activities of environmental groups towards companies has in some cases led to systematic and broad patterns of interaction between state, market and civil society with an interpenetration character.

> Societal interdependence and inter-penetration affect each other varyingly, according to orders of governance. The influence from inter-penetration to interdependence is stronger in processes of institutionalisation; in meta governance the influence seems to be the other way around, and in problem-solving or opportunity-creation influence in both directions might be expected.

Inter-penetration between state, market and civil society

One may further wonder if something can be said about the way the three societal institutions 'interact'. We already encountered this in the manner, according to Habermas and others, civil society was 'colonised' by the state and the market. I use the more neutral terms interdependence and inter-penetration. Here I give an idea how such interdependencies and inter-penetrations between the societal institutions might look. It is assumed that not all three societal spheres have all needed governing elements in the same quality or quantity at their disposal, either on the intentional or on the structural level. To hypothesise in a simplified manner: the state is 'strong' in mobilising action potential that can be expressed in support of a particular problem to be solved or an opportunity to be created. The market is 'strong' in disposing of all kinds of societal resources other institutions might need. Civil society also has action (potential) but arguably its strongest asset is knowledge and values, that is to say, the image condition for governing. Interdependence and interpenetration means mutual use of these assets or capabilities in governing interactions at both levels. This might be called 'exchange', but more is usually involved than just exchange. In these processes 'identities' are also at stake, which can be seen when we go into the 'inter' relations between the three societal institutions in more detail. Indications such as given for 'inter-sectors' and inter elements never can be seen as end-states but always to some extent reflect temporary balances between forces looking for change and forces wanting relations to stay as they are.

Table 13.2   Interdependence and inter-penetration between state,
market and civil society

	Inter-intentional	Inter-structural
Institutions		
State – Civil Society	action # image	Political society
State – Market	action # instrument	Public management
State-market – Civil Society	action # instrument # image	Sustainable society

Civil society – state interdependence and inter-penetration: political society

Earlier, I mentioned the role of civil society in the liberalisation or demo-cratisation of developing countries as an aspect of its dynamics. This line of thinking can be advanced one step further by introducing the concept of 'political society'. Political society is the overlapping sphere between civil society and politics, based on ideas by Gramsci.[3] In this line of think-ing, political society can be seen as a sphere of actors and institutions 'mediating, articulating and institutionalising the relation between the state and civil society'.[4] Political parties are a key element of political society. In this literature civil society is related with liberalisation and political society with democratisation. The state, political society and civil society together form 'public life' and should be analysed closely together. For instance should political society be either banned or absorbed by the state, civil society can react as a source of protest and action.[5] So in a dynamic way there is a constant tension within political society in which balances shift between the state and civil society. Seen from the side of civil society, the state can be inter-penetrated (build and consolidate political society) by means such as of building the foundations of a civil society, building alliances, developing intermediary channels, opening up trans-national space and building citizenship. Stages of democratisation can be distinguished according to the shifting balance between civil society and the state and the role and influence of political society as the 'space of inter-penetration'.

Market – state interdependence and inter-penetration: public management

An inter-penetration in which governing images played an important role was the introduction of management ideas from the market sector into government. In the 1980s a wave of reform emerged in the public sector that was strongly influenced by ideological actors, who believed that the provision of public services was inefficient and that reform must involve the public sector adopting elements from the market. This wave of reform – well defined as a movement or as a doctrine – came to be known as the 'new public management'.[6] The essence of this movement and the administrative practices it brought to bear 'was [of] creating institutional and organisational contexts, which, in as many respects as possible, were to mirror what were seen as critical aspects of private-sector modes of organising and managing' with as a key factor the creation of so-called 'quasi-markets' in which public services were to be 'produced' and 'sold' and in which contracting was the main institutionalised tool.[7] Although other motives played a role, there is no doubt that the main thrust for this inter-penetration of market thinking into the state sector had – at least in the beginning – a highly ideological undertone that has since changed ideas of governing the public sector in many countries. This certainly raises important governance questions, such as 'competition, how far can you go?'[8]

State, market and civil society inter-penetrations: sustainable society

An example of a high interdependence with light inter-penetration can be found in the changing relations between state, market and civil society in the area of environmental protection or more broadly formulated towards a sustainable society.[9] Under modern conditions public matters can no longer be the exclusive responsibility of the state. All the spheres have a task here. Therefore, the market can no longer be a sphere of limited public responsibility, some responsibility has to be transferred to the market, and civil society ought to be more involved in the governmental process.

There are good reasons to accept the differentiation between the spheres. While trying to link them more adequately, we ought also to be cautious to preserve their distinctions and their singularity. One might say that more classical ideas on the separation between these spheres need to be complemented with new and alternative ideas. With regard to the linkage between the state and civil society the ways in which civil society can influence the state ought to be extended. However, the state and civil society ought to keep a certain distance, and ways of influence beyond the stubbornly insisted-upon idea of democracy as participation need to be found. With regard to the relation between the market and the state there may be advantages in all kinds of co-arrangements, although improved co-operation between public officials and companies does involve some dangers. These are the classical corporatist dangers, the blurring of responsibilities, the entwining of interests and the centralisation of power. 'Co' has to be complemented by the more classical strategy of keeping the state and the market at a distance. The relation between the market and civil society is a typical one from this perspective. Here more interaction is necessary, particularly for a new political channel to supplement the consumer-producer relation that nowadays exists.

> Interdependence and inter-penetration between the three societal institutions lead toward 'new' structural arrangements: between state and market towards 'public management'; between state and civil society towards 'political society'; and between state, market and civil society towards 'sustainable society' as examples.

Varieties of societal interactions and modes of governance

In modern society, an enormous variety of interactions can be observed. They vary from quite informal ones such as in families, to formalised ones as between states. The most spontaneous and least organised ones I called *interferences*, the more 'horizontally' inter-organised and often semi-formalised types I referred to as *interplays*, and the most formal and 'vertically' organised ones I labelled *interventions*. In this section I will continue examining these three types of interactions in relation to the three governance modes, self-, co- and hierarchical. This relation helps me to further develop the theorising on governance.

For the purpose of synthesising, I see self-governance as related to societal interferences, co-governance to interplays, and hierarchical governance to interventionist interactions. These relations concur with my general views on the relation between the intentional and structural level of all interactions (see Chapter 2). Insights such as on the enabling or constraining character of this relation, unintended effects within them, and forces influencing them institutionally as well as ideologically also apply to the three varieties of interactions, and the governance modes linked to them. I see the governance modes, as it were, 'embedded' in these societal forms of interactions; they form their 'breeding' ground, as a realm where societal experiences can be 'translated' into forms of governance.

Interferences and self-governance

The distinction between the intentional and structural levels of inter-actions reveals the relation between interferences as societal medium and self-governance as a mode of governance. Intentional interferences influence their own self-governing structures, 'upward' within, and across organisations, sectors or even societies. Trends may be discovered in which inferential interactions, enabled by structural conditions, become more widespread and in this process new patterns of self-governance may develop. Or conversely: interferential interactions may become constricted by structural conditions controlling them, resulting in new patterns of limited self-governance.

On the basis of the dualistic character of these interferences, and the self-governing interactions embedded in them, general notions about the character of this embedding can be formulated. So one might expect that many interferences in primary processes are becoming more and more complex. Interweaving of economic, technological, juridical and informational aspects in many of these processes may have controlling rather than enabling options and thus limit their self-governing nature at the structural level. However, because of social-cultural influences opposite trends can be noticed also: individualisation tendencies in societal interferences may embody a higher potential for self-governance, and thus the relation between the intentional and structural level of interferences and self-governing interactions may become more enabling. Interferences and self-governing interactions can thus be considered subjects of governance.

Interference and, for that matter, self governing can also be seen as governing objects. This might be the case when in societal domains certain (categories of) interferences at the intentional level, the structural level, or the relation between the two get social-political attention. Self-governing codes of conduct may raise questions of an ethical or juridical nature, these codes may become controlling ones, resulting in interventions. In principle, all interferential interactions (social, technical, cultural) can be of interest for social-political governing. As argued in the chapter on first-order governing, every subject, whatever it may be, can become a social-political issue. To what extent interferences, and the self-governing interactions embedded within them can be considered as such, depends partly on historical and broader societal considerations, partly on matters of perspective. Usually, societal interferences with their basically spontaneous and fluid character, occur in a random fashion. However, a generalised 'trigger', either on the intentional or the structural level, will start organising and formalising them, developing them into other sorts of interactions, which also may have an impact on their self-governing nature, either in scale or moving them into another governance mode. It calls attention to their 'qualities' as governance subjects, their contribution to and place in the broad governance spectrum, and as governing objects in the way they might have to be governed – to add a normative note. Here, the dualistic notion between government as the 'governor' and society as 'being governed' has not been set aside, but is approached in a nuanced way. The first substantive step is to elaborate on the notion that to govern and to be governed is to regard both as a social-political capacity, shared between governments and other more or less formalised social-political governing entities in societies at large. This is the appearance of the self-governance mode with its own possibilities and limitations, and always to be seen in mixes with the two other types, co- and hierarchical governance.

> Experiences with interferential interactions basically point at the why, if, and how of the self-governing capacity in modern societies.

Interplays and co-governance

In theorising governance, co-governance can be considered to be especially related to the kind of societal interactions I have termed interplays. In modern societies these forms of societal interactions abound, and at the level of societal sectors or institutions we can see particular inter-organisational patterns, showing ways in which organisations and other societal entities try to overcome the far-reaching effects of societal differentiation and specialisation. This is, as I argued above, not only the case within institutions such as the state, the market and civil society, but also between them. Interplays as horizontal, semi-formalised patterns of societal interactions are the clearest expression of tendencies in modern societies, believed by many (including myself) to be related to growing interdependencies in major societal processes. I see co-governing, as a conceptual category, as being embedded within those interplays. Similar to the conceptual relation between self-governing and interferences, I see interplays within the broader realm of horizontal societal interactions, producing experiences on which forms of co-governing can be built, developed or grown. Therefore interplays can be considered as the propensity of societal entities to do things together in an organised, but equalised, manner. Similarly co-governance can be considered as the propensity of governing entities to do something together, and from the governance point of view those across sectors or institutions are the most important, and theoretically the most interesting ones.

For the moment, it may be sufficient to say that interplays, and co-governing interactions as their main governing expression, are typically 'intermediate', 'in-between' phenomena, as are the concepts applied to map them. Interplays are, so to say, clamped between interferences on the one hand and interventions on the other. This is not to say they do not deserve a special place; they do, as they are a societal 'growth' phenomenon. However, in contrast to interferences and interventions, which have a long history, interplays seem to be a more recent phenomenon. The examples given in the chapter on co-governance modes underline this view. As argued above, interplays may have developed as more organised and formalised versions of interferences. Alternately they can be seen as less formalised and 'horizontalised' forms of interventions. Actors interacting in interferential forms, may need more organisation and continuity to cope with their internal or external diversity, complexity and dynamics. This is where interplays enter the fray. The same, if in the opposite direction, can be said with respect to interventions. There are many situations where direct interventions do not work: they might be too specific or too general; directed towards too narrow or too broad an audience; or their time frame may be too short or too long. In such situations intervening actors might consider approaching those they intervene with in a different way, more sharing than controlling, more guiding than directing, more inter than top-down. Interplays, then, can be conceptualised as this 'mid-field' between interferences on the one hand and interventions on the other.

Interplays and co-governing interactions embedded within them are of special importance if we look at the interrelations between state, market and civil society. As argued earlier in this chapter, the interdependency and inter-penetration tendencies between these institutions are to be seen as a central characteristic of modern societies coping with (growing) diversity, complexity and dynamics. Although interplays and co-governing within these three societal domains are interesting, their major importance lies in the relation between them: therefore I have developed theoretical notions on this relationship.

Interplay forms of societal interactions form the basis for co-governing; for governance they are particularly important at the crossroads between societal sectors and domains.

Interventions and hierarchical governance

Interventions are not simply top-down, one-sided governing relations, they are two-sided interactions binding both governors and governed. As do all interactions they have an intentional and a structural level and relations between these two levels can be distinguished. Questions can be raised about the diversity of those participating in these interventions (intentional level), we can look at interventions in their complexity dimensions (structural level) or about tensions within and between these levels 'causing' their dynamics. I already hinted at the possibility that in modern societies societal diversity may make governing by interventions problematic. Legal interventions, for example, are considered to be based upon principles such as 'equality before the law'; on the other hand however, this 'equality' is constantly being eroded by tendencies to refine rules for special cases enhancing their effectiveness. Dilemmas such as these not only beset public intervening. Often in the private sector cycles between interventions as preferred means of governing are alternated by other governing practices. We also know that intervention-systems have dynamics of their own: their involuntary and obligatory nature implies a conflictual element in them, resistance may be expected, and tensions will arise around them. The more guarantees inbuilt, the more energy invested in their implementation, the more difficult it will be to adapt and develop them in an evolutionary manner, the more likely are 'positive feedback' phenomena to appear around them, and crises may be the consequence. Systems of interventions can also be analysed in their complexity. Each intervention by itself may be considered an efficient way of governing considering the goal pursued, however, in a systemic perspective this may not be the case at all. One intervention may be followed by another to combat side-, or other unforseen or unwanted, effects. True or false as it may be, in many cases (public) interventions applied to and seen from the point of view of specific subjects, have become so intertwined that the whole of them becomes over-complex, counterproductive and their effectiveness put in doubt.

This brings the hierarchical mode of governance to the fore. In Chapter 8 I alluded to the fact that although the hierarchical model as an 'ideal' one has lost some of its glory, it still is, and probably will remain, an important mode of societal governance. What can be noticed in the public sphere is that next to its central and hard core, large 'grey' areas of delegated authority to semi-public, semi-private, organisations for partic- ular forms of interventions have been created. In the European continen- tal tradition we find (neo) corporatist arrangements, while in English usage 'quangos' (quasiautonomous-non-governmental organisations) are the expression of this grey area. Whatever they are called, they basically belong to the hierarchical mode of governance, and many of their inter- actions in the fields they have authority in, are of an interventionist nature. From a governance perspective they can be seen as the long arm of hierarchical governance, located in the state as well as in the market domain. As argued for the areas in between interferences (self-governance) and interplays (co-governance), there are also grey areas between inter- plays and interventions or between co-governance and hierarchical governance. I already mentioned in Chapter 9 co-management schemes, which tread a thin line in differing from corporatist arrangements. These phenomena can also be found in networks, which may devolve in the direction of hierarchy, and regimes evolving in dominant ruling actor ones. A discriminating factor between all those mixed forms of public and private interventions are their degree of formalisation and the question of whether sanctions are available to them. We also should keep in mind that even interventions and hierarchical governing interactions are social constructions at different levels of societal aggregation with qualities and boundaries fluctuating all the time. As with all societal and governing interactions there are always general forces at work to change them or to keep them as they are. These can find their initiation at the intentional as well as at the structural level of societal interventions and hierarchy, subjects requiring serious and systematic attention, certainly in relation with the two other governance modes.

> Societal interventions and hierarchical governing remain an important subject of governance attention in their central core, in their boundary areas, as well as in their mixes with other modes of governance.

Types of interactions, modes of governance and cybernetic qualities

Modes of governance and the spheres of interactions they are embedded in can be used to formulate propositions about qualities inherent in them which may be of interest from a governing point of view. The use of their 'cybernetic' qualities to create governing opportunities can serve as an example. Here I refer to the well-known distinction between feedback, feed-forward and feed-while forms of (cybernetic) steering. Feedback is based on the idea of steering after a mistake has been detected, in particular in situations with many unknowns and where learning from experience is a necessary quality. Feed-forward is based on the principle that mistakes cannot be tolerated, so all possible mistakes are calculated beforehand: this in particular applies to 'high-risk' operations. Feed-while falls in between these two: it is in fact steering by doing. This is done in situations where the 'variables' can be relatively easily manipulated during an implementation process.

If we take the three forms of governing interactions into consideration, it is easily understood that the following distinction as a general principle can be made (other conditions being kept equal).

Since I have positioned the three modes of governance (self-, co- and hierarchical) within the three spheres of these interactions, these three varieties of steering or cybernetic governance can be seen as fitting within the three governance modes, and thus they can be seen as best representing those qualities. When these combined forms of representation as indicated in Table 13.3 are present, optimal steering (cybernetic governing) may be expected.

Table 13.3   'Cybernetic' qualities of types of interactions
and governance modes

	Modes		
	Self-governance	Co-governance	Hierarchical governance
Types of interactions			
Interferences:	feedback		
Interplays:		feed-while	
Interventions:			feed-forward

Types of governing interactions and the modes of governance that are embedded within them show different cybernetic qualities.

Governability and relations between aspects of governance

At the start of Chapter 12 I defined governability of a social-political system or entity as a quality of this system or entity as a whole, that whole being more than the sum of the parts. In this section this quality will be discussed as can be deduced from the relation between the different aspects distinguished in the previous chapters. All governance aspects contribute to this quality: elements, modes and orders. To express it normatively: the better that governing elements fit with governing modes and orders, the higher the quality of its governability. The same applies to the relation between governing modes and governing orders. And the governability of modern society also depends greatly on the way the state, market and civil society 'contribute' to its governance. The following propositions, and the way they are argued, are final examples of how a systematic approach to the governability of social-political systems can be built.

Elements of governing and modes of governance

The three elements of governing, image formation, choice of instruments and action, and the structural conditions they are nested in, respectively. value systems, resources and social-political capital, can be supposed to not be equally distributed for governance purposes. Table 13.4 serves as a basis for phrasing a proposition about the emphasis of the use of these elements distributed across the three governance modes.

Table 13.4 Elements of governing and modes of governance

	Modes		
	Self-governance	Co-governance	Hierarchical governance
Governing elements			
Value systems/images	X		
Resources/instruments		X	
Capital/action			X

From what has been discussed in earlier chapters, the relation between these elements and modes of governance can be deduced quite easily. The dominant motive for co-governing arrangements is of a resource/ instrumental nature, allegedly based upon growing interdependencies and inter-penetration tendencies in modern societies. Therefore that relation can be assumed to be a dominant one. Hierarchical governance, as we have seen in Chapter 8, finds its base in controlling and steering capacities. Although for the state domain these capacities are on the decline to take action based upon action capital is still the main resource hierarchical governance is based upon. Therefore that relation can be hypothesised as being a strong and direct one. The relation between self-governance and fact and value systems as its main governance base may be less evident at first sight. However, it can nevertheless be assumed that self-governance with its 'internal' orientation around primary processes is strongly influenced by existing and developing fact and value systems. Its autonomous, partly *autopoietic* nature makes it, so the theory assumes, greatly dependent on communication as its primary way of governing. Distilling and internalising facts and values from the societal environment are the key to self-governing possibilities.

> Modes of governance have differentiated relations with elements of governing: self-governance with facts and value systems (images), co-governance with resources (instruments), and hierarchical governance with social-political capital (action).

Elements of governing and orders of governance

In an elaboration of the connection between the different governing elements and other governing aspects, we can also observe the way that the image, instrumental and action condition of governing relate to the governing orders, respectively problem-solving and opportunity-creation

Table 13.5   Elements of governing related to orders of governance

	Image/values	Instrument/resources	Action/capital
Orders of governance			
First order (challenges)	High	Medium	Low
Second order (institutions)	Low	Medium	High
Meta (principles)	High	Low	Medium

(first order), care for institutions (second order) and phrasing normative principles (meta). In Table 13.5 my suggestions at this point are summarised.

Image formation and problem or opportunity creation are closely linked. In dealing with the diversity, dynamics and complexity of such problem-solution and opportunity-strategy systems (proper) images are of primary importance. It is clear that the same applies to the fact and value systems in which those images are embedded. For example, ideological or systematic combinations of facts and values such as in scientific disciplines, can be important factors in the way problems and opportunities are approached, thus having a dominant influence on the way the diversity, complexity and dynamics of certain governing situations are handled. I did not systematically discuss the instrumental/resource and action/capital component of first-order governance, but I suspect that the instrumental/resource element is the second important one, followed, in this governance order, by the action component. For second-order governance forming adequate images will not be the biggest problem. Finding the proper instruments and in particular mustering sufficient action potential to overcome institutional resistance will be the crucial governing element. For meta-governance it seems quite clear that this is first and foremost a question of image formation. This has to be complemented, however, with a certain amount of willpower for these meta notions to have an impact on actual governance affairs.

Governing elements and orders of governance relate distinctively: image and instruments to first-order governance, instruments and action to second-order governance, and image and action relate to meta governance.

Modes of governance and societal institutions

Finally, two propositions are formulated on the role of the three societal institutions, state, market and civil society in governance, and their contribution to governability is questioned. Table 13.6 summarises the

**Table 13.6   Relation between modes of governance
and the three societal institutions**

	Modes		
	Self-governance	Co-governance	Hierarchical governance
State	Low	Medium	High
Market	High	Low	Medium
Civil Society	High	Medium	Low

supposed dominant relation between the three societal institutions and the three governance modes.

The pattern emerging from Table 13.6 hypothesises that each societal institution is characterised by a particular mix of governance modes. For the state the dominant one is hierarchical governance, while co-governance is on the rise and self-governance is not a particular feature of this institution. The market is basically self-governing, although within it the hierarchical mode is certainly not missing and co-arrangements are present but remain relatively rare. For civil society also, self-governance is the dominant feature, but here hierarchical governance is relatively rare and co-governing – as with the state – seems to be on the rise.

There is a dominant relation between each of the societal institutions and particular modes of governance. Dominant for the state are the hierarchical, for the market and civil society are self-governance. The market and civil society differ mainly in their secondary and tertiary governance mode.

Orders of governance and societal institutions

This final proposition on the three societal institutions is about their role in the three governing orders, that is to say first-order (problem-solving and opportunity-creation), second order (care for institutions) and meta (discussing and establishing principles). The state is predominantly seen as the problem solver and institutional care taker, the market takes care of its own institutions and civil society acts as a forum for meta-considerations (see Table 13.7).

In problem-solving civil society should become much more involved and the market to some extent, while the role of the state can be reduced in this activity. Certainly, in opportunity-creation civil society, but also the state, could play a more outspoken role. In institutional care the govern-ing activities of the state should be more complemented by civil society

Table 13.7   Orders of governance and the three societal institutions

	First order (problems)	First order (opportunities)	Second order (institutions)	meta (principles)
State	↓	↑	=	↑
Market	↑	=	↑	↑
Civil society	↑	↑	↑	=

and market parties. Finally, in the responsibility for meta governance the role of civil society should become more systematically and be shared by the two other institutions.

> In societal governability a larger role for the market in institutional matters and somewhat in phrasing governance principles seems appropriate, as well as a more outspoken role for civil society in problem-solving or opportunity-creation and in institutional care.

Conclusion

In this last chapter the concept of governability has been placed central stage. I see governability as the most all-encompassing concept used, because it indicated the governance situation of social-political systems as wholes. The question arises of course if in this chapter the concept has opened up its potential richness, and the answer has to be a qualified 'no'. This is, in the first place, due to the limitations I imposed on myself, by remaining within the boundaries of the concepts used so far for its exploration; and they are far from complete. In second place, the method of squaring the different separate dimensions provided insights, but again far from a complete picture. Still, exploration of the concept has shown that in principle it is able to fulfil its promise, and serve as an image for the governance quality of social-political systems as wholes, at different levels of societal aggregation.

This is expressed in the fact that without too much difficulty all the major aspects of the governance perspective as an analytical exercise could be given a place in its use as a synthetic concept. From the assumptions made on the societal features diversity, complexity and dynamics, via the introduction of the concepts of interdependence and inter-penetration, to successively introducing the different aspects of governing itself, a survey could be given of the major dimensions of the approach in terms of their (potential) contributions to an insight of what governability of social-political systems is about. This oversight gives – with the limitations as mentioned above – an idea of the richness and the variety of aspects that together form the governability of those systems. So they form, as it were, the *diversity* element of the governability of social-political systems. The matrices in which these elements are related and the formulated propositions as summaries of relating these dimensions can be considered as the backbone of what might be seen as the *complexity* dimension of governability. They express how these aspects hang together and in these inter-relations form its complexity in summary. And thirdly to the *dynamics* of governability. This can be found in some matrices from which I deduced ideas about patterns of change, and statements like 'this is not an end state' or 'these are tendencies in this or that direction' demonstrate this. They can be found in the inter-penetrations taking place between societal institutions, which may give rise to new structural arrangements such as public management, political society or sustainable society. Together these three dimensions give a synthetic conceptual idea of what governability as a governance quality of social-political systems as a whole might have to offer.

In Chapter 1 I started by using governability as a descriptive tool, as a guide showing the main subjects to be treated in this study. In this final chapter I returned to it but instead as a closing concept for the book as a whole. I consider the summaries and their argumentation as statements for the outcome of the book. At the same time they are the first step towards the formulation of a more coherent theoretical statement about social-political governance. I see as one of the contributions of this book that it has made such on endeavour conceivable. Elements of such a theory have been conceptualised, and a number of hypothetical relations between them have been sketched. A more complete elaboration remains a task for the future, however.

A few words about concepts not discussed as components of the governance approach is required. There are several I used here and there in the text, without defining them, or treating them properly. Of those, three in particular, culture, power and democracy were originally going to be used explicitly, but during the process of working on this book I kept postponing giving them the place they probably deserve. Not because I consider them as unimportant, on the contrary. Introducing them more fully into the framework would have enriched the perspective, on the other hand adding them would have meant another layer of concepts to give a proper place. Culture, power and democracy belong to the category of concepts one really needs to pay careful attention to. However, they are such broad, difficult and often misused categories, that I decided to consider them 'silhouettes hovering in the background' rather than as 'active figures in the foreground' of my effort to understand what governance and governability is about.

Finally, a few words on the outcome of the book in light of the ambition with which I started it. I had two things in mind: in the first place to develop a conceptual scheme able to cope with what I consider to be some major features of modern governance. The edited volume with this title[10] was a first exercise in this direction, and my aim with this study was to further this exploration in a more systematic manner. Secondly it was my purpose, as explained in Chapter 1, to try to give a conceptual answer to a number of questions raised about the increasing interest in governance in the literature and in practice. These centre around two main issues. In the first place, does the rising interest in governance have to do with societal developments, which ask for a re-thinking of what governing and governance is about, in other words do we have to look for this rising interest in the first place to modern society, and from there reason towards governance. Or secondly, do we primarily search for this rising interest in the governance realm itself, such as expressed in a phrase like 'more governance, less government'. In other words do we start or search at the other end, by looking at the governance system in the first place and from there reason towards modern society. Looking back now to my intentions with this book, the purposes I had in mind merged: in developing the conceptualisation the answer to these questions grew at the same time. But at the same time more questions arose during this exercise. With this publication I formally close a phase in an ongoing process, showing that there is enough in it to be shared. Hopefully it stimulates others to pursue their quest to find out what governance is about.

Notes

1 Luhmann, 1984; Münch, 1987a.

2 Münch, 1987b; 1988; Etzioni, 1968. Münch also includes non-interactional types such as domination and submission in these processes, Etzioni relates them to isolation and alienation.

3 Gramsci, 1971.

4 Biekart, 1999, p. 33.

5 *idem*, pp. 36–43.

6 For a recent overview, see Pollitt and Bouckaart, 2000.

7 Dawson and Dargie, 1999, p. 461.

8 Röber, 2000.

9 Adapted from Dubbink, 1999.

10 Kooiman, 1993.

GLOSSARY

Governance
Governance: theoretical conceptions on governing interactions.
Governability: quality of governing interactions of a social-political system/entity as a whole.
Governing: interactions to solve societal problems or create societal opportunities, care for institutional aspects of these interactions, and setting normative principles for them.

Interactions
Interaction: a mutually influencing relation between two or more actors or entities. In an interaction an action/intentional level and a structural/contextual level are distinguished.
Interference: a relatively open, flexible and spontaneous societal interaction.
Interplay: a 'horizontal' and semi-formalised societal interaction.
Intervention: a 'vertical' and formalised societal interaction.

Elements
Action: will-power available in governing interactions.
Factual and evaluative system: potential (cultural) pictures available for governing interactions.
Image-building: process of creating mental pictures as guidelines for governing interactions.
Instrument choice: process of selecting available means for governing interactions.
Resource: potential means available for governing interactions.
Social-political capital: potential will-power available in governing interactions.

Modes
Co-governance: a mode of governing consisting of collaborating or co-operating governing entities (interplays).
Hierarchical governance: a mode of governing consisting of authoritative relations between societal entities (interventions).
Self-governance: a mode of governance consisting of predominantly autonomous governing entities (interferences).

Orders
First order governing: governing interactions for solving societal problems or creating societal opportunities.
Meta governing: governing interactions setting the normative principles of rationality, responsiveness, performance and responsibility for governance itself.

Second order governing: governing interactions to take care for and maintain governing institutions as contexts for first order governance.

Societal features
Complexity: multitude of often overlapping interactions.
Diversity: qualitative differences of interacting societal entities.
Dynamics: tensions within and between interactions.
Interdependence: mutual dependence of societal entities at the intentional level of societal interactions.
Inter-penetration: mutual dependence of societal entities at the structural level of societal interactions.

REFERENCES

Abbott, A. (1988) *The System of Professions*. Chicago: Chicago University Press.

Ahrne, G. (1998) 'Civil Society and Uncivil Organizations', in J.C. Alexander (ed.), *Real Civil Societies*. London: Sage, 84–95.

Alexander, J.C. (ed.) (1998a) *Real Civil Societies*. London: Sage.

Alexander, J.C. (1998b) 'Citizen and Enemy as Symbolic Classification: on the Polarization Discourse of Civil Society', in J.C. Alexander (ed.), *Real Civil Societies*. London: Sage, 96–114.

Almond, G.A. and Verba, S. (1963) *Civic Culture*. Princeton: Princeton University Press.

Andrain, C.F. and Apter, D. (1995) *Political Protest and Social Change*. Houndsmille: McMillan.

Archer, M.S. (1988) *Culture and Agency: the Place of Culture in Social Theory*. Cambridge: Cambridge University Press.

Archer, M. (1990) 'Human Agency and Social Structure: A Critique of Giddens', in J. Clark, C. Modgil and S. Modgil (eds), *Anthony Giddens: Consensus and Controversy*. London: Falmer Press, 73–84.

Arend, A.C. (1999) *Legal Rules and International Society*. New York: Oxford University Press.

Argyris, C. (1992) *On Organizational Learning*. Cambridge: Blackwell.

Ashby, R.W. (1958) 'Requisite Variety and its Implications for the Control of Complex Systems', *Cybernetica*, 1: 83–99.

Ayres, I. and Braithwaite, J. (1992) *Responsive Regulation*. New York: Oxford University Press.

Axelrod, R. (1984) *The Evolution of Cooperation*. New York: Basic Books.

Axelrod, R. and Keohane, R.O. (1986) 'Achieving Cooperation under Anarchy: Strategies and Institutions', in K.A. Oye (ed.), *Cooperation Under Anarchy*. Princeton, NJ: Princeton University Press, 226–254.

Bandemer, S. von and Hilbert, J. (1998) 'Vom expandierender zum aktivierender Staat', in B. Blanke, S. von Bandemer, F. Nullmeier, G. Wewer and J. Hilbert, (Hrsg) *Handbuch zur Verwaltungsreform*. Opladen: West Deutscher Verlag, 25–32.

Bateson, G. (1972) *Steps to an Ecology of Mind*. New York: Ballantine Books.

Bechmann, G. (1993) 'Risiko als Schlüsselkategorie der Gesellschaftstheorie', in G. Bechmann, (eds) *Risiko und Gesellschaft*. Opladen: Westdeutsche Verlag, 237–276.

Beck, R.J., Arend, C.J. and Vander Lugt, R.D. (eds) (1996) *International Rules*. New York: Oxford University Press.

Beck, U. (1992) *Risk Society*. London: Sage.

Benhabib, S. (ed.) (1996) *Democracy and Difference*. Princeton: Princeton University Press.

Bellamy, C. and Taylor, J.A. (1998) *Governing in the Information Age*. Buckingham: Open University Press.

Bendel, P. and Kropp, S. (1998) 'Zivilgesellschaft – ein geeignetes Konzept zur Analyse von Systemwechseln?', *Zeitschrift für Politikwissenschaften*, 8: 39–67.

Benz, A., Scharpf, F.W. and Zintl, R. (1992) *Horizontale Politikverflechtung*. Frankfurt: Campus.

Berger, J., Eyre, D.P. and Zelditch Jr, M. (1989) 'Theoretical Structures and the Micro/Macro Problem', in J. Berger, M. Zelditch Jr and B. Anderson (eds) *Sociological Theories in Progress*. Newbury Park: Sage, 11–32.

Berting, J., d'Anjou, L. and Steijn, B. (eds) (1997) *De Tirannie van het Beeld*. Meppel: Boom.

Berting, J. and Villain-Gandossi, C. (eds) (1994) *The Role of Stereotypes in International Relations*. Rotterdam: Erasmus University, RISBO.

Berting, J. (1996) 'Over Rationaliteit en Complexiteit', in P. Nijkamp, W. Begeer and J. Berting (red), *Denken over Complexe Besluitvorming*. Den Haag: SDU, 17–30.

Berting, J. (in press) *Europe Adrift*. Oxford: Berghahn Publishers.

Beyme, K. von (1995) 'Steuerung und Selbstregelung', *Journal f. Sozialforschung*, 35: 196–217.

Biekart, C.H. (1999) *The Politics of Civil Society Building*. Utrecht: International Books.

Blanke, B. (2001) 'Verantwortungsstufung und Aktivierung im Sozialstaat', in H.-P. Burth, A. Görlitz (eds), *Politische Steuerung in Theorie und Praxis*. Baden-Baden: Nomos, 147–166.

Blom, A. (1997) *Complexiteit en Contingentie*. Kampen: Kok.

Börzel, T.A. (1998) 'Organizing Babylon: on the Different Conceptions of Policy Networks', *Public Administration*, 76: 253–273.

Boudon, R. (1996) 'The "Cognivist Model"', *Rationality and Society*, 8: 123–150.

Boulding, K.E. (1956) *The Image*. Ann Arbor: University of Michigan Press.

Bourdieu, P. (1986) 'Three Forms of Capital', in J.G. Richardson (ed.), *Handbook of Theory and Research in the Sociology of Education*. New York: Greenwood Press, 241–258.

Bourdieu, P. (1991) *Language and Symbolic Power*. Oxford: Polity Press.

Bourdieu, P. and Wacquant, L.J.D. (1992) *An Invitation to Reflexive Sociology*. Chicago: Chicago University Press.

Brah, A. (1992) 'Difference, Diversity and Differentiation', in J. Donald and A. Rattansi (eds), *Race, Culture and Difference*. London: Sage, 126–148.

Brans, M. and Rossbach, S. (1997) 'The Autopoiesis of Administrative Systems: Niklas Luhmann on Public Administration and Public Policy', *Public Administration*, 75: 417–439.

Bressers, J.Th.A. and Klok, P-J. (1987) 'Grondslagen voor een Instrumententheorie', in *Beleidswetenschappen*, 1: 77–97.

Bruijn, J.A. de and Heuvelhof, E.F. ten (1991) 'Policy Instruments for Steering Autopoietic Actors', in R.J. in 't Veld et al. (eds), *Autopoiesis and Configuration Theory*. Dordrecht: Kluwer, 161–170.

Buchner-Jeziorska, A. and Evetts, J. (1997) 'Regulating Professionals', *International Sociology*, 12: 73–92.

Buechler, S.M. (1995) 'New Social Movements Theories', *The Sociological Quarterly*, 36: 441–464.

Bühl, W. (1990) *Sozialer Wandel in Ungleichgewicht*. Stuttgart: Enke.

Bühl, W. (1995) 'Internationale Regime und Europäische Integration', *Zeitschrift für Politik*, 42: 122–148.

Burkart, R. (1998) *Kommunikationswissenschaft*. Wien: Böhlau.

Burns, T.R., Baumgartner, Th. and Deville, Ph. (1985) *Man, Decisions, Society*. New York: Gordon and Breach Publishers.

Burns, T.R. and Flam, H. (1987) *The Shaping of Social Organizations*. London: Sage.

Burrage, M., Jarausch, K. and Siegrist, H. (1990) 'An Actor-based Framework for the Study of the Professions', in M. Burrage and R. Torstendahl (eds), *Professions in Theory and History*. London: Sage, 203–225.

Calhoun, C., LiPuma, E. and Postone, M. (eds) (1993) *Bourdieu: Critical Perspectives*. Cambridge: Polity Press.

Campbell, C. (1996) *The Myth of Social Action*. Cambridge: Cambridge University Press.

Campbell, C. (1999) 'Action as Will-Power', *Sociological Review*, 47: 48–61.

Campbell, J.L., Hollingsworth, J.R. and Lindberg, L.N. (eds) (1991) *Governance of the American Economy*. Cambridge: Cambridge University Press.

Castells, M. (1996) *The Network Society*. Oxford: Blackwell.

Cerny, P.C. (1990) *The Changing Architecture of Politics*. London: Sage.

Chemers, M.M. (1997) *An Integrative Theory of Leadership*. Mahwah, NJ: Erlbaum.

Chisholm, D. (1989) *Coordination without Hierarchy*. Berkeley: University of California Press.

Cohen, B.P. and Silver, S.D. (1989) 'Group Structure and Information Exchange: Introduction to a Theory', in M. Berger, B. Zelditch Jr. and B. Anderson (eds), *Sociological Theories in Progress*. Newbury Park: Sage, 11–32.

Cohen, J.L. and Arato, A. (1992) *Civil Society and Political Theory*. Cambridge: MIT Press.

Coleman, J. (1990) *Foundations of Social Theory*. Cambridge: Belknap Press, 300–321.

Collin, S-O. and Hansson, L. (2000) 'The Propensity, Persistence and Performance of Public-Private Partnerships in Sweden', in S. Osborne (ed.), *Public-Private Partnerships*. London: Routledge, 201–218.

Conger, J.A. and Kanungo, R.N. (1998) *Charismatic Leadership in Organizations*. Thousand Oaks: Sage.

Costain, A.N. (1992) 'Social Movements as Interest Groups: the Case of the Women Movement', in M.P. Petracca, (ed.), *The Politics of Interests*. Boulder: Westview, 285–307.

Cotterell, R. (1992) *The Sociology of Law*. London: Butterworths.

Crespi, F. (1992) *Social Action and Power*. Oxford: Blackwell.

Crowley, D. and Mitchell, D. (eds) (1994) *Communication Theory Today*. Oxford: Polity Press.

Curran, J. (1991) 'Rethinking the Media as Public Sphere', in P. Dahlghren, C. Sparks (eds), *Communication and Citizenship*. London: Routledge, 27–57.

Dahl, R.A. and Lindblom, C.E. (1953) *Politics, Economics, and Welfare*. New York: Harper.

Dahlgren, P. (1991) 'Introduction', in P. Dahlgren and C. Sparks (eds), *Communication and Citizenship*. London: Routledge, 1–24.

Dahrendorf, R. (1964) *Homo Sociologicus*. Köln: Westdeutscher Verlag.

Dawson, S. and Dargie, C. (1999) 'New Public Management: An Assessment and Evaluation with Special Reference to UK Health', *Public Management (Review)*, 1: 459–482.

Delden, A.Th. van and Kooiman, J. (1983) *Adviesorganen in de Politieke Besluitvorning*' Gravenhage: Wetenschappelijke Raad voor het Regeringsbeleid, Rapport V 41.

Derksen, A.A. (1992) 'Wat is Rationaliteit & Wat is er zo Goed aan?', *Algemeen Nederlands Tijdschrift voor Wijsbegeerte*, 84: 258–286.

Dery, D. (1984) *Problem Definition in Policy Analysis*. Lawrence: Kansas University Press.

Deutsch, K. (1963) *The Nerves of Government*. New York: Free Press.

Diani, M. and Eyerman, R. (eds) (1992) *Studying Collective Action*. London: Sage.

Dijkzeul, D. (1997) *The Management of Multilateral Organizations*. Deventer: Kluwer.

DiMaggio, P. (1997) 'Culture and Cognition', *Annual Review of Sociology*, 23: 263–287.

Douglas, M. and Wildavski, A. (1982) *Risk and Culture*. Berkeley: University of California Press.

Douglas, M. and Hull, D. (eds) (1992) *How Classification Works*. Edinburgh: Edinburgh University Press.

Dubbink, W. (1999) *Duurzaamheid als Patstelling*. Delft: Eburon.

Dubnick, M.J. (1996) 'Challenges to American Public Administration: Complexity, Bureaucratization, and the Culture of Distrust', *International Journal of Public Administration*, 19: 1481–1508.

Duff, A.S. (2000) *Information Society Studies*. London: Routledge.

Duff, R.A. (1998) 'Responsibility', in E. Craig (ed.), *Encyclopedia of Philosophy*. London: Routledge, 288–294.

Dunsire, A. (1993) 'Modes of Governance', in J. Kooiman, (ed.), *Modern Governance*. London: Sage, 21–34.

Dunsire, A. (1996) 'Tipping the Balance: Autopoiesis and Governance', *Administration and Society*, 28: 299–334.

Easton, D. (1953) *The Political System*. New York: Knopf.

Edwards, B. and Foley, M.W. (1998) 'Civil Society and Social Capital beyond Putnam', *American Behavioral Scientist*, 42: 1 and 124–139.

Eeden, C.J.M.A. van and Kooiman, J. (1995) *Wisselwerkingen*. Rotterdam: Erasmus Universiteit, Rotterdam, School of Management, Erasm Management Report Series, No. 243.

Eeden, C.J.M.A. van (2001) *Waarnemen als Besturingsopdracht*. Rotterdam: Faculteit Bedrijfskunde, Erasmus Universiteit, Vakgroep Business Society Management, Ph D. Diss.

Eijlander, Ph., Gilhuis, P.C. and Peters, J.A.F. (1993) *Overheid en Zelfregulering*. Zwolle: Tjeenk Willink.

Eisenstadt, S.N. (1989) 'Culture and Structure in Recent Sociological Analysis', in H. Haferkamp (ed.), *Social Structure and Culture*. Berlin: Walter de Gruyter, 5–14.

Ester, P., Halman, L. and Moor, R. de (eds) (1994) *The Individualizing Society*. Tilburg: Tilburg University Press.

Etzioni, A. (1968) *The Active Society*. New York: Free Press.

Evans, M. (1995) 'Elitism', in D. Marsh and G. Stoker (eds), *Theory and Methods in Political Science*. London: Macmillan, Chapter 12.

Evers, A. and Nowotny, H. (1987) *Über den Umgang mit Unsicherheit*. Frankfurt a.M: Suhrkamp.

Fligstein, N. (1996) 'Markets as Politics', *American Sociological Review*, 61: 656–673.

Foley, M.W. and Edwards, B. (1999) 'Is it Time to Disinvest in Social Capital?', *Journal of Public Policy*, 19: 141–173.

Fornaess, J. (1995) *Cultural Theory and Late Modernity*. London: Sage.

Fraser, N. (1989) 'Talking about Needs: Interpretive Contests as Political Conflicts in Welfare-State Societies', *Ethics*, 99: 291–313.

Freidson, E. (1994) *Professionalism Reborn*. Cambridge: Polity Press.

Friedrich, C.J. (1963) *Man and His Government*. New York: McGraw-Hill.

Früh, W. and Schönbach, L. (1992) 'Der dynamisch-transaktionale Ansatz', in R. Burkart, (Hrsg), *Wirkungen der Massenkommunikation*. Wien: Braumüller, 86–100.

Fuchs Epstein, C. (1992) 'Tinkerbells and Pin-ups: the Construction and Reconstruction of Gender Boundaries at Work', in M. Lamont and M. Fournier (eds), *Cultivating Differences*. Chicago: Chicago University Press.

Galston, W.A. (1991) *Liberal Purposes*. Cambridge: Cambridge University Press.

Gastelaars, M. and Hagelstein, G. (eds) (1996) *Management of Meaning*. Utrecht: University, ISOR/CBM, 1–8.

Gellner, E (1992) *Reason and Culture*. Oxford: Blackwell.

Geraets, T.F. (ed.) (1979) *Rationality Today*. Ottawa: The University of Ottawa Press.

Gerding, G. (1991) *Unit-Management bij de Rijksoverheid*. Delft: Eburon.

Geus, M. de (1989) *Organisatietheorie in de Politieke Filosofie*. Delft: Eburon.

Giddens, A. (1984) *The Constitution of Society*. Berkeley: University of California Press.

Goodin, R.E. (ed.) (1996) *The Theory of Institutional Design*. Cambridge: Cambridge University Press.

Goodin, R.E. (1998) 'Collective Responsibility', in D.R.E. Schmidtz and R.E Goodin (eds), *Social Welfare and Individual Responsibility*. Cambridge: Cambridge University Press, 145–154.

Gordon, J.E. (1978) *Structures*. Harmondsworth: Penguin.

Gormsley, W.T. (1994/1995) 'Privatization Revisited', *Policy Studies Review*, 13: 215–234.

Grabher, G. (ed.) (1993) *The Embedded Firm*. London: Routledge.

Gramsci, A. (1971) *Prison Notebooks*. London: Lawrence and Wishart.

Grandori, A. and Soda, G. (1995) 'Inter-Firm Networks: Antecedents, Mechanisms and Forms', *Organization Studies*, 16: 183–214.

Granovetter, M. (1985) 'Economic Action and Social Structure: the Problem of Embeddedness', *American Journal of Sociology*, 91: 481–510.

Greca, R. (2000) 'Institutional Co-governance as a Mode of Co-operation between Various Social Service Carriers and Providers', *Public Management (Review)*, 2: 379–398.

Gross, N., Mason, W.S. and McEachern, A.W. (1964) *Explorations in Role Analysis*. New York: Wiley.

Grote, J.R. and Gbikpi, B. (eds) (2002) *Participatory Governance*. Opladen: Leske & Budrich.

Grusky, D.B. (1994) *Social Stratification*. Boulder, Co: Westview.

Gunsteren, H.R. van (1985) 'Het Begrip Sturing', in M.A.P. Bovens, W.J. Witteveen (eds), *Het Schip van Staat*. Zwolle, W.E.J. Tjeenk Willink, 277–296.

Gupta, J., Wurff, R. van der and Junne, G. (1995) *International Policies to Address the Greenhouse Effect*. Amsterdam: Free University, Institute for Environmental Studies.

Gusfield, J.R. (1981) *The Culture of Public Problems*. Chicago: Chicago University Press.

Habermas, J. (1984, 1987) *The Theory of Communicative Action*. Boston: Beacon Press, Vols I and II.

Habermas, J. (1989) *The Structural Transformation of the Public Sphere*. Cambridge, MA: MIT Press.

Hall, P. and Taylor, R.C.R. (1996) 'Political Science and the Three New Institutionalisms', *Political Studies*, XLIV: 936–957.

Hannerz, U. (1992) *Cultural Complexity*. New York: Columbia University Press.

Hardin, G. (1968) 'The Tragedy of the Commons', *Science*, 162: 1243–1248.

Hasenclever, A., Mayer, P. and Rittberger, V. (1997) *Regimes as Links between States*. Tübingen: Center for International Relations, Nr 29.

Hawkins, K. (1989) '"FATCATS" and Prosecution in a Regulatory Agency', in F. Short, J.F. Junior and L. Clarke, (eds) *Organizations, Uncertainties, and Risk*. Boulder: Westview, 275–298.

Hayek, F.A. (1994) 'The Theory of Complex Phenomena', in M. Martin and L.C. McIntyre (eds), *Readings in the Philosophy of Social Science*. Cambridge, MA: MIT Press, 55–70.

Held, V. (1982) 'The Political "Testing" of Moral Theories', in P. A. French, T.E. Uehling Jr and H.K. Wettstein (eds), *Midwest Studies in Philosophy*. Minneapolis: University of Minneapolis Press, 342–363.

Hisschemöller, M. (1993) *De Democatie van Problemen*. Amsterdam: VU Uitgeverij.

Höreth, M. (1998) *The Trilemma of Legitimacy-Multilevel Governance in the EU and the Problem of Democracy*. Bonn: Center for European Integration Studies, Discussion paper C 11.

Hofstadter, D.R. (1985) *Metamagical Themes*. Harmondsworth, Penguin.

Hollander, J. den (1995) *Sturen op Afstand*. Utrecht: Lemma.

Hood, C.C. (1983) *The Tools of Government*. London: Macmillan.

Hood, C.C. (1976) *Limits of Administration*. New York: Wiley.

Hoogerwerf, A. (1987) 'Beleid Berust op Veronderstellingen: de Beleidstheorie', in P.B. Lehning and J.B.D. Simonis (eds), *Handboek Beleidswetenschap*. Meppel: Boom, 23–40.

Hoogerwerf, A. (1989) 'De Beleidstheorie uit de Beleidspraktijk: een Tussenbalans', *Beleidswetenschap*, 3, 320–341.

Hoppe, R. (1989) *Het Beleidsprobleem Geproblematiseerd.* Muiden: Coutinho.

Humphreys, P.J. (1996) *Mass Media and Media Policy in Western Europe.* Manchester: Manchester University Press.

Huxham, C. (ed.) (1996) *Creating Collaborative Advantage.* London: Sage.

Huxham, C. (2000a) 'Ambiguity, Complexity and Dynamics in Membership of Collaboration', *Human Relations,* 53: 6, 771–806.

Huxham, C. (2000b) 'The Challenge of Collaborative Governance', *Public Management Review,* 2: 337–357.

Huxham, C. and Vangen, S (2000) 'Leadership in the Shaping and Implementation of Collaborate Agendas', *Academy of Management Journal,* 43: 1159–1175.

Jansen, D. (1995) 'Interorganisationforschung und Politiknetzwerke', in D. Jansen and K. Schubert, (eds), *Netzwerke und Politikproduktion.* Marburg: Schürren Verlag, 95–110.

Jentoft, S. (1989) 'Fisheries Co-management, Delegating Government Responsibility to Fishermen's Organisations', *Marine Policy,* 2: 137–154.

Jentoft, S. and McCay, B. (1995) 'User Participation in Fisheries Management, Lessons Drawn from International Experiences', *Marine Policy,* 19: 227–246.

Jentoft, S., Friis, P., Kooiman, J. and van der Schans, J.W. (1999) 'Knowledge-based Fisheries: Opportunities for Learning', in J. Kooiman, et al. (eds), *Creative Governance: Opportunities for Fisheries in Europe.* Aldershot: Ashgate, 239–258.

Jervis, D. (1993) 'Systems and Interaction Effects', in J. Snyder and J.D. Jervis (eds), *Coping with Complexity in the International System.* Boulder: Westview, 25–46.

Johnson, T.J. (1972) *Professions and Power.* London: Macmillan.

Jordan, G. and Schubert, K. (1992) 'A Preliminary Ordering of Policy Network Labels', *European Journal of Political Research,* 30: 7–27.

Kaase, M. and Marsh, A. (1979) 'Political Action Repertory', in S. Barnes and M. Kaase (eds), *Political Action.* Beverly Hills: Sage.

Kahn, R.L., Wolfe, D.M., Quinn, R.P., Snoek, J.D. and Rosenthal, R.A. (1964) *Organizational Stress: Studies in Role Conflict and Ambiguity.* New York: Wiley.

Kaplan, A. (1964) *The Conduct of Inquiry.* San Francisco: Chandler.

Kaplan, S. and Garrick, B.J. (1993) 'Die quantitative bestimmung von Risiko', in R. Bechmann (eds), *Risiko und Gesellschaft.* Opladen: Westdeutsche Verlag, 91–124.

Kasperson, R. (1992) 'The Social Amplification of Risk', in S. Krimsky and D. Golding (eds), *Social Theories of Risk.* Westport: Praeger, 153–178.

Katz, D. and Kahn, R.L. (1966) *The Social Psychology of Organizations.* New York: Wiley.

Kaufmann, F-X, Majone, G. and Ostrom, V. (eds) (1986) *Guidance, Control, and Evaluation in the Public Sector.* Berlin: de Gruyter.

Keane, J. (ed.) (1988) *Civil Society and the State.* London: Verso.

Kenis, P. and Schneider, V. (1991) 'Policy Networks and Policy Analysis', in B. Marin, and R. Mayntz (eds), *Policy Networks.* Frankfurt a M: Campus.

Keohane, R.O. and Nye, J.S. (1989) *Power and Interdependence,* 2nd ed. Glenview: Scott, Foresman.

Keohane, R.O. and Ostrom, E. (eds) (1995), *Local Commons and Global Interdependence.* London: Sage.

Kickert, W.J.M. (1979) *The Organization of Decision-making.* Amsterdam: North Holland.

Kickert, W.J.M. (1993) 'Autopoiesis and the Science of (Public) Administration', *Organization Studies,* 4: 261–278.

Kickert, W.J.M. (red) (1993b) Veranderingen in Management en Organisatie bij de Rijksoverheid. Alphen ad Rijn: Samson, H.D. Tjeenk Willink.

Kickert, W.J.M., Klijn, E.-H. and Koppenjan, J.F.M. (eds) (1997) Managing Complex Networks. London: Sage.

Kitschelt, H. (1991) 'Resource Mobilization Theory', in D. Rucht (ed.) Research on Social Movements. Frankfurt: Campus, 325–354.

Klandermans, B. (1997) The Social Psychology of Protest. Oxford: Blackwell.

Klijn, E.-H. (1996) Regels en Sturing in Netwerken. Delft: Eburon.

Koelega, D. and Noordegraaf, H. (1994) Moet Moraal Weer? Kampen: Kok.

Kolk, A., Tulder, R. van and Welters, C. (1999) International Codes of Conduct and Corporate Social Responsibility. Rotterdam: Erasmus University, Rotterdam School of Management, Report Series, No. 10.

König, T., Rieger, E. and Schmitt, H. (eds) (1996) Das Europäische Mehrebenensystem. Frankfurt: Campus Verlag.

Kooiman, J. (1988) Besturen: Wisselwerking tussen Overheid en Maatschappij. Assen: van Gorcum.

Kooiman, J. (ed.) (1993) Modern Governance. London: Sage.

Kooiman, J. (1996) 'Stapsgewijs Omgaan met Politiek-maatschappelijke Problemen', in P. Nijkamp, W. Begeer and J. Berting, (eds) Denken over Complexe Besluitvorming. Den Haag: SDU Uitgevers, 31–48.

Kooiman, J., Vliet, M. van and Jentoft, S. (eds) (1999) Creative Governance: Opportunities for Fisheries in Europe. Aldershot: Ashgate.

Kooiman, J. (1999) 'Social-Political Governance: Overview, Reflections and Design', Public Management (Review), 1: 67–92.

Kooiman, J. (2000a) 'Societal Governance: Levels, Modes and Orders of Social-Political Interaction', in J. Pierre (ed.), Debating Governance. Oxford: Oxford University Press, 138–164.

Kooiman, J. (2000b) 'Working with Governance'. Special Issue of Public Management Review, Vol. 2, No. 3.

Kooiman, J. (2002) 'Governance: A Social-Political Perspective', in J.R. Grote and B. Gbikpi (eds), Participatory Governance. Opladen: Beske and Budrich, 71–96.

Kooiman, J. (in press) 'Activation in Governance', in H. Bang (ed.), Culture Governance as Political Communication. Manchester: Manchester University Press.

Kooiman, J. (in press) 'Societal Governance', in I. Katenhusen and W. Lamping (eds), Demokratien in Europa. Opladen: Beske and Budrich.

Kooiman, J. and van Vliet, M. (2000) 'Self-governance as a Mode of Societal Governance', Public Management Review, 2, 359–378.

Kouwenhoven, V.P. (1991) Publiek-Private Samenwerking. Delft: Eburon.

Kouwenhoven, V.P. (1993) 'Public-Private Partnership', in J.Kooiman (ed.), Modern Governance. London: Sage, 119–130.

Krabbendam, H. and Ten Napel, H.-M. (eds) (2000) Regulating Morality. Antwerpen-Apeldoorn: Maklu.

Krasner, S.D. (1982) 'Structural Causes and Regime Consequences', International Organization, 36: 185–205.

Krause, E.A. (1996) Death of the Guilds. New Haven, CT: Yale University Press.

Krimsky, S. and Golding, D. (eds) (1992) Social Theories of Risk. Westport: Praeger.

LaPorte T.R. (ed.) (1975) Organized Social Complexity. Princeton: Princeton University Press.

Larson, M.S. (1977) *The Rise of Professsionalism.* Berkeley: University of California Press.

Leeuw, A.C.J. de (1994) *Besturen van Veranderingsprocessen.* Assen: van Gorcum.

Longstaff, P.H. (1999) 'Regulating Communications in the 21st Century', in B.H. Compaine and W.H. Read (eds), *The Information Resources Policy Handbook.* Cambridge: MIT Press, 453–481.

Lowi, T.J. (1972) 'Four Systems of Policy, Politics and Choice', *Public Administration Review,* 32: 298–310.

Lowndes, V. (1996) 'Varieties of Institutionalism: a Critical Appraisal', *Public Administration,* 74: 181–197.

Luhmann, N. (1974) *Soziologische Aufklärung II.* Köln/Opladen: Westdeutscher Verlag.

Luhmann, N. (1982) *The Differentiation of Society.* New York: Columbia University Press.

Luhmann, N. (1984) *Soziale Systeme.* Frankfurt: Suhrkampf.

Luhmann, N. (1995) *Social Systems.* Stanford: Standford University Press.

Lukes, S. (1991) *Moral Conflicts in Politics.* Oxford: Clarendon Press.

MacDonald, K.M. (1995) *The Sociology of the Professions.* London: Sage.

McGlade, J. (1999) 'Bridging Disciplines', in J. Kooiman, S. Jentoft and M. van Vliet (eds), *Creative Governance.* Aldershot: Ashgate, 175–185.

McQuail, D. (1984) *Communication,* 2nd edn. Harlow: Longman.

McQuail, D. (1994) *Mass Communication Theory.* London: Sage.

McIntyre, L.C. (1994) 'Complexity and Social Scientific Laws', in M. Martin and L.C. McIntyre (eds), *Readings in the Philosophy of Social Science.* Cambridge, MA.: MIT Press, 131–143.

McQuaid, R.W. (2000) 'The Theory of Partnership', in S.P. Osborne (ed.), *Public-Private Partnerships.* London: Routledge, 9–35.

Majone, G. (1997) 'From the Positive to the Regulatory State', *Journal of Public Policy,* 17: 139–167.

Majone, G. (1999) 'The Regulatory State and its Legitimacy Problems', *West European Politics,* 22: 1–24.

March, J.G. and Olsen, J.P. (1984) 'The New Institutionalism', *American Political Science Review,* 78: 734–749.

March, J.G. and Olsen, J.P. (1989) *Rediscovering Institutions.* New York: Free Press.

Marin, B. and Mayntz, R. (eds) (1991) *Policy Networks.* Frankfurt a M: Campus.

Marin, B. (ed.) (1990) *Governance and Generalized Exchange.* Frankfurt a M: Campus.

Marsh, D. (ed.) (1998) *Comparing Policy Networks.* Buckingham: Open University Press.

Martinelli, A. (1994) 'Entrepreneurship and Management', in N.J. Smelser and R. Swedberg (eds), *The Handbook of Economic Sociology.* Princeton: Princeton University Press, 475–503.

Mason, H.E. (ed.) (1996) *Moral Dilemmas and Moral Theory.* New York: Oxford University Press.

Mayntz, R (Hrsg) (1968) *Bürokratische Organisation.* Cologne: Kipenheuer & Witsch.

Mayntz, R. (1990) *The Influence of Natural Science Theories on Contemporary Social Science.* Köln: Max-Planck-Institut für Gesellschaftsforschung, MPIFG Discussion paper 90/7.

Mayntz, R. (1993a) 'Modernization and the Logic of Interorganizational Networks', in J. Child et al. *Societal Change between Market and Organization.* Avebury: Ashgate, 3–18.

Mayntz, R. (1993b) 'Governing Failures and the Problem of Governability: Some Comments on a Theoretical Paradigm', in J. Kooiman (ed.), *Modern Governance.* London: Sage, 9–20.

Mayntz, R. (1993c) 'Policy-netzwerke und die Logik von Verhandlungssysteme', in A. Héritier (Hg) *Policy- Analyse, PVS,* Sonderheft 24: 39–56.

Mayntz, R. (1999) 'Organization, Agents and Representation', in M. Egeberg and P. Laegreid (eds), *Organizing Political Institutions*. Oslo: Scandinavian University Press, 81–91.

Mayntz, R. and Scharpf, F. (eds) (1995) *Gesellschaftliche Selbstregelung und politische Steuerung*. Frankfurt/New York: Campus.

Mayntz, R. (1997) *Soziale Dynamik und Politische Steuerung*. Frankfurt/New York: Campus.

Meijs, L. (1997) *Management van Vrijwilligersorganisaties*. Utrecht: NOV Publicaties.

Melucci, A. (1992) 'Frontier Land', in M. Diani and R. Eyerman (eds), *Studying Collective Action*. London: Sage, 238–258.

Melucci, A. (1996) *Challenging Codes*. Cambridge: Cambridge University Press.

Merlin, P. (1997) *Overheid en Verzekeringsmarkt in Wisselwerking*. Delft: Eburon.

Merton, R.K., Gray, A., Hockey, B. and Selvin, H.C. (eds) (1952) *Reader in Bureaucracy*. New York: Free Press.

Messner, D. (1997) 'Netzwerktheorien', in E. Altvater, A. Brunnengrase, M. Haake and H. Walk (Hrsg), *Vernetzt und Verstrickt*. Münster: Dampfboot Verlag, 27–64.

Metcalfe, L. (1994) 'International Policy Co-ordination and Public Management Reform', *International Review of Administrative Sciences*, 60: 271–290.

Morgan, D. and Shinn, C. (1999) 'Community Capital, Social Trust and Public Administration', *Administrative Theory & Practice*, 21: 11–22.

Morgan, G. (1986) *Images of Organization*. London: Sage.

Müller, W.C. and Wright, V. (1994) 'Reshaping the State in Western Europe', *West European Politics*, 17: 1–11.

Münch, R. (1987a) *Theory of Action*. London: Routledge.

Münch, R. (1987b) 'The Interpenetration of Microinteraction and Macrostructure in a Complex and Contingent Institutional Order', in J.J. Alexander et al. (eds), *The Micro-Macro Link*. Berkeley: University of California Press, 356–387.

Münch, R. (1988) *Understanding Modernity*. London: Routledge.

Nelson, B., Roberts, D. and Veit, W. (eds) (1992) *The Idea of Europe*. New York: Berg.

Nijkamp, P., Begeer, W. and Berting, J. (1996) *Denken over Complexe Besluitvorming*. Den Haag: SDU.

Nonet, P. and Selznick, P. (1978) *Law and Society in Transition*. New York: Harper.

Oberschall, A. (1993) *Social Movements*. New Brunswick: Transaction Publishers.

Oksenberg Rorty, A. (1992) 'The Advantages of Moral Diversity', in E. Frankel Paul, F.D. Miller, Jr and J. Paul (eds), *The Good Life and the Human Good*. Cambridge: Cambridge University Press, 38–62.

Olsen, M.E. (1993) 'Sociopolitical Pluralism', in M.E. Olsen and M.N. Marger (eds), *Power in Modern Societies*. Boulder: Westview, 146–152.

Olson, M. Jr (1965) *The Logic of Collective Action*. Cambridge: Harvard University Press.

Osborne, S.P. (ed.) (2000) *Public-Private Partnerships*. London: Routledge.

Ostrom, E. (1986) 'A Method of Institutional Analysis', in F.-X. Kaufmann et al. (eds), *Guidance, Control, and Evaluation in the Public Sector*. Berlin: de Gruyter, 495–510.

Ostrom, E. (1990) *Governing the Commons*. Cambridge: Cambridge University Press.

Ostrom, E. (1992) 'Institutions and Common-Pool Resources', Introduction of Special Issue, *Journal of Political Theory*, Vol 4, No. 3.

Ostrom, E., Gardner, R., Walker, J. et al. (1994) *Rules, Games, and Common-Pool Resources*. Ann Arbor: University of Michigan Press.

Ostrom, V. (1986) 'A Fallabilist's Approach to Norms and Criteria of Choice', in Kaufmann, F.-X., Majone, G. and Ostrom, V. (eds), *Guidance, Control, and Evaluation in the Public Sector*. Berlin: de Gruyter, 229–244.

Outshoorn, J. (1986) *De Politieke Strijd rondom de Abortuswetgeving in Nederland 1964–1968*. Amsterdam: Vrije Universiteit, PhD Diss.

Oye, K.A. (ed.) (1986) *Cooperation under AnarCchy*. Princeton: Princeton University Press.

Peters, B.G. and van Nispen, F.K.M. (eds) (1998) *Public Policy Instruments*. Cheltenham: Edward Elgar.

Peters, B.G. (2000) 'Governance and Comparative Politics', in J. Pierre (ed.), *Debating Governance*. Oxford: Oxford University Press, 36–53.

Pichardo, N.A. (1997) 'New Social Movements', *Annual Review of Sociology*, 23: 411–430.

Pierre, J. (ed.) (2000) *Debating Governance: Authority, Steering, Democracy*. Oxford: Oxford University Press.

Pitkin, H. (1967) *The Concept of Representation*. Berkeley: University of California Press.

Pollitt, C. and Bouckaert, G. (2000) *Public Management Reform*. Oxford: Oxford University Press.

Portes, A. (1998) 'Social Capital', *Annual Review of Sociology*, 24: 1–24.

Powell, W.W. and Smith-Doerr, L. (1994) 'Networks and Economic Life', in N.J. Smelser and R. Swedberg (eds), *The Handbook of Economic Sociology*. Princeton: Princeton University Press, 368–402.

Powell, W.W. and DiMaggio, P.J. (eds) (1991) *The New Institutionalism in Organizational Analysis*. Chicago: Chicago University Press.

Presthus, R. (1962) *The Organizational Society*. New York: Vintage.

Prigogine, I. and Stengers, I. (1984) *Order out of Chaos*. New York: Bantam.

Pröpper, I.M.A.M. and Steenbeek, D.A. (1998) 'Interactieve Beleidsvoering: Typering, Ervaringen en Dilemma's', *Bestuurskunde*, 7: 292–301.

Pullin, R.S.V., Bartley, M. and Kooiman J. (eds) (1999) *Towards Policies for Conservation and Sustainable Use of Aquatic Genetic Resources*. Manilla: ICLARM, Conf. Proc. 59.

Putnam, R.D. (1993) *Making Democracy Work*. Princeton: Princeton University Press.

Raab, C. (1993) 'The Governance of Data Protection', in J. Kooiman (ed.) *Modern Governance*. London: Sage, 89–104.

Raab, C. (1999) 'From Balancing to Steering: New Directions for Data Protection', in C. Bennett and R. Grant (eds), *Vision of Privacy*. Toronto: Toronto Press, 68–93.

Radaelli, C.M. (1995) 'The Role of Knowledge in the Policy Process', *Journal of European Public Policy*, 2: 159–183.

Rayner, S. (1992) 'Cultural Theory and Risk Analysis', in S. Krimsky and D. Golding (eds), *Social Theories of Risk*. Westport: Praeger, 83–116.

Reed, M.I. (1992) *The Sociology of Organizations*. New York: Harvester/Wheatsheaf.

Renn, O. (1992) 'The social arena concept of risk debates', in S. Krimsky and D. Golding (eds) *Social Theories of Risk*. Westport: Praeger, 179–196.

Rhodes, R.A.W. (1997) *Understanding Governance*. Buckingham: Open University Press.

Richardson, J.J. (1995) 'The Market for Political Activism: Interest Groups as a Challenge to Political Parties', *West European Politics*, 18: 116–139.

Ringeling, A.B. (1987) 'Beleidstheorieën en Theorieën over Beleid', in P.B. Lehning and J.B.D. Simonis (eds), *Handboek Beleidswetenschap*. Meppel: Boom, 41–53.

Ringeling, A.B. (1983) *De Instrumenten van het Beleid*. Alphen a.d.Rijn: Samson.

Rist, R.C. (1994) 'The Preconditions of Learning: Lessons from the Public Sector', in F.L. Leeuw, R.C. Rist and R.C. Sonnichen (eds), *Can Governments Learn?* New Brunswick: Transaction Publishers, 189–206.

Ritzer, G. (1992) *Sociological Theory*, 3rd edn. New York: McGraw-Hill.

Röber, M. (2000) 'Competition: How Far Can You Go?', *Public Management Review*, 2: 311–336.

Rochefort, D.A. and R.W. Cobb, (eds) (1994) *The Politics of Problem Definition.* Lawrence: Kansas University Press.

Rogers, D.L. and Whetten, D.A. (1982) *Interorganizational Coordination.* Ames: Iowa State University Press.

Sabatier, P.A. and Jenkin-Smith (eds) (1993) *Policy Change and Learning: An Advocacy Coalition Approach.* Boulder, CO: Westview Press.

Saxenhouse, A.W. (1992) *Fear of Diversity.* Chicago: Chicago University Press.

Schans, J.W. van der (2001) *Governance of Marine Resources.* Delft: Eburon.

Scharpf, F.W. (1973) *Politische Durchsetzbarkeit innerer Reformen im pluralistisch-demokratischen Gemeinwesen der Bundesrepublik.* Berlin: International Institute of Management.

Scharpf, F.W., Reissert, B. and Schnabel, F. (1976) *Politikverflechtung.* Kronberg/Ts: Scriptor.

Scharpf, F.W. (ed.) (1993) *Games and Hierarchies in Networks.* Frankfurt: Campus.

Scharpf, F.W. (1994) 'Community and Autonomy: Multi-level Policy-making in the European Union', *Journal of European Policy*, 1: 219–242.

Scharpf, F.W. (1997) *Games Real Actors Play.* Boulder: Westview Press.

Scharpf, F.W. (1999) 'Legitimacy in the Multi-actor European Polity', in M. Egeberg and P. Laegreid (eds), *Organizing Political Institutions.* Oslo: Scandinavian University Press, 261–289.

Scheffler, S. (1995) 'Individual Responsibility in a Global Age', in E. Frankel Paul, F.D. Miller Jr and J. Paul (eds), *Contemporary Political and Social Philosophy.* Cambridge: Cambridge University Press.

Schmidt, L. (2000) 'Variante des Konstruktivismus in der Soziologie sozialer Probleme', *Soziale Welt*, 51: 153–172.

Schuppert, G.F. (2000) *Verwaltungswissenschaft.* Baden-Baden: Nomos.

Scott, W.R. (1995) *Institutions and Organizations.* London: Sage.

Scott, W.R. (1992) *Organizations: Rational, Natural and Open Systems*, 3rd edn. Engelwood Cliffs: Prentice Hall.

Sewell, W.H. Jr. (1992) 'A Theory of Structure: Duality, Agency, and Transformation', *American Journal of Sociology*, 98: 1–29.

Shimanoff, S.B. (1980) *Communication Rules.* Beverly Hills: Sage.

Sibeon, R. (2000) 'Governance and the Policy Process in Contemporary Europe', *Public Management Review*, 2: 289–310.

Simon, H.A. (1957) *Models of Man: Social and Rational.* New York: Wiley.

Simon, H.A. (1962) 'The Architecture of Complexity', *Proceedings of the American Philosophical Society*, 106: 467–482.

Simon, H.A. (1983) *Reason in Human Affairs.* Stanford: Stanford University Press.

Sklair, L. (1988) 'Transcending the Impasse: Metatheory, Theory and Empirical Research in the Sociology of Development and Underdevelopment', *World Development*, 16: 697–709.

Smircich, L. and Morgan, G. (1982) 'Leadership: the Management of Meaning', *The Journal of Applied Behavioral Science*, 18: 257–273.

Smith, M.J. (1990) Pluralism, Reformed Pluralism and Neopluralism: the Role of Pressure Groups in Policy-making', *Political Studies*, 38: 302–322.

Smith, M.J. (1995) 'Pluralism', in D.Marsh and G.Stoker (eds) (1995), *Theory and Methods in Political Science*. London: Macmillan, 209–227.

Smith, S. (1988) 'Belief Systems in the Study of International Relations', in R. Little and S. Smith (eds), *Belief Systems in International Relations*. Oxford: Basil Blackwell, 11–36.

Smith, T.A. (1975) *The Comparative Policy Process*. Santa Barbara: CLIO-Books.

Snyder, J. and Jervis, D. (eds) (1993) *Coping with Complexity in the International System*. Boulder, CO: Westview.

Somers, M.R. (1995) 'Narrating and Naturalizing Civil Society and Citizenship Theory', *Sociological Theory*, 13: 230–274.

Sorokin, P.A. (1937–41) *Social and Cultural Dynamics*. New York: Bedminster Press, Vol. I–IV.

Sowell, T. (1991) 'A World View of Cultural Diversity', *Society*, Nov/Dec: 37–44.

Starr, P. (1992) 'Social Categories and Claims in the Liberal State', in M. Douglas and D. Hull (eds), *How Classification Works*. Edinburgh: Edinburgh University Press, 154–179.

Stinchcombe, A.L. (1965) 'Social Structure and Organizations', in J.G. March (ed.), *Handbook of Organizations*. Chicago: Rand McNally, 142–193.

Swartz, D. (1997) *Culture and Power: the Sociology of Pierre Bourdieu*. Chicago: Chicago University Press.

Swedberg, R. (1994) 'Markets as Social Structures', in N.J. Smelser and R. Swedberg (eds), *The Handbook of Economic Sociology*. Princeton: Princeton University Press, 255–282.

Taylor, I. (1996) 'Who is enabled by whom to do what', Paper IRSPSM Symposium. Aston University, Birmingham, 25–26 April.

Teubner, G. (1993) *Law as an Autopoietic System*. Oxford: Blackwell.

Tilly, C. (1978) *From Mobilization to Revolution*. Reading: Addisson-Wesley.

Torstendahl, R. and Burrage, M. (eds) (1990) *The Formation of Professions*. London: Sage.

Toulmin, S. (1990) *Cosmopolis*. Chicago: Chicago University Press.

Touraine, A. (1994) 'European Countries in a Post-National Era', in C. Rootes and H. Davis (eds), *Social Change and Political Transformation*. London: UCL Press.

Turner, F. (1997) 'Chaos and Social Science', in R.A. Eve, S. Horsfall and M.E. Lee (eds), *Chaos, Complexity and Sociology*. Thousand Oaks: Sage, xi–xxvii.

Turner, J.H. (1988) *A Theory of Social Interaction*. Cambridge: Polity Press.

Veld, R.J. in't., Schaap, L., Termeer, C.J.A.M. and Twist, M.J.W. van (eds) (1991), *Autopoiesis and Configuration Theory*. Dordrecht: Kluwer.

Vliet, L.M. van (1992) *Communicatieve Besturing van het Milieuhandelen van Ondernemingen*. Delft: Eburon.

Vliet, L.M. van (1993) 'Environmental Regulation of Business', in J. Kooiman (ed.), *Modern Governance*. London: Sage, 105–118.

Vught, F.A. van (1987) 'Verklaringsmodellen bij Beleidsevaluatie', in P.B. Lehning and J.B.D. Simonis (eds), *Handboek Beleidswetenschap*. Meppel, Boom, 154–176.

Wallace, W.L. (1994) *A Weberian Theory of Human Society*. New Brunswick: Rutgers University Press.

Warner, J. (1996) *Regimes*. Unpublished working document.

Weaver, W. (1948) 'Science and Complexity', *American Scientist*, 36: 536–544.

Weaver, R.K. and Rockman, B.A. (1993) *Do Institutions Matter?* Washington, DC: The Brookings Institution.

Wessels, W. (1997) 'An Ever Closer Fusion?' *Journal of Common Market Studies*, 35: 267–299.

White, S.K. (1995) *The Cambridge Companion to Habermas*. Cambridge: Cambridge University Press.

Whitmeyer, J.M. (1994) 'Why Actors are Integral to Structural Analysis', *Sociological Theory*, 12: 153–164.

Wilden, A. (1987) *The Rules are no Game*. London: Routledge and Kegan.

Williamson, O.E. (1975) *Markets and Hierarchies*. New York: Free Press.

Willke, H. (1992) *Ironie des Staates*. Frankfurt: Surkamp.

Willke, H. (1993) *Systemtheorie*. Stuttgart: G.Fischer Verlag.

Wirth, W. (1986) 'Control in Public Administration', in F.-X. Kaufmann et al. (eds), *Guidance, Control and Evaluation in the Public Sector*. Berlin: de Gruyter, 595–624.

Witteveen, W.J. (1985) 'Dokteren aan het Schip van Staat', in M.A.P. Bovens and W.J. Witteveen (eds), *Het Schip van Staat*. Zwolle, W.E.J. Tjeenk Willink, 23–52.

Wolfe, A. (1992) 'Democracy versus Sociology: Boundaries and their Political Consequences', in M. Lamont and M. Fournier (eds), *Cultivating Differences*. Chicago: Chicago University Press, 309–326.

Zentner, H. (1957) 'Sorokin's Analysis of Time and Space' in P. Owen (ed.), *Social and Cultural Dynamics*. London: Routledge.

Zetterholm, S. (ed.) (1994) *National Cultures and European Integration*. Oxford: Berg.

Zimmerman, M.J. (1992) 'Responsibility', in L.C. Becker (ed.), *Encyclopedia of Ethics*. Chicago: St James Press, 1089–1095.

INDEX